Wilmington Memories...

CHASING THE ICE TRUCK

A LIVING HISTORY OF WILMINGTON
IN THE GOOD OLD DAYS

OTHER BOOKS FROM HOMETOWN MEMORIES

Claremont Tales
Taylorsville Tales
Burke County Tales
Catawba County Tales
Cleveland County Tales
Blue Ridge Tales
Foothills-Piedmont Tales
Memorable Tales of the Smokies and Blue Ridge Mountains
Caldwell County Tales
Albemarle Tales
Lincolnton Tales
Montgomery County Tales
Lee County Tales
Rowan County Tales
Cold Biscuits and Fatback and other Richmond County Tales
Skinnydipping in the Mule Trough and other Rockingham County Tales
Lunch in a Lard Bucket and other Cabarrus County Tales
Rooster in a Milk Well and other Moore County Tales
A Prayer for the Baby Goat and other Alamance County Tales
Mill Village and the Miracle Bicycle and other Gaston County Tales
Wilmington Tales
Asheville Tales
Guilford County Tales
The Elegant Tarpaper Shack - Tales from the North Carolina Heartland
The Class of '47 Was Me - Tales from the Coast
Outhouse Spiders and Tin Tub Baths - Tales of the Blue Ridge Mountains
Wringer Washers and Ration Stamps - Tales from Forsyth County
Front Porch Stories, Back Porch Bathrooms - Tales from Alexander, Davie, Iredell, Rowan and Yadkin Counties
Crank Victrolas and Wood Cook Stoves - Tales from Greene, Lenoir, Pitt and Wayne Counties
Mules, Mud and Homemade Soap - Tales from Anson, Stanly and Union Counties
Life in the Good Old Days in Alamance, Caswell and Rockingham Counties
Life in the Good Old Days in Catawba, Lincoln and Gaston Counties
Life in the Good Old Days in Buncombe and Henderson Counties
Two Holers and Model T Fords and other Randolph County Tales
Ain't No Bears Out Tonight and other Cabarrus County Tales
Ham Biscuits and Baked Sweet Taters and other Montgomery, Richmond and Scotland County Tales
Steam Whistles and Party Line Phones and Other Memories from Roanoke
Possum Hunters, Moonshine and Cornshuck Dolls and Other Memories from Wilkes County

Wilmington Memories...
Chasing the Ice Truck

A TREASURY OF 20TH CENTURY MEMORIES
Compiled and edited by Bob Lasley and Sallie Holt

HOMETOWN MEMORIES PUBLISHING COMPANY
Hickory, North Carolina

Wilmington Memories...
CHASING THE ICE TRUCK

Senior Editor: **R. T. Lasley**
Design and Graphic Arts Editor: **Sallie Holt**

Copyright © 2007

All rights reserved by Hometown Memories Publishing and by the individuals who contributed articles to this work. No part of this work may be reproduced in any form, or by any means, without the written permission of the publisher or the individual conntributor. Exceptions are made for brief excerpts to be used in published reviews.

ISBN 978-0-9799199-1-6

Published by

Hometown Memories Publishing Company
1030 15th Avenue N.W.
Hickory, N. C. 28601
(828) 324-7446

Printed in the United States of America

INTRODUCTION

History books are usually a chronological record of events. They describe these events, list important dates and provide names of historical characters. They are usually written by a single author.

This book is not intended to be that kind of history. Rather than listing historical events, it attempts to explain how people reacted to one of the most change-filled eras ever known to man. And rather than one author, it has literally dozens of them.

Instead of facts, dates, events and politics, it focuses on living conditions, morals, traditions and customs. In it, you will find humor, adventure, romance, heroism, even a little suffering.

This is a *living* history; it's history as it was experienced by those who survived it.

Most of the people represented in this book grew up around New Hanover County, North Carolina. The stories of those who aren't natives often provide an entertaining contrast.

We hope this book will entertain today's readers, especially those who grew up back in the "good old days" and who can identify with the stories. But its real purpose is to provide a unique window into the past, to let future readers know that their forefathers were real people, with thoughts, emotions and actions common to people everywhere.

Acknowledgements

To those New Hanover County old-timers (and to those few who "ain't from around here") who took the trouble to write down your memories and mail them in to us, we offer our heartfelt thanks. And we're sure you're grateful to each other, because together, you have created a wonderful book.

We also thank those who trusted us with their family photographs, some of them very old and rare. We asked contributors to this book to furnish photos of themselves during their younger days. We tried to include as many of them as possible because they, too, are important historical documents, true relics from a forgotten era. We believe that one day, in the distant future, these photos, along with their accompanying stories, will reveal that those of us who survived the good old days were real people, not just names slipping from memory.

We regret that some of the photos were not of the best quality. We did our best to reproduce them as clearly as possible. A few of them weren't identified, but we included some of them with the name of the person who submitted them. We hope those of you who submitted such photos will identify them by writing in the margin of this book. Your descendents will thank you.

Some of you, our Associate Editors, deserve special thanks. Not only do you have stories of your own, but through your efforts in encouraging others to submit memories to us, you have increased the content and the quality of this book. These Associate Editors are James Allen Willard, Bill Annarino, Emily Barber, Mary Blanton, Frank Bowen, Kathleen Ellis, Charles Hart, Virginia Kelley, Mildred Navarro, Porter Robbins, Florence Simmons, Elsie Smiley, Gladys Thomas and Hulda Willett. We'd like to especially thank Karen Dolan, who not only has her own story in this book, but who solicited and wrote stories for many residents of the Autumn Care facility. You'll find these folks, and their story titles, in the Table of Contents.

To encourage participation, we offered cash awards to the contributors of the five most appealing stories. These awards were not based upon writing ability or historical knowledge, but rather upon subject matter and interest. The winners were Rosie Boyd, Sylvia Crippen, Milton Domler, Jay Wilcox and Glenn Williams. You'll also find these folks in the Table of Contents. It was extremely difficult to choose these winners because almost every story in this book had its own special appeal.

Table of Contents

Ruth Agee	Cornbread and Milk	83
Christina Annarino	Memory Minders	109
V.C. (Bill) Annarino	Boards of Education	66
Bill Baker	Cider Hard and Sausage Old	122
Linda Baker	Walking the Circle	67
Emily Barber	Notes to the Milkman	19
Lois Basiliere	Last Trip to Utica	142
Ruby Beavers	The Things in the Net	184
Mary Blanton	Black Dog Woman	95
Obbie Blanton	A Quiet Hero	60
Frances Blizzard	Pretty Decent Folks	202
Hazel Bloodworth	A Tale From the Mountains	120
Ervin Boswell	An Honorary Fireman?	119
Frank Bowen	Hits the Spot	137
Rosie Boyd	The Hobo's Letter	180
Camille Bridger	Sand Castles of Memory	13
Peggy Canady	I Remember Mimi	143
Sue Creech	Green Stamps, Tobacco and Hogs	102
Sylvia Crippen	Patriotic Cattails	58
Richard Cushman	Freedom from Knickers	73
James Davis	Charlie and the War Injuries	78
Nettie Deasy	When a Penny Was a Treasure	196
Kristy Dixon	The Missed Wooden Doll	173
Myrtle Dixon	The Honor System	140
H. Mike Dolan	Hanging Out on the Corner	91
Karen Dolan	Penny Candy and the Cold War	100
Milton Domler	The Feather Bed, Rum Runner and the Cobbler	135
Darlene Drescher	City Girl, Country Girl	54
Betty Duncan	The Rooster and the Eyeglasses	117
Mary Duncan	The Zoo Keeper's Son	146
Karen Edwards	Azalea Queens and Air Shows	74
Kathleen Ellis	Iceman and Lumina Farewell	166
Margaret Ann Faison	Remembering the Duck Biscuits	195
Douglas Flynn	Five Buttons at the Bijou	178
Juanita Gibson	Scratch Biscuits	131
Ester Gillis	Green Worms with Red Horns	46
Robert Goff	Those Days Are Gone	62
Julia Gower	Southern Cooking at the Bus Station	33
Becky Gregory	The Little Sister's Rare Name	19
Betty Lou Gurganious	The Blanket in the Field	47
Barbara Guy	Two Sips at Grandma's House	111
Lois Hardison	Drinking Cobie	49
Charles Hart	Picking Up Coal	172

Author	Title	Page
Stanley Harts	Woods That Are No More	76
Colo Hayes	A Snowy New England Romance	114
Houston Hendrix	A Good Place to Croak	98
Helen Higley	Grandma's Kitchen	17
Gaynelle Hinson	The Greek Blessing	88
Mary Hodge	Too Short for School	44
Clara Jane Hodges	Remembering the Maco Light	130
Sandra Huddle	The Lost Anchor	168
Anita Jezewski	An Enviable Childhood	190
Virginia Kelley	A Successful Career	81
Walter Kelly	The Girl at the Toilet Goods Counter	128
Shirley King	When the Railroad Left Wilmington	118
Elizabeth Knight	Ride the Bus or Walk	51
Odessa Koen	Castle Street Memories	84
Lew Kurtzman	The Proof's in the Pantyhose	16
Mary Lange	The Obvious Other	128
Barbara Liles	The Backseat Pot	163
Dianne Lynch	Cotton Wads and Scorched Duds	141
Willie Mae Mattocks	Same Water, Different People	119
Garry McDaniel	The Judge's Trees	172
Thelma McGuire	Victrola Waltzing	24
Mary Mitscher	Again Next Summer	28
Ann Montgomery	Old Joe's Bottom	92
Cindy Morrison	The Forecaster	194
Bette Motley	Wilmington Saturdays and the Empie House Ghost	30
Mildred Navarro	Bringing Home the Paycheck	150
Janet Nelson	Going to Town	64
Natalie Nicholas	The Church in the Wildwood	201
Nancy Oakley	The Yo-Yo Champ and the Streaked Butter	76
Roberta Painter	The Deer at the Well	126
Carolyn Parrish	Wedge and Sledge	144
Dorothy Pastis	Wilmington's Protective Charm	121
Mary Pearson	Seeing This Day	153
William Pepe	A Generation of Heroes	98
Nancy Potts	Hazel, Hand-Me-Downs and Biscuits	149
Julia Pridgen	An Unusual Luxury	36
Charles Register, Jr.	Dry Pond Memories	34
John Rehder	The Days of Pinecone Ball	22
Porter Robbins	Nine Cents Change	36
Dianne Roof	Granny Vann's Bonnet	178
John Russell	Twenty-Eight Memories	57
Betty Sanders	Mr. I Got 'Em	194
Mona Scott	A Variety of Pumps	104
Florence Simmons	Overflowing Beds	79
William Small	Spooks, Elephants and Alligators	94
Elsie Smiley	Salty Water and Trolley Rails	73
Cody Smith	A Toddle House Romance	72
Silas Sneeden	The Vanished Communities	112

Millie Solomon	Caruso in the Groove	152
June Stannus	Grandpa's Smoking Jacket	88
Mary Suchsland	A Lover of Books	48
Mary Swain	Comic Book Sundays	103
Lyman Taylor	Oscar's Money and the Pencil Sharpener	189
Audrey Teachey	A Lot of Dreaming	106
Gladys Thomas	Line Dried Laundry	139
Virginia Wallace	Ration Stamps and Wind-Up Victrolas	109
Forrest Walton	Wartime Wilmington	39
Adelaide Ward	The Green Hornet and Feather Beds	188
Thurston Watkins	Remembering Charlie "Barrel" Niven	156
Ellen Wells	A Ham Radio Baby	127
Gwendolyn West	The Garden Spot of the World	53
Marie Whitman	Upgrading from an Outhouse	108
Jay Wilcox	The Purpose of Little Red Wagons	155
Hulda Willett	The Ragged Beggar, Sleeping	132
Glenn Williams	The Source of Milk	185
Shirley Williams	The Doc Who Prescribed Ice Cream	164
Susan Williams	The Exploring Shoes and the Movie Man	175
Maxine Wright	Singing in the Swing	179
Steven Wright	The Cowboys	132

The Memories ...

Sand Castles of Memory
by
Camille ("Mimi") Bridger of Virginia Beach, Virginia

Rarely have we seen a description of "home" as elegantly done as this one. Mimi Bridger describes the Wrightsville of her youth as a lovely village where strangers were few and pleasures were many. This one will pluck the heartstrings of those who remember the days of Lumina and the time before Hazel.

My family has owned a home on East Columbia Street in Wrightsville Beach for over 60 years. It was owned first by my grandparents, Myrtle and Henry Bridger, and then by my parents, Sarah and MacRae Bridger. I was born in 1947.

Columbia Street was a special place; the same people came to those homes year after year. The Huggins of Wilmington, the Allens, the Evans, the Walkers, the Alpers, the Bellamys, the Clarks were owners. The street was unpaved, and was one of the last to be paved.

As small children, Mary Allen and I would build sand castles there. Very little traffic came up the street, but we looked forward to the ice cream truck in the afternoons, and the ice truck in the morning. The iceman would hook a big block of ice and take it into our house. Usually, he would give us a piece to suck on.

The vegetable man would also come up the street, selling local produce, ringing his bell.

A special memory is of sitting underneath those great homes on the beachfront. They were built upon high pilings, only yards from the ocean. Our mothers would sit there to protect themselves from the sun's rays, while all of the kids swam nearby. And in the after-

Lumina Avenue after Hurricane Hazel (October, 1954). On the left is the Neptune Restaurant. A little further down on the left is Robert's Grocery Store. Across the street on the right is Crest Theater.

The O'Brien/Allen home on Columbia Street after Hurricane Hazel hit in 1954.

noon, Mary Allen and I would go there and build sand castles.

Hurricane Hazel took those homes, and the next few rows of homes, away.

There were wonderful jetties up and down the beachfront. They were a block or so apart. The ocean currents were not as they are now that they are all gone. We used to float for hours in essentially the same spot, and we would catch a bushel of crabs in no time, using only our crab nets with no bait.

Wrightsville was low in population, so children played freely. Hugh McManus, Mary Allen and I would frequently walk across the inlet between Shell Island and Wrightsville at low tide. Shell Island was so beautiful, with no homes…just sea grass, birds, dunes, shells and sea creatures. It was a haven, a place to really feel close to nature. We knew to get back to the inlet before the tide started washing in.

The main street at Wrightsville was filled with family fun. There was the Crest Theater on the corner of Columbia Street, a favorite meeting place. And 25 cents to get in! There was a bingo parlor where I often played with my grandmother. Newell's was a beach store, with the best soda fountain ever. It was a place where all of the kids loved to go, and Mr. Newell seemed to always be there—and knew our names. Wings now occupies that building.

Roberts Grocery Store was located diagonally across the street from the current one. The owner, Mrs. Dorothy Roberts, lived upstairs. She was a lovely, gracious woman. She did not work in the store, but Mr. and Mrs. Cross did. They were the managers, and their son Billy seemed to always be there with them. Occasionally, he would take time out to swim with my sister Jeanne and other friends.

The big baskets of fruits and vegetables (all local) lined the entrance to the front door of the store. Once inside, you were greeted by old wooden floors, a warm family atmosphere with Mr. Cross at the meat counter, and Mrs. Cross at the front counter.

There was Shooney's, which was across the street from the now Jerry Allens (where the theater was). They would throw open the windows, had stools outside and a juke box, too. It was a gathering place for us in our early teens.

One landmark that I miss so much is the Edgewater Hotel, located on the sound at West Columbia Street. It was so welcoming, a big old cottage with a big porch and lots of rocking chairs. Both guests and locals gathered there to share stories and lots of laughs. Mrs. Edna Kelly, the owner, loved children and would let us dock our boat there anytime we wanted. We would ski early in the morning, take a break from the sun in the middle of the day, then go back again.

I was never without Mary Allen and Hugh McManus. There was no such

The sound between Wrightsville and Harbor Island before Hurricane Hazel hit in 1954.

thing as a no-wake zone, so we skied around Harbor Island frequently. We would fill up our gas tanks at Pennington's (on Harbor Island) and were always greeted with a smile from Allen. Sometimes he would pull Mary and me on a board behind his powerful boat. We'd hang on for dear life. Pennington's was a fun place to stop for gas.

Everyone loved the Lumina at the south end. We went to dances there and we skated there, too. My grandparents used to dance to music from some of the best big bands of their time at that place. It was a glorious place for a very long time.

My cousins, Joe, Elizabeth and Chris Stone, lived on the sound just over from Columbia Street on Harbor Island. Our parents would cook fresh fish, while Chris, Beth (my sister) and I would jump off the pier and swim till dark.

Camile Bridger with uncle, Barry Bridger, in 1947.

Many friends come to mind as I think back on early Wrightsville days: Hugh McManus; Mary Allen; Becky Lilly; Penny Cromartie, Susan Brewer; Lynn Hooks; David Scott; Jimmy Thornton; Bruce Bryant: Jakie Marsh: Chris Stone; Billie Corbett; Laura Fonville: Jimmy Burgess; Terry Turner; John Elmore; Emmitt and Harry Stovall; Jean and Frances Evans; Rusty Clark; and more than I could mention. We all enjoyed Wrightsville as a relatively untouched paradise.

My memories of my grandmother playing bridge in the house with her friends, Mrs. Longley, "Aunt" Melva Pearsall and Mrs. Lilly are so vivid. And Maggie, her chef, was always in the kitchen whipping up a great lunch for them.

I have to expand on Maggie Hall, who lived with and worked for my grandparents. She was a gem of a person, a great cook, and a lover of people. Much of our downstairs was open to the salt air, with white latticework all around. On Saturday nights, Mary Allen and I would sit there with Maggie and

Camile (Mimi) Bridger in 1961 on one of the jetties that used to be on Wrightsville Beach.

Camile (Mimi) Bridger in the early 1950s.

Camile's home on Columbia Street in 1990 which has changed very little since the 1940s.

her friends. They would laugh, tell stories, shell beans, and have that radio on, listening to good music. I loved listening to them; it was a night that Mary and I looked forward to, and will never forget. Maggie always had a flower in her hair.

I live in Virginia Beach, and have since 1982; but all of my family live in or near Wrightsville Beach. My daughter, Elizabeth Hart, lives in Wilmington and my son, Kevin Hart, lives on Wrightsville. Our family continues to enjoy the cottage on Columbia Street. My mother, Sarah, still lives there during the summer, and I visit year 'round as often as I can. I sit downstairs in the open air where Maggie and her friends once did, and it all comes back clearly. Just like yesterday. All of the wonderful memories can never be erased. I continue to love to swim in the saltiest, cleanest water on the east coast—Wrightsville Beach.

The Proof's in the Pantyhose
by
Lew Kurtzman of Wilmington

This story centers, of all things, around airports, a far cry from most other tales in this book. Yet it has a definite place here, because it succinctly reminds many of us of the simplicity of the good old days. Lew Kurtzman was born, in 1943, in Quincy, Massachusetts and also grew up there. We're glad that he made Wilmington the location of his final luggage carousel.

As a Wilmington transplant from Boston, Massachusetts, I have fond memories of my first few visits to Wilmington in the early 1980s. At the time, the purpose of my trips to Wilmington was to consult for and train a start-up pharmaceutical services company.

My normal travel itinerary was to locations like Tokyo, Bombay, Sydney and cities throughout Europe. As I recall, I figured that travel to Wilmington would be simple. Little did I know that flying from Logan Airport to Wilmington's Blumenthal Field would be an adventure to remember.

Piedmont Airlines was the carrier that serviced Wilmington from Boston. Of course there were no direct flights (and still aren't) so my change of planes was in Norfolk, Virginia. Then there was a stop in Kinston, North Carolina, followed by another stop in Jacksonville. The flight from Jacksonville to Wilmington couldn't have taken more than fifteen minutes, but it seemed to be much longer. The entire trip took about eight hours.

On my first visit, upon arriving at the old terminal, I was told that my luggage would be unloaded and brought to the baggage pick-up area. Looking around for a conveyer belt, I realized that there was none, and that I had to retrieve my suitcase outside the terminal building in a fenced-in pick-up zone. There was a slight drizzle, so people stayed under cover until they saw their respective luggage.

Through the confusion of sifting through the baggage, I finally spotted mine. Well, at least I thought it was mine.

When I got to my hotel, a Holiday Inn on Market Street, I opened the black and tan luggage case, only to find clothing that was totally unfamiliar to me. The nylon pantyhose were a giveaway that the bag belonged to a woman who probably took possession of my bag by mistake in the chaos of the luggage retrieval area. Checking the nametag, I found that the case, indeed, belonged to a woman from Detroit.

I contacted the airport and was informed that my bag was returned and a taxi would be sent to my hotel to drop it off and retrieve the lady's bag.

In 1991 I returned to Wilmington and to my delight, there was a single plane change in Charlotte, and a quick US Air jet flight to Wilmington International Airport. Best of all there was a new terminal building; this time with an indoor luggage area with a real luggage conveyer. (Today there are two luggage retrieval conveyers to handle the ever increasing passenger traffic at ILM.) Wilmington had come of age and was blossoming into a charming yet modern small city.

A few months later, I returned to Wilmington once again. This time to stay!

Grandma's Kitchen
by
Helen Higley of Wilmington

Helen Higley, born in Johnston County in 1943, writes of visits to her grandparents' home. You'll encounter twinkling Christmas lights, an aromatic cellar and a frightening upstairs bear. But most of all, you'll find a kitchen, magical to a little girl.

I was a young girl in the late forties. I had both my grandparents, Grandpa and Grandma Medlin, then and relish the fond memories of them during this time in my life. Our family didn't own a car, so we relied on an uncle or the train taking us to Grandma's house from Selma to Garner, North Carolina.

Grandma's house was an old two-story farmhouse with a cellar. Pull chains for light, period furniture, old wall pictures and a menagerie of interesting dust collectors. Rugs were carefully placed on the wood floors and beaten outside to clean them.

Grandma was a kindly, gentle soul. She was my pick of anyone's grandma. Seems she almost always wore an apron, but my guess would be she was in the kitchen a lot.

There existed a dank, dark cellar that had strange odors like tobacco, but for some reason I found this damp smell likeable. The porch had nearly a wraparound look with rocking chairs being the source of seats. My Gran loved to rock. And babies were being born, so I know she put those old rockers inside and outside to be used to their fullest potential.

The area leading upstairs was narrow and steep. Only a pulled drawstring curtain separated the big "bear" and me. In an effort to keep me from climbing those stairs, I was told a big bear stayed up there. Still, I dared to sneak to the top. When I caroused around the room looking and checking all the neat array of "stuff" in the rooms, I saw a sight which scared the living daylights out of me. I saw the big "bear" and had to be rescued. Some

Helen Higley with Grandma Medlin in the center.

time years later, I learned the bear was my Aunt Neen's fur coat. What a blast every time I think about it.

But Grandma had a favorite place, at least for me. Grandma's kitchen was a glorious mixture of a big eating table, old pots and pans, a pie safe filled with assorted dish patterns, glasses, cups and bowls. To this day, I have a few choice pieces of her Blue Ridge.

Then there was the stove. Cut wood was its source of getting the stove hot enough to use, and the cute little warming bins held biscuits, pies and all the delicious things Grandma and "I" made. I can still smell ham in the old frying pan, teaming with scents of eggs and golden brown biscuits. Large, puffy biscuits were a treat for me. Grandma made her own butter and it was my privilege to "assist" her in making the butter, kneading the biscuit dough and intertwine the two for a pleasant surprise.

I thought her specialty was making cakes and frostings from scratch. Of course, I didn't know what scratch was at six, but Grandma reached for and placed her big blue bowl on the eating table. Gently laying all the ingredients aside, she put a pinch of this and that and I got my special wooden spoon. I was really waiting to lick the bowl clean, which I did. She carefully stirred it to the right pitch, poured the batter in cake pans and baked it in the oven. One could smell the awesome odor of baking cake layers mixed with the burning crackling scent of wood.

She began the ardent task to make perfect fudge icing. I watched it boiling on the front burner. As hot as it was, I knew I would be the one to lick yummy dark chocolate with my wooden spoon.

The cake layers were perfected, removed and laid to cool. Not long then, I watched her ice the cake; salivating the delicious drippings of chocolate spill over. Needless to say, we enjoyed her desserts with meals.

Speaking of meals, Gran canned and froze veggies fresh from their garden. Oh! Peas, butterbeans, corn, okra and homegrown tomatoes complimented the table before the wonderful dessert.

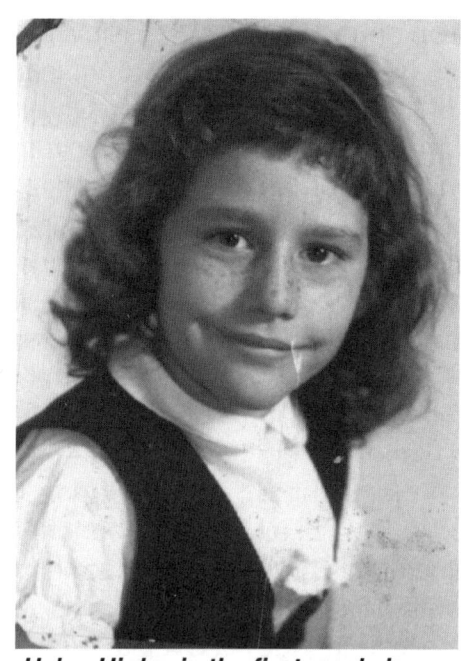
Helen Higley in the first grade in 1949.

And Christmas: from Grandma's kitchen drifted smells of ham nestled in those huge buttered biscuits, cakes, pies, fudge and all the delicious food that delighted the senses. At Grandma's house all visits and occasions seemed to be special. But the crisp air at Christmas time, a big cedar tree showing off real old-time bubbling lights and holding decorations of years gone by was a main event.

Years ago, I moved to Wilmington. I love this city. I've created many sweet and delightful memories. Loving to decorate in and around our home at Christmas, I think often of days gone by. I remember the hand-me-down desserts and a plentiful table. I feel thankful and blessed. But no matter where I am or what I may be involved in, I stop in the eve of a cold night and watch twinkling lights on frosted panes. I can see that little girl, standing on a kitchen chair, underneath Grandma's smile. I see her helping her stir batter for cakes in the big blue bowl. All this time, I see me holding my wooden spoon in gleeful anticipation.

Grandma is gone now. I miss her gentleness, kindness and love. There will always remain sweet innocent memories for me when having downtime with my Grandma in her beloved kitchen. She lived to a ripe age, but her wisdom and loving legacies have, and will, endure in my heart forever.

The Little Sister's Rare Name
by
Becky Rivenbark Gregory of Rocky Point

We believe the guilty cousin's name in this tale is Sandra (shame on you, Sandra!). But guilt aside, Becky Gregory, who was born in Wilmington in 1942, tells a very entertaining story as proof of that universal truth: you just can't pull anything over on Mama.

In the summer of 1958, I was a rising junior at New Hanover High School. My family lived on Market Street and I was fortunate enough to land a job at Morton's Service Drugstore. In the afternoon after school, lots of students from NHHS would hang out in the drugstore, where we had a soda fountain, booths and dip ice cream.

I have a first cousin who grew up in Rocky Point, and who would come and spend some days with me. One of the guys who worked in the drugstore became sweet on my cousin, and oddly enough, he had a convertible. He asked us to go to the Miljo drive-in one night and I knew my mother wouldn't hear to that. So, after a lot of thinking, we came up with a plan. We said we were going to walk to the Manor Theater to watch a movie. However, we had to take my sister, Mary Clark Rivenbark, who is two years younger.

We met Manford Taylor [*probably the young man sweet on the cousin. Ed.*] at the drugstore and off we went.

Back then, at night, Bill Weathers had a radio show from the Miljo, taking requests for your favorite song. Being so stupid as we were, we had Bill play a song for Sandra, Becky and Mary Clark.

Everything seemed to be going well...until we got home that night and Mama quizzed us about the movie. "Oh, it was wonderful," we said.

Mama, however, didn't share our enthusiasm. Seems she had been ironing, listening to the radio and heard our names announced. She said the name Mary Clark gave us away since the name "Mary Clark" is rare.

We lived through it, but learned to leave Mary Clark home after that.

Notes to the Milkman
by
Emily B. Barber of Wilmington

Emily Barber writes very interestingly about all the sales and delivery folks who used to show up at our doors back in the good old days. But that's only for starters. In her story you'll also find frozen clothes, green cake and penny candy, among many

Making pine baskets at the John C. Campbell Folk School in 2000.

other anecdotes. Mrs. Barber was born in 1922 and grew up in New Jersey.

Thank you for the opportunity to tell you about some of the many things I remember in my lifetime. I am an 85 year old lady and still enjoy life. I was married to a wonderful man for over 51 years. I have been a widow for 14 years. I am very active, have many wonderful friends, and enjoy fairly good health.

I do certainly remember the iceman. We had a card to place in the window when we wanted him to stop, and it had numbers on it as to the size piece wanted. That way, the man would not have to make two trips to the back door.

Many things were delivered to the house when I was growing up. The milkman came every day except Sunday and if you wanted more than the usual delivery, or less, you would place a note In the empty bottle. One lady that I knew was in the habit of using both sides of paper, being very thrifty, but the side the milkman got, said. "I am next door, come on over." The milkman wrote back, "I came over but nobody was home."

The bread man and the dry cleaners would come to the door, and a sign was placed in the window for them too. Door to door salesman were popular: Fuller Brush, American Tea Company, insurance men would collect on policies weekly.

Of course, in those days many of the women stayed at home. Also, few women drove cars or smoked cigarettes.

I well remember wringer washers, and set tubs in the basement, also hanging clothes on the line in the yard. In the wintertime the clothes would freeze, and many times would need to be re-hung in the basement.

Earl Barber in Hawaii in 1944.

Since I lived in the north then, most everyone had a basement. We kids would play in the basement, when we could not go outside, and roller skate down there. One time we were going to have a Halloween party in our basement, and we kids waxed fall maple leaves and strung them on string, to decorate. My father took the Christmas lights with the leaves and hung them to the rafters. It sure was pretty. However, we waxed the leaves in another girl's kitchen, heated the wax on the stove, while her mother was not home. I can't imagine how dangerous that must have been. Fortunately it all turned out well.

My brother had the same birthday as me. He was two years younger and he is now deceased. Since the day is March 15, remember many a cake with green icing and green candles. My mother always made the cake, no cake mixes or electric mixers. I also have a sister, she is 89.

I lived in Trenton New Jersey, the capital of New Jersey, and we had wonderful places to visit in the capital area. There was a great museum, and at Christmas time we would go and see the Christmas tree at the Capital building. We had trolley cars in the city, and a ticket you could purchase on Sunday, that was good for a whole week on any trolley. My girlfriend and I would many times go for a ride on the trolley, and go to the end of the line. The trolley would not turn around, but the conductor would just go to the other end of the trolley to drive it. He would also turn all the seats in the other direction, as the backs were loose.

We had a confectionery store in our neighborhood, called Charlie's, and Charlie must have had a lot of patience, as we kids would go to the store with just a couple of pennies, and stand in front of the counter trying to decide what we wanted to purchase. I remember you could get six spearmint leaves or seven licorice babies for a penny. Charlie would place them in a little bag for us. I would also go there to purchase a White Owl cigar for my father, cost five cents. My father would say, "Go get me a stogie."

Many a hand-me-down I had, from my sister and also from cousins, but I was happy to get them, and my mother would make them fit me. Women used to mend clothing, and especially socks. I still have a wooden darner that I used to put in the sock over the hole, making it easier to sew.

The mailman would deliver the mail right to the house in a box on the outside or a slot In the door, dropping the mail right into the house. We had delivery twice a day, and at Christmas time and on Sunday too. My husband was in the Navy during World War II and I would not hear from him weeks at a time. When mail finally came, the mailman would ring the doorbell, as there would be a number of letters for me.

I well remember flypaper, especially in grocery stores. It sure was nasty looking. Most stores would just have the doors standing open in nice weather, no air conditioning in those days. Many places would have fans; ceiling fans were in many buildings, but not in homes.

We would listen to stories on the radio. I remember a program called "First Nighter." They would announce, "The people are rushing down the aisle to their seats, a hush comes over the audience, Act One." You would almost feel that you were there. At the intermission, they would say, "Smoking in the outer lobby only, please," and would repeat it several times.

Elsie, Robert, Mother, Grandma Bullosh and Emily at Ocean Grove, NJ, in 1926.

Another program my brother listened to was "Buck Rogers." The minister was coming to dinner, and my mother told my brother he could not listen to Buck Rogers that night. The minister asked my brother if he ever listened to it, and of course he said yes. I guess the minister listened to it too. Perhaps it was turned on, I do not remember.

I do remember the party line telephone. We usually had a two party line in New Jersey. But in 1963 we moved to Ohio, and had a ten party line. It was terrible. People would listen in when you were talking, and you would know that was happening. Also, every time another party picked up the phone, it would make a click and some of them would keep picking it up to see if you were still talking.

Emily Barber, age seven months.

At Christmas time we would hang our own socks on the mantle. We usually did not get very much in them, always an orange or apple, and perhaps a piece of candy. Many times the toys you would get were not new, but that was fine, it was new to us.

I had a play table given to me, from a cousin, and she did not even know I had it.

Barber family around 1915.

Many years later I told her I still had it, and arranged to give it back to her. It was oak, with drop leaves, perhaps someone had made it. It looked homemade. She was so pleased to get it for her grandchildren, and gave me some of her mother's fine china.

The Days of Pinecone Ball
by
John B. Rehder of Knoxville, Tennessee

John Rehder was born in Wilmington in 1942 and grew up there. He shares some especially appealing memories of a carefree boyhood, including snow cones, the skeeter fogger, leeches and snakes. And we'd like to imagine that Dr. Rehder's chosen profession might have arisen from his days of exploring the shoreline of Greenfield Lake.

For the first fourteen years of my life, I lived in several places in and around Wilmington. We first lived in Lake Forest in the cinderblock duplexes, then moved to Riverside into the brick apartments there. Then to Carolina Beach on Harper Avenue, and finally (for me between the ages of seven in 1949 to fourteen in 1956) to Lake Village in a small wooden single unit at 68 West Drive on a finger of Greenfield Lake.

Lake Village was one of the "Projects" for government-subsidized housing. We were poor but didn't know it. My dad was a flying instructor who earned $100 a month. Rent was $25 a month.

After my parents divorced when I was eleven, my mom worked in a garment factory. Clothes and most toys were hand-me-downs from my older cousin. However, my grandfather, "Grampy" (Mom's dad), and great grandfather "Pop" made me wooden toys in their woodworking/rod-and-reel shop at Carolina Beach.

The adult males in Lake Village were mostly blue collar workers: city bus drivers, gasoline tanker drivers, Coca-Cola® delivery truck drivers, telephone and utility linemen, gas station attendants, and my dad—the flying instructor who later became a pilot for Piedmont Airlines.

In the summer, kids played outside from dawn to past dusk, only coming home to eat. All summer long, we went barefoot and often tangled with sandspurs that seemed to grow everywhere. We often played in the street on white sand-covered black asphalt; playing pinecone ball—a form or stickball baseball—with a pinecone ball and a broomstick bat. We skated on rough metal skates and rode old bicycles in the street. At night we played hide and seek using the telephone pole with a streetlight for home base.

There was a crippled man on a three-wheeled motorcycle who came to the neighborhood to sell us snow cones. I can just taste them now; my favorite flavors were pineapple, grape, and cherry.

Another summertime activity was to run behind the mosquito fogger truck as it sprayed an oily cloud of surely dangerous "skeeter killer stuff" in the air around dusk. The skeeter truck and my wading in Greenfield Lake worried my mom the most.

Greenfield Lake was the best place for a kid my age to grow up around. There were interesting critters like alligator gar fish and huge turtles—some of them dangerous snapping turtles. I never saw an alligator or any poisonous snakes around the lake, but there surely had to be some there. The good Lord was watching over us because I never heard of any child being bitten by a poisonous snake. Southeastern North Carolina was notorious for rattlesnakes, copperheads, cottonmouth water moccasins, and coral snakes but we didn't encounter them directly at Greenfield Lake.

The cola colored water enticed me to wade in it all year long. Leeches attached themselves to our legs. We tested our courage by tentatively stepping into small quicksand places on the creeks that fed into the lake. The lakeshore had great trees to climb via wisteria vines. Spanish moss, gum tree leaves, and pine needles could be used for camouflage when we played "Army." Poison ivy, poison oak, and the worst one yet—poison sumac—became natural environmental enemies.

Lake Village had no organized sports, no Boy Scout troops, no Boys and Girls Club. A kid at age eleven to fourteen could ride a bike anywhere and everywhere; my friends Wilbur, Mac, Billy, Skippy, Gene, and twins Ray and Jay, and I did this often. So for a few months, some of us joined a Boy Scout troop located near 17th and Market Street. At night, we rode our bikes the long distance from Greenfield Lake to the Scout hut through rough neighborhoods where other kids threw dirt clods and sticks at us as we ran the gauntlet to Scouts. We quit Scouts because we realized that the journey there was just too doggone dangerous.

During the summer, we sometimes thumbed rides (hitchhiked) to Wrightsville Beach. I shudder to think about anyone trying these crazy stunts now.

We attended school at Lake Forest School for grades one through nine. The principal was Mrs. Manley Williams. Occasionally, Mrs. Williams would call on the intercom for me to come to the office; my classmates sometimes wondered if I was in trouble. She would call me in to say that my grandparents (Dad's folks) had invited me to come eat lunch with them. I would walk the four blocks to their house, have a prayer, eat lunch, and listen to Paul Harvey's news program on the radio. I can't believe it but Paul Harvey is still broadcasting now in 2007 over fifty years later! I would return to school with a rose that my grandparents cut for Mrs. Williams, thanking her for allowing their grandson to visit them at lunchtime.

Lake Forest School was especially constructive for my musical upbringing. I began drumming in the sixth grade band, then moved up to the junior high band where we had real honest-to-goodness red and white uniforms. Mr. "Red" Dobson was the band director and a terrific one at that. He worked us hard in the junior high band and we made trips to band contests across the state. I recall that our little Lake Forest Junior High School Band won a major band contest in Greensboro in about 1954 or 1955. We always marched smartly in the Azalea Festival Parades. Even the sixth grade band marched, but it once took two kids to carry the bass drum: one in back to play it and one strapped to the front to help carry it.

In 1956, I moved away from New Hanover County for good. I did my high school years in Winston-Salem, my undergraduate college degree at East Carolina, and Masters and PhD Degrees at Louisiana State University. For the past four decades, I've been a geography professor at the University of Tennessee in Knoxville, Tennessee.

Such memories and so many more are what life in New Hanover County was about.

Victrola Waltzing
by
Thelma Taylor McGuire of Wilmington

Thelma McGuire, who was born in 1924, weaves an enchantingly nostalgic tale about what it was like to be young during the pre-World War II years. You'll find anecdotes about grapevine smoking, snuff dipping grandmas and nickel hotdogs. You'll read about innocent romance and a first kiss. And we hope you'll feel the patriotism with which Mrs. McGuire ends her recollections.

I was born in Roanoke Rapids, N.C. in Halifax County. It was mainly a textile and paper mill town. There were very few wealthy people there, but a wonderful hospital, fire department and an ever vigilant police department. Only the two main streets had electricity or running water. We had a pump in the backyard, and that was good clear pure tasting water. We had a dipper in the water bucket, and we all drank from that mostly. (We had no paper cups that I can recall.)

We finally got running water on our streets in 1932 and electricity the next year. Before then, in the summertime, my mother would put a washtub filled with water out in the sun and me and my little brother and sister would enjoy pretending we were in swimming, as well as washing ourselves.

It was so great to have a bathtub and toilet inside and to be able to see by the electric light instead of a kerosene lamp. Of course we got a radio then, and I loved to listen to Amos and Andy, Little Orphan Annie, the Grand Ol Opry, and Major Bowes Amateur Hour. That's where I heard Kate Smith sing "God Bless America" for the first time. Some songs never die and that is one that has lived on. I still love to hear it, or sing it myself.

I was one of four children—an older brother and a younger sister and brother. We played all kinds of games like jump rope, Tisket Tasket, marbles and cowboys and cowgirls with a stick for a horse. I loved to go swimming and I liked to play ball, too. One of the wealthy mill owners installed a swimming pool for us and we went every day. I learned to swim and to dive a little. We called it the "Frog Pond" because only part of the bottom of it was cemented in, and little frogs would get in sometimes.

My father and mother, Mattie Pierce and Howard Taylor, were very musically gifted. They both sang and danced and she could play the ukulele. My daddy would stand me on his shoes and we would waltz and two-step to a record player called the Victrola. Then my little sister would have her turn learn-

Thelma McGuire with her two children, Rebecca and Danny, in 1946.

ing to dance. Sometimes we would sit on the front porch in the late evening and sing as the ukulele played songs like "Shanty Town," and "When the Moon Comes Over the Mountain," and I especially liked "Five Foot Two."

We had a wonderful high school, also backed by the same wealthy mill owner. It was rated the best in the state, and the teachers were tops in their field. We had to be attentive and there was nothing like drugs or smoking or chewing gum in class…or anywhere else. Our female teachers were required to be single, or resign if they did marry. (Some archaic notion that they might get pregnant.) We didn't ever use the word "pregnant," but instead, we said "expecting" or "PG." So proper we had to be. Our parents would only whisper about an expectant mother.

My sister, Shirley, cousin, Sylvia, and I took tap dancing lessons for 25 cents from a lady who moved in from Richmond, Virginia. I borrowed a pair of tap shoes that were too small, and finally we ordered a pair of shoes C.O.D. from Sears and Roebuck for $2.98. I was an excited little girl when I went to the post office to get them. I skipped all the way home.

We used to put on shows in the backyard or the neighbors' garage. We sang and danced and pretended we were big stars, like Shirley Temple. We always wanted to be in the movies, didn't you?

Once, on Easter Monday, my favorite friend, Helen, and I decided to have a picnic in the woods nearby. We built a fire on a big piece of tin so as not to burn the leaves nearby. Paying no mind that the wind was brisk that day, that fire blew right off that tin and immediately set the leaves on fire. No matter how hard we stamped we were no match for that fire. Nearby was a house and Mr. Gray's cow, too. We were scared out of our minds, but soon Mr. Gray and other adults in the vicinity came running and they yelled at us, "You younguns get home!" You bet we did, with our hearts pounding out of our chests. We never told our parents, who were at work, and we left the wieners and chocolate rabbits there, too.

Thelma, her father, Thomas Taylor, and her two grandchildren, Michael and Gina Hardee, in 1966.

Once or twice we practiced smoking. We had heard that dried grapevines were good, and dried corn silks rolled up in paper, as well as rabbit tobacco. Anyway, we tried them all. When I tried the corn silks, the paper blazed up and nearly burnt my mouth, so that was the end of that. I don't even smoke now...

Another great adventure was when Evelyn, my older cousin, and I would go down to a nearby canal and walk across the train trestle—scary! Then we'd climb through a barbed wire fence into a pasture to pick great, big blackberries so our mothers could make a cobbler. The only catch was that there were bulls in that pasture. We had to pick the berries fast and keep one eye on those bulls. Then on down to the riverbank to pick long-stemmed violets to take to our favorite teacher.

We always went barefoot in the summer and it was a set rule that we had to wait until May First. When we did wear shoes and the soles wore out, my mother would send us down the street to Mr. Tanner's house. He would trace my shoes on a new piece of leather and then cut it out and put my shoes on a last and tack on the new soles. He charged 25 cents. I would feel like I had a new pair of shoes on as I wore them back home. Remember when your shoe sole would come loose and would flap? My brother-in-law said his grandfather would take a fine piece of wire and wire them back together.

We only had one pair of shoes at a time, and a special dress or pants for Sunday.

My mother was an excellent seamstress. She made all our dresses and petticoats and nightgowns, and some of my brother's shirts. She didn't even need patterns. She made my first evening gown for a birthday party. It was lavender organdy and was as pretty as any of the store-bought ones that some wore. I still have one of her dresses that she designed. It is pale green dotted Swiss.

We liked to see the iceman coming on his wagon. We would run out to the street and sometimes he would chip off a small piece of the ice and give it to us. What a treat! A small block of ice was a nickel and a large piece was a dime. Once I had to go to the iceman's home for ice and he tied a string tightly around it and I carried it home, dripping all the way. It was so heavy for my little skinny arms.

Our doors to our homes were never locked. While my parents worked, we played all over the neighborhood. We had a nice maid named Callie and she was paid $3.00 a week, the same as we paid to rent the house. Later, we moved to a bigger house and the rent was $4.25. Altogether, my parents earned about $25.00 a week. They would never dream the prices of rent or food today.

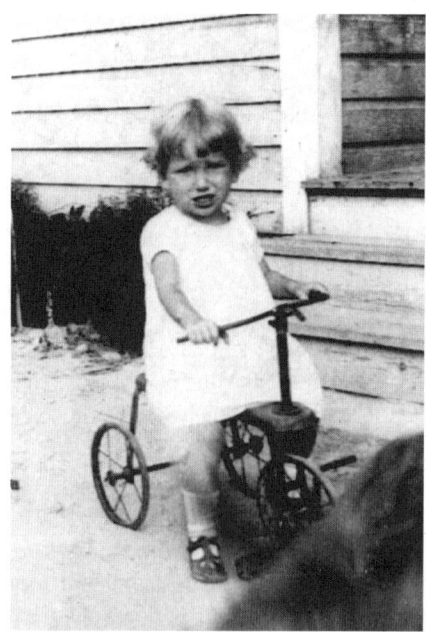

Thelma Taylor at age three in 1927.

At Christmas time, my brother and my father would go out and cut a pretty little pine tree, and my mother would decorate it with red garlands and ornaments—no lights then. We were delirious on Christmas Eve for Santa to come. We always got a baby doll, maybe some new socks, and a nice bag of candy, nuts, and fruit. My brothers got cowboy suits or an air rifle for the older one. We were happy, and thankful.

Almost everyone had a vegetable garden and maybe a few chickens, and a lot of the vegetables and fruits were canned and preserved. I liked the pickled peaches best. We always had biscuits or cornbread and a loaf of store bread was a treat. At first, it was even un-sliced.

A man named Mr. Riggan used to come by and sell fresh buttermilk and butter for 15 cents. One day he asked me if I was "courting." It embarrassed me to pieces. Most of us teenage girls didn't really date boys, but we had sweethearts, or boys that we liked. We usually just saw them at the movies, or the skating rink, or we would ride our bicycles together.

I didn't get a bike until I was thirteen and shared it with my sister. Nowadays, the kids are all ready to take driving lessons.

The first time I drove a car, I almost ran into the front porch before I could get the brakes on. I was grown before I drove again—didn't have a car, anyway.

When people died, their caskets were brought to the homes and people visited there. My grandmother, Josie Pierce, came to live with us when my mother unexpectedly died. It was just the way people were. She made no complaints, just took us over like a mother.

She was so cute. She wore a starched apron over her dress every day, and she also wore a laced-up corset every day, and black laced-up shoes with cotton stockings. In her apron pocket was a little silver snuffbox with a little dipping brush made from a stem off a sweetgum tree. Yes, so many people dipped snuff back then.

Thelma's grandmother, Josie Pierce, holding Thelma's first born, Rebecca McGuire, in 1943.

I don't know what would have become of us if we hadn't had a special grandmother like her to encourage, support and discipline us, too. She was a saint, and we loved and respected her.

We always walked to school. Only the kids who lived over a mile away rode the buses, but we loved walking together and laughing and talking, even in the rain or snow.

When I was fifteen, some of my classmates "voted" to have a party at my home. It was so exciting. My mother made simple refreshments and punch. We played the radio and then some games. Then someone said, "Let's play spin the bottle." So that was my first experience of being kissed by boys. They were shy, too, but it was so exciting. Do kids ever play post office or spin the bottle now? I doubt it—too juvenile, I guess.

I borrowed an evening gown for my senior prom. It was pink, and I and five or six other neighborhood girls rode the city bus to the school. Hardly anyone came with a date back then, but we finally danced with them and even with each other. Most of the boys had two left feet, so to speak, but it was fun anyway, even when they stepped on our toes. Just thrilled to be there, dancing, and having an innocent time.

We didn't know what TV dinners were and had no really fancy restaurants, maybe one or two, but we loved the little cafes that sold delicious hotdogs for five cents and a big Pepsi Cola for five cents. The boys called the Pepsi a "gut buster." We used to save the bottles and return them for two cents deposit. When we got ten cents we would go to the Saturday western movies to see Buck Jones, Roy Rogers, Gene Autry or Bob Steele. We were lucky to have an extra nickel for a bag of popcorn. And of course we never missed a Shirley Temple movie.

When World War II began, good food was hard to find. The best of it went to the armed forces. We went everywhere trying to get washing powder, canned milk, etc. Automobile tires were not to be found and even film for picture taking. We had ration books with coupons in them for meat buying, etc. You had to stand in line to get them.

The Taylor Family just after moving to Carolina Beach in 1942: Howard, Shirley, Thelma, Edward and Thomas.

Thelma's mother, Mattie Pierce Taylor, with Thelma and her oldest brother, Edward, in 1928.

I had just moved to Carolina Beach when I was seventeen. I missed my friends from back home, but they soon caught the bus to see us and they were as thrilled as could be to be on the beach swimming and suntanning and meeting cute boys. There were hundreds of boys because the shipyard was hiring so many and also Camp Davis was full of young soldiers. We danced our feet off on the boardwalk. That was wonderful music, too: Glenn Miller, Tommy Dorsey and Artie Shaw, etc. We learned to jitterbug and do the "Big Apple." Oh boy!

I will never forget my first permanent wave. The beautician rolled it up and put clamps with wires on the rollers. Sitting under that wire-up hood, I looked like I was being electrocuted. I thought my hair would never get long again. I still hate to get permanents.

In the letters I received from classmates back home, I found that most of the boys I knew had gone into the service. World War II had started the year before. Some of those boys never came back, and now when I go to class reunions, the ones who are left have some very sad memories. I still see them as the wonderful, young, innocent boys that I knew—and so brave. I could cry. And now our young men and women are leaving again.

God Bless America, our wonderful homeland.

Again Next Summer
by
Mary Mitscher of Rocky Mount, Virginia

Mary Mitscher was born in Brazil, Indiana in 1919. Her story interestingly relates a child's viewpoint of summer...and the summers to follow.

My name is Mary Irene Ervin Mitscher. I want to tell you about some of the good ole days I remember when I was a child.

I was born in Brazil, Indiana, the fifth child in a family of six children. My father, Joseph Clifford Ervin, worked in a clay factory as a fireman of a kiln that made sewer pipe. We lived in what they called a company house that was owned by the plant my father worked for. We moved into town when I was two years old where the sixth of the children was born, a little baby sister. We named her Anna Marie.

I lived in Brazil all my life until I married Carl F. Mitscher on November 28, 1934 at the age of fifteen and a half. We had a baby girl in 1936 and gave her the name of Carmen Joan.

As children, we didn't have much money, like a lot of people at that time, but we had a lot of fun and lots of love. Our house was the gathering place of the neighborhood children. They all liked to come to our house. We used to like to make Taffy. We had lots of fun trying to see how fast we could pull it and how thin we could pull it.

Then we sometimes made donuts for a church youth group to sell to help our church budget. Boy, did our kitchen smell good! We did these things with the help of my mother who had as much fun as we did.

We also made popcorn balls just for the fun of it. You would have to work fast or burn your hands on the hot syrup. We used oleo to keep from burning our hands. These are some of the things we did for fun.

Then it was summertime. My dad would take all the kids who were old enough to walk a fair distance and carry a pail or bucket down a railroad track and pick blackberries. We went early in the morning when it was cool and filled our containers before it got too hot. We ate about as many as we put in our containers. Boy, they were juicy and sweet! Our hands and mouths were purple by the time we started back home. Those containers got pretty heavy to carry home, but we all knew the blackberry cobbler Mom would make for supper was going to taste real good.

Of course the berries weren't all we brought home with us. Even the kerosene rags we tied around our pant legs and sleeves were never enough to keep the chiggers away, and if you ever had chiggers I'm sure you know what I'm talking about. Even after we all had a salt water bath, we didn't get much sleep that night because they let us know they had found a nice place to get a good meal at our expense. Ouch itch oh. But we were always ready to do it again next summer. I guess you forget what comes home with you.

Then we also could go out after supper, after we got the dishes washed and the dishes, pots and pans put away. We could go down on the corner under the street light with all the kids in the neighborhood and play Simon Says, kick the can, hide and seek, jump the rope. We thought we had the world by the tail. Didn't take much for us to think we had it all.

In daytime when we had our chores done, we went to the schoolyard and played a game of ball. That ball would make more hits on our bodies than home runs. We thought that went with the game and laughed it off.

My dad had a Model A Ford and Dad and Mom would load that Ford with a large tent and food and go down on Eel River and pitch the tent. Then Dad would dig a hole for our cook stove. We had a big flat sheet of iron to put over the hole to cook on. We kids had to look all around to find wood to build a fire and to keep wood up so we always had a woodpile. Next was the most important thing of all: find a place for our toilet. Dad would look for two trees close enough so he could nail a board between them, the comfort of home.

Then he dug a hole for the icebox where we kept milk, butter, bread. We knew there was an ice truck and bread truck and milk truck that came by. We bought eggs from the farmers who lived around there. There was a big field of corn between us and the road and the farmer told us we could get some to eat, so we had corn on the cob, too.

We stayed on the river for two weeks at time. My dad put out trot lines in the river and ran them three times a day, morning noon and midnight. We caught all kinds of fish and had them for every meal if we wanted to. There isn't any better food to eat than fried taters, navy beans and fish in the outdoors.

Dad always marked the river where us kids could go swimming.

We always thought the two weeks went by too fast, but we always knew we would do it again next summer.

Back home again in our usual roles, school started and we could hardly wait for the first frost. We knew we would drive out on the country road and pick up walnuts.

I told you my dad had a Model A Ford. Dad would take the back seat out and all the kids who wanted to go, which was usually four or five of us, got in back of the Ford and went looking for walnut trees. We usually filled the back area until there was just enough room for us kids to ride on the walnuts to go back home. When we came to much of a hill, we had to get out and help push that Ford full of nuts up the hills but we didn't think of it as work because we all knew those walnuts were going to taste real good in the candy, cakes and cookies during the cold winter. Even the nut meat was so good by itself. You get a brick or a piece of railroad track or anything that's hard enough to crack the nut on, and hit it with a hammer.

There is so much more I could write about, but maybe I better stop. As I said in the beginning, we didn't have much money but we sure had a lot of love.

I spend a lot of my 88 years thinking of the past and wondering if the young people of this time could stand to live in the times that are gone. I have to believe they would pass the test.

Wilmington Saturdays and the Empie House Ghost
by
Bette Suzi Motley of Wilmington

If you remember mid-century Wilmington, you'll immediately recognize the places, events and emotions in this beautiful tale of long ago. But there's also possibly some startling new information concerning a well known Wilmington landmark. Read this story and decide for yourself. You may want to investigate personally.

Porter Alex Robbins home in the 40s or 50s.

Being born (1948) and raised in Wilmington all my life, my fondest memories revolve around this wonderful town. I can't imagine living anywhere else. And as always, childhood memories are the best.

I lived most of my youth in downtown Wilmington. One home we lived in was the old Purnell-Empie House at 319 South Front Street, built in 1851. (Hannah Block purchased and restored the house in 1966.) There were several apartments that rented in this old home and the rent was cheap. (Back in the 1950s, the downtown area served a lot of the lower Income families.)

In the backyard of this house there were several fig trees. Two of the other children who lived in this house along with me became young salesmen. We would pick the figs, box them and take them down to the old Stemmerman's Grocery and sell them. The owners always gave us a little more money than they should have—I know that now. We made a little pocket change, which helped us enjoy our great Saturdays downtown.

We all could hardly wait for Saturday mornings so we could take off and head downtown to the old Manor Theatre. The Manor was located on Market Street between Second and Third Streets. Back then, we never locked our doors and parents did not have to worry about their children being abducted or street gangs when the children were out on their own.

Every Saturday morning was the "Kiddie Show" that started at 9:30. The line would stretch around the building by that time. One of the best parts of this show was you could get in FREE with an empty 25 cent bag of Gordon's potato chips! (We all made sure that our moms had a least one bag in her cart when we went to Joe's Market on Fourth and Nun Street each week.) Saving the admission fee assured us of popcorn and a drink.

We would all receive a numbered ticket that we held onto so tightly. They would draw numbers for the kids to participate in games and contests. I remember the hula-hoop contest. I was so excited when my number was called and ran to the stage. I won! And I had that teddy bear prize clutched to me every night for many years.

After the stage show came the cartoons and the weekly cliffhanger serial. And then we watched the movie of the week. All great clean fun—no ratings back then. Parents didn't have to worry about what their children were watching.

After the show we would all go to the Kress 5 & 10, which was on Front Street between Market and Princess Streets, and go sit on the tall bar stools at the soda fountain. We would all order cherry Cokes and they were the best ever. I can close my eyes and still taste those wonderful drinks.

We all made sure that we were very good the next week so we could come back downtown. My mom would not let me go if I had gotten into trouble. (Of course I was always good.) I would have rather had a spanking than be told I was not being allowed to go downtown the next Saturday.

Oh what great memories I have of living in this wonderful town!

Every time I go by the Old Manor Theatre I feel a tug in my heart. This old building has seen many changes in the last 50 years. There are no more sounds of children's laughter echoing in the theatre any longer. But I remember when it was filled with happy sounds. This was truly one of the best memories I had as a child.

Another happy memory of the good ole days of the 1950s and '60s is of Greenfield Lake. My mom would load up the car on a hot Saturday or Sunday with all the children in the block and take us there. This was going to be a great day for swimming. And, yes, people used to swim in Greenfield Lake before all the pollution, algae and unknown critters of the deep.

The Purnell - Empie House was built in 1851 by Governor Edward Dudley for his daughter, Eliza Purnell. She sold the house in 1857 to Adam Empie who added the north wing. This house, restored by Hannah Block in 1966, was the first preservation in the city.

We would all pile out of the car with our towels and food and head for a spot close to the water. We would see who could get wet first, and spend hours in that lake. We all came out of the lake shriveled.

There was a rope that was used to show that this was as far as you could go out into the lake. You were not allowed to go past that rope. Well, you know kids: dare and double dare! We would go out to the rope and dive under the rope and then come back ASAP. All the while holding on for dear life to that rope. We all thought there was something in the water on the other side of the rope that might "get" us.

I always took a bag of potato chips to feed the ducks. There was a large group of ducks that lived on the lake and they had become so tame they would eat out of your hand. And they were the fattest ducks in the city.

After we were tired of swimming, we would head across the park to the zoo. We never got tired of visiting the animals. It was so much fun.

There was also a little train that ran through the zoo. We would probably ride that train a dozen times in a day. Then we would head back to the lake and start all over again until my mom came to pick us up.

Of course we never wanted to go home. We wanted to swim and play some more. Mom would say that we were tired and needed to go home. Tired? Us? Never! But within a few minutes of leaving the lake, all the kids were sound asleep in the car.

I do love the beach but Greenfield Lake was magical to me.

While I was living in the Purnell-Empie home during the early 1950s, something very strange happened to me one hot August night when I was about six years old. We lived in the far back left side apartment, which was adjacent to the driveway. In front of the bedroom window was my bed. I could sit there and look out the window up and down the driveway.

I was supposed to be asleep this night, but it was very hot and muggy so I sat in front of the window, hoping to a catch some breeze. I was playing with my dolls and my parents were in the living room, which was at the back of the house. It was a very dark night—no moon or stars.

I looked out the window and saw a man walking up the driveway. His shoes made no noise. He looked liked he glowed. A light was shining down on him from above. He had longish blond hair and was wearing a light blue or gray long sleeve coat with front buttons all the way from the neck down. It seemed strange to be wearing a coat on this hot August night.

I said hello but he never turned his head. I called to my dad and said there was a man walking up the driveway. My dad ran out the door but there was no one to be found. It was like the man disappeared.

Alex at Station I in 1949.

Dad searched all over the yard. He even had a flashlight but never saw the mysterious stranger.

My parents said I was dreaming but I knew I had not been asleep. It was very unsettling for me because I knew I had been awake and saw this man. But there was no arguing with my parents.

I can recall every detail like it was yesterday. For many years after I would dream about this stranger who walked up our driveway.

A few years ago my friends and I went on the History-Mystery tour that included the Purnell-Empie house. (We have gone every year since this tour started—they are wonderful.) The tour started to the right of the house with the storyteller telling of stories of the yellow fever epidemic and the history of the home. The last stop was right by my old bedroom window.

The storyteller told of some restoration work that had to be done on this beautiful old home. In 1966, while digging right by my bedroom, they uncovered some very old bones. After a forensic examination, it was determined that the bones were over 100 years old. Also they found a few bits of clothing—gray in color. The examiner believed that these bones were that of a person who died in the 1860s and most likely he was a Civil War soldier.

I was stunned and said that this must be my mysterious visitor. Of course everyone wanted to know what I was talking about. I then became the storyteller. The people in my group were very interested in what I saw.

After a few days I dreamed of my visitor again. This time as he walked up the driveway, he turned and smiled at me. I have not dreamed about him since.

Was this a childhood dream or did I really have an encounter with someone from the past? All I know is that this encounter was, and still is, very, very real to me.

Southern Cooking at the Bus Station
by
Julia Gower of Wilmington

Julia Gower was born in Durham County in 1941, but grew up in Carolina Beach. Hers is the kind of story we like to get for our books, one about a specific location that is no more. In her story, she speaks with nostalgia about the famous Fort Fisher Hermit. Several tales about this elusive individual, including one from a lady who used to cut his hair, can be found in our earlier book about the Wilmington region, Wilmington Tales.

From 1956 until around 1966, my parents owned and operated the Carolina Beach bus station. Most people who came in called them Paul and Mary **[last names not given]**. I will refer to them as Mom and Daddy.

Daddy operated the bus station side, selling bus tickets to and from Wilmington, and running the telegraph station, delivering messages sent to area residents. The telegram had to be delivered in that yellow envelope. I just remember words, and the word "stop" as a period at the end of a sentence.

The north end of this beach flooded very easy, especially if a nor'easter came through.

I would go with my daddy in that small black Austin car, thinking if he flooded out, I could save him and I couldn't even swim well.

On the other side, my mom operated the grill restaurant with good cooks, who served up Southern comfort food and Mom always liked to pile the food high.

During annual Azalea Festivals in Wilmington, many folks would crowd onto Carolina Beach. The boardwalk running along the ocean was a beehive of much activity. An amusement park at the southern end of the boardwalk gave off a carnival atmosphere. Many parents watched the joyful, smiling faces of their children. The Ferris wheel gave one a good view of the ocean. Our local youth came down from Wilmington to have a good time on all of the rides and to play games at booths along the boardwalk going down to the Landmark Grill, which now has been demolished.

At that time, a crowd of people would line up outside the bus station to the aromas of Southern food. I would think and say to some of my friends my mom had hired to help me serve and bus tables, "Maybe some of these people will go across the street to eat." We were tired, but these words were never said to my mom.

The Air Force Station at Fort Fisher was in operation back then and many officers and servicemen came up to the restaurant to eat, speaking well of the food that was served and cooked by a good kitchen staff. I remember the great tips I made in the fall when many fishermen came to fish from the piers on Carolina Beach. Late afternoons, I would sit and do homework, jump up and wait on a table. Most fall business came from a few locals, servicemen, and fishermen.

Marines from Jacksonville crowded the beach to go to the Ocean Plaza Ballroom, which now has been demolished. They would party on the boardwalk and on Sunday mornings, head back to Camp Lejune before their leave was up.

The Ocean Plaza hosted big name bands and many Wilmington adult residents went there to dance the night away with groups such as Chuck Berry and his band singing and performing such oldies but goodies as *Maybellene*, *Roll Over Beethoven* and *My Ding-a-Ling*, which was a very raunchy song for back then.

One Saturday night after performing at the Ocean Plaza, Chuck Berry and band came into the back of the bus station. That is where African-Americans were located back then. There was a large window where they gave me their orders for hamburgers, French fries and drinks. We wanted to go see these bands perform on stage, but yet we wanted them to remain in the back of the bus station. Chuck Berry did travel on his own bus.

The site of the old bus station is now a BB&T Bank. It has a lot of the same shape, but one can't smell the aroma of Southern cooking or see a long line of people standing in line or the Fort Fisher Hermit walking by pushing his cart. Some people will tell you he never left Fort Fisher, but he would walk up to Carolina Beach.

I do hope someone will send in a letter about the Fort Fisher Hermit. It deserves to be in this book. Much has been written about him. Life was active but so different from today on Carolina Beach, North Carolina.

Dry Pond Memories
by
Charles Register, Jr. of Wilmington

Almost universally, youthful memories are the fondest, particularly when those memories arise from an environment like that described below. Charles Register, who was born in New Hanover County in 1927, shares many interesting anecdotes about the early years in Dry Pond.

During early 1930, the health care in Wilmington was nothing like it is today, but I had the greatest baby doctor in town, Dr. Auley Crouch, whose office was in his home on Dock Street, between Fifth and Sixth Streets. In 1932, something lodged in my windpipe and my mother rushed me to his office. Unfortunately, he did not have the facilities to take care of the problem. He immediately called a doctor in Kinston, N.C. and explained the situation, and was told to get me there as soon as possible. Not only did the doc drive us up there in his car, but he stayed during the surgery, paid the bill, and brought us back home. I was told later that this was the first tracheotomy done in the state of North Carolina.

Growing up in Wilmington during the 30s, living in Dry Pond, attending William Hooper School where everyone was your neighbor and friend made for a wonderful childhood. The area was composed of firemen, policemen, building contractors, janitors, and a pharmacist at the corner drugstore; a time and place where no one locked their doors, day or night; and a streetcar which ran from Third Street to Sunset Park, then back to downtown Wilmington.

My father was a fireman on the fireboat which docked at the foot of Grace Street. When the streetcar passed near my house on Third and Mears, I would put my father's dinner on the streetcar (at a pre-determined time) and my father would meet the car at Front and Grace Streets and pick up his dinner. The conductors were always friendly and helpful.

Christmas was always special to us. Our neighborhood was far from being rich, but we were thankful for whatever we got. Every Christmas, the City would close two blocks on Mears Street between Front and Third, for the entire neighborhood to join together and let the kids ride their new bikes, skate, play with their wagons, whatever they had received for Christmas, in complete safety. Those living on these streets who had cars gladly parked on the side streets.

Summers in Dry Pond consisted of visiting the animals in cages across from Greenfield Lake on Third Street. There were live bears, monkeys and other animals. There was also a "spring tap" which furnished quick water for thirsty little boys. This tap also was used by many people for filling up gallon jugs of fresh spring water to be used in their homes. Swimming in the lake was another favorite in the summertime. But it was not always fun. Accidents happen, and one boy, diving from a tree into the water, broke his neck, yet he lived for several years after.

Attending William Hooper School was a blast! For seven years, my friends and I (besides being educated) spent time trying to dodge the principal. You didn't want to end up in her office; she had a paddle, which, unlike today, she was not afraid to use on the palms of your hands. (Now that smarted!) When you got home, you received another paddling most effectively, "elsewhere."

Couple years later, I started delivering groceries for seventy-five cents a week, this being every day after school and on Saturday. Later, I worked at the corner drugstore for $3.00 a week, including Saturdays and Sundays. Whenever the pharmacist needed drugs, he would send me to Bellamy Drugs at Second and Market to pick them up. There was never any question that I would take them anyplace but back to the drugstore. Total trust. Not only was this the place to go for the best milkshakes in town, but for five cents Buttercup ice cream, cherry Cokes, chocolate nut sundaes, and Nehi Orange drinks.

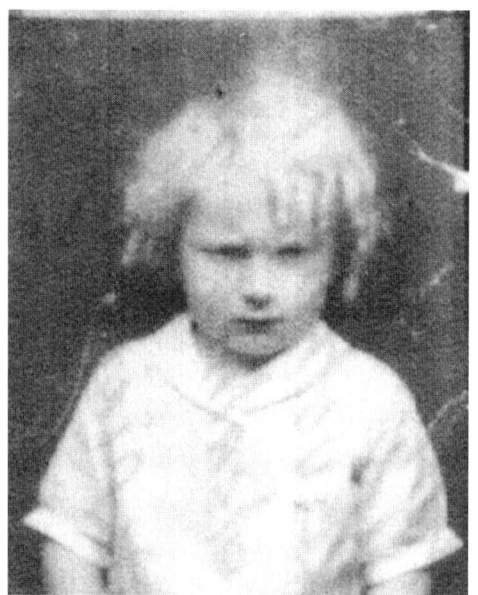

Charles Register, age six.

The pharmacist, Dr. J. Hanson, Sr., also treated local cuts, bruises and even once in a while, broken arms. This pharmacist was indeed a man of many talents. While in business, he patented and produced a medicine called Dr. Hanson's Indigestion Remedy, which was delivered and sold in many of the drugstores in the city.

While working there, I observed the pharmacist treating a man with a very serious sore on his leg which would not heal. After many weeks of going to the drugstore and letting the druggist treat him (with his homemade salve which he applied on the man's leg twice a week), the wound healed. I believe to this day that this man had some form of skin cancer and the druggist had a cure, but he died taking his secret with him.

Neighborhood baseball—another joy of my youth. On Saturdays, around ten or twelve of us boys would get together and go to an open field, really a sand bed, at Seventh and Martin. There, the young blacks in the neighborhood would meet us and we would play ball all morning long. Arguing and fighting was unheard of...it was just good clean fun between a bunch of boys who got along great and loved baseball.

A group of boys around 17 or 18 years of age from the area formed a real ball team. We put our monies together and joined a semi-pro league in town (Cape Fear League) and named ourselves the Greenfield Tigers. We played ball till the league was discontinued several years later.

So much for growing up in Dry Pond.

An Unusual Luxury
by
Julia H. Pridgen of Rocky Point

We think one of the greatest marketing schemes ever was when a livestock feed company packaged its product in colorful cloth bags. This material was of excellent quality, and those who wore clothing created from it were often envied by others who had no livestock. Julia Pridgen, born in 1942 in Rocky Point, remembers those days with pride. She also adds a brief anecdote about the machine that washed her dresses.

My beautiful feed bag dresses is my best memory of growing up.

I remember going to the local country store for anything you needed. We could purchase groceries, hardware, garden supplies, medical needs as well as animal feed packed in beautiful bags. I remember going to the store with Daddy, begging him to buy certain bags because I liked the beautiful material the feed came in.

After emptying the feed in a large barrel, Mama carefully washed the bag, ironed the material, placed the dress pattern on top of the material. Once it was cut out, she sewed it to perfection. She put lace, rickrack or embroidered it. After it was tried on, she starched it heavy, so it stood out. I would come home after a day at school with chapped skin where the starch had eaten me up under my arms.

But I was proud of those beautiful dresses.

I remember the first electric washing machine my mom went and bought. Boy, what a disaster! My brother, C.H., was curious and he turned the wringer on and decided to stick his arm between the wringers. We were so scared when his arm was pulled through we did not think of turning it off. All we could do was holler for Mama to come. She came and turned the wringer in reverse and out came his arm, as good as new.

Nine Cents Change
by
Porter A. Robbins of Wilmington

We always look forward to receiving stories like this one because they entertain us just as much as they will you, our reader. Porter Robbins, who was born in Wilmington in 1932, spins a tale ranging from adventure to introspection. You'll find a pair of noisy goats, very chilly skinny dipping and a not so complimentary discourse on those horrible corduroy knickers with which many of us old-timers were once inflicted. And you'll discover the meaning of nine cents change.

Racing goats. When I was eight years old my grandfather, Porter Hufham, died and part of his estate was the old Hufham home place in Delco, North Carolina. My mother was given the home as part of her inheritance. The family moved to Delco, approximately 30 miles from Wilmington.

When my dad was a boy, his dad built him a small wagon and bought two goats to pull the wagon. Well, Dad thought my brother and I would like a goat just as he had, so he bought two. We had a big chicken yard on the property which was fenced in, naturally, with chicken wire. He placed the goats in the chicken yard after he got them home, and that very night the goats chewed right through the chicken wire as if it wasn't there. The home place had a porch on three sides of the house and these two goats started chasing each other around the porch on a moonlit night. You can't imagine the noise of two goats' hooves clomping on the wooden porch.

Well, mom got up in her nightgown, got a

broom and chased the goats around and around the porch. Dad finally got up and locked them in the garage. Needless to say they disappeared the next day.

We also moved back to Wilmington at 2500 Princess Place Drive because of gas rationing due to the war.

Flypaper. Yes, I can remember as a teenager seeing flypaper hung up in the house, especially at entrances. We had to keep the windows open since we did not have air conditioning. There is very little that will keep out flies and bugs when kids are running in and out of the house all day.

As a kid, I didn't think anything of it. With windows opened and screens getting holes punched in them by us kids playing, the flypaper was a tremendous help in combating flies. We also had a hand held pump sprayer that was used to kill all sorts of flying bugs.

Mentioning the screens reminds me of the screen repair kits that were sold in the hardware stores. They were small patches used to repair little holes in the screens. Air conditioning was a definite improvement.

Knickers: a curse. One thing that I remember as a child was that I really despised wearing knickers. They were pants that came just below the knees with elastic to keep the bottoms of the pants bloused out when the elastic worked. When the elastic band became stretched, the pants would fall down and become very irritating, and I was constantly pulling them up. It was a good day when this fad ended.

Skinny dipping in January. I

Porter's sister, Pat Robbins Voss, their dad, James A. Robbins, Sr. and their 1950 Desoto.

will never forget, when attending grammar school at Chestnut Street School (now Annie Snipes School), some of us boys went across the street (Chestnut Street) one January lunch period to the rock quarry located on Mr. Salmon's property to go swimming. This was initiated on a dare by one of my buddies, Ray Pittman. He, Don Piver, Dick Plott and I pulled off all our clothes and dived in. The water was ice cold, and I don't think anyone ever knew how deep the quarry was. Well, Mr. Salmon heard noise from his store on Princess Place Drive and came over to see what was going on. He saw us in the water naked, took our clothes and told us we could pick them up at his store. He then turned and walked away. This turn of events ended our interest in swimming, so we got out of the water and talked Don Piver into going after our clothes. He wrapped some branches

Porter Robbins' family: Vergia, mother; James A., father; Vinie, grandmother; cousins, and Maurice Robbins, brother.

around himself and ran to Mr. Salmon's store to get our clothes. Fortunately, Mr. Salmon let Don have all our clothes. He did tell Don that the next time this happened he was taking the clothes to our mothers. Needless to say we never went swimming in the rock quarry again.

A case of missing horsemanship. I lived one block from the city limits, which was then Williams Street, but is now 25th Street. Zoning was not overly enforced. I say this because one of my buddies, Ted Blake, had a horse stable and pasture behind his house on Kenwood Avenue. Another buddy, Ray Pittman, had a horse at his home on 23rd Street. Ted had a little pinto horse and an Arabian horse at his home. He allowed me to ride them anytime I wanted to.

Porter Alex and Maurice C. Robbins at the Chestnut Street School in 1953.

One day I took Billy (the pinto) across Princess Place Drive, which was at that time (40s and 50s) fields and woods all the way to Smith Creek. Having had no experience with horses prior to this period of time and knowing very little about them, it didn't keep me from enjoying my rides.

On this day, I was riding Billy across the fields and the bit in his mouth got turned up causing it to have no effect on him and I'm convinced he knew it. He took off running toward home with me pulling on the reins to no avail.

My real concern at the time, since I did not have enough sense to loosen the reins and let the bit drop down where it would have some effect, was that we were approaching Princess Place Drive and Kenwood Avenue at full speed. These streets were paved and I was afraid that once Billy's horseshoes hit the pavement we would go flying in all directions.

Fortunately, this did not happen and Billy turned into the driveway to his pasture. My next concern was that he would try to jump over the fence. Not to worry: he stopped at the gate on a dime and gave me nine cents change as I went flying over the gate myself. Billy knew who was in charge.

Painless chores. On Saturdays I would have to mow the grass or do other outside chores. The mower we had was a push reel mower. Naturally, as a teenage boy I would much rather be doing something else, like playing ball or cowboys and Indians. Since I

Porter's wife, Barbara, at Wrightsville Beach in 1956.

would not dare disobey my parents, I proceeded to place my radio on the front porch and turn up the volume. While mowing the yard or doing other chores, I would listen to North Carolina University and Charlie "Choo Choo" Justice or Notre Dame and Johnny Lujack playing football. Some Saturdays while mowing, I could listen to the Army football team with Doc Blanchard and Glenn Davis romping over their opposition. I played every minute of the game while doing my chores. It sure made time pass faster…and the chores less painful.

More radio. When I arrived home from Chestnut Street Grammar School, I would get a big glass of milk, a big slice of Merita cake, sit down in front of the radio (no TV back then), and listen to programs like Terry And The Pirates, Hop Harrigan, Green Hornet and The Lone Ranger. One of the great things about listening to the radio was that each person visualized in their own minds what was happening. It made one think while listening.

Youthful ingenuity. In my days growing up as a kid, there were no stores such as Toys R Us with every conceivable toy and game available. There might have been one shelf in the five and dime store with toys and games. What I am leading up to is that we had to improvise and make our own toys. I whittled my own pistol out of a piece of wood, made slingshots, peashooters and used a broomstick as a horse when playing cowboys. It was just as much fun and made us kids use our imaginations. I will have to admit that one Christmas, when I received as a present Lone Ranger pistols and holster, along with a black mask and white hat, I felt I was truly in the old West helping stop the bad guys. These were great days and it kept us outside and very active.

Beaches: a great place for young people. Growing up in a coastal community and being so close to Wrightsville and Carolina Beach, it was pretty normal for young people to gravitate toward the sand and surf. I for one was a worshiper of the "sun and fun" at Wrightsville Beach Station 1 location.

Depending on which generation one is talking about determined what area of the beach was frequented. Generally, our 1940s and 1950s group spent our days on the beach at Station 1. Those of us who had fair skin and blond hair would rub our bodies with baby oil and iodine to get a quick tan. We used peroxide and lemon juice to get our hair lightened even more. We would take our portable radios to the beach, spread out our blanket, catch the sun rays and watch the girls go by. Sometimes the guys would play tag football on the strand, trying to impress the girls. It was a great time to be alive.

By the way, my wife Barbara and I continued to spend many hours at Station 1 soaking up the sun. We now sit in lounge chairs, under an umbrella, covered in sun screen and reading a good book.

Wartime Wilmington
by
Forrest L. Walton of Southport

Many of us old-timers remember the war years. Those years in Wilmington were more intense than in many other locations because of the region's importance to the war effort. Forrest Walton, born in 1933, recalls those years intimately. His is a story of blackouts, enemy submarines and the hurricane of 1944, among many other memories.

My family moved to Wilmington in 1942 so my dad could work at the shipyard helping build dry docks. He worked as a carpenter, building the forms for concrete. My parents were Asa James and Maybelle Walton.

Our first home was an apartment in a home owned by Uncle Jack Bradshaw's mother. The home was located on Walnut Street between Second and Third street. There was a service station on the corner next door at the intersection of Walnut and Third Street. My first payphone experience happened there.

The entrance to the house was from the sidewalk by way of a large ornate stairway to the second floor porch which led to a center hallway and back porch. There were apartments on both sides of the hallway and a bathroom located at the right end of the back porch. There was a latticework screen across the back porch and stairs down to the ground level. The front, side and back yards were tiny. Especially for a boy who had just moved from a country village named Maple Hill located near Camp Davis in Pender County. To a third grader, who had just enrolled in Hemingway Elementary School in Wilmington, sidewalks, curbs of granite, stone fences with glass embedded in the top, indoor bathrooms with claw foot tubs and lots of people was a real adventure.

Dad bought me a pair of roller skates that clamped to the soles of your shoes and was further secured by a leather strap across the instep. The skates and my bicycle were the focus of my life.

Also enjoyed, almost every day, was a two block trip down third street to the railroad bridge where I spent many hours watching steam powered trains puff into the station, unload passengers and freight, and turn around in something called a roundhouse. I was told that the white splashes on top of freight cars was a result of bomb practice using small flour sacks. Who knows?

As time passed and I met playmates, swapping comic books featuring Superman, Plasticman, Batman and Robin and many more became a real pastime. Listening to radio programs every day after school was also big.

In the summer of 1942, Dr. Kasaruba removed my tonsils. The procedure was done in his office while I was under ether. No fond memories of that adventure. I do remember I could not eat watermelon and hated the smell of ether which was prevalent at all doctor offices and hospitals.

Other memories of that time include searchlights at night playing along the base of low clouds, blackout shades pulled down at night to keep any light from windows showing, car headlights painted black except for narrow horizontal slits, open highway speed limits of 35, coupon books for most foods, shoes and gasoline, iceboxes, ice delivered to homes, milk deliveries to homes, milk bottle deposits of five cents, war bond stamp books for children (each stamp was ten cents and you could exchange the book when full ($18.75) for a War Bond and soft drink bottles had a two cent deposit.

Several of my favorite pastimes as a nine-year-old was to go to the bus station, a block away at the corner of Second Street and Walnut, to watch soldiers, sailors and visitors come and go. I was free to go most anywhere during this time period and I did. You could ride your bike, catch a bus or thumb a ride with someone lucky enough to have a car.

Another favorite activity was to collect milk bottles for their deposit value, take the money and head for the movies. I would start with the Bijou on Front Street which usually showed double feature westerns and allowed you to sit through as many showings as you wanted. The cost was nine cents to get in, popcorn and sodas (referred to as drinks) were five cents each. It was very noisy since most patrons were children. I would sit on the front row if possible since my vision was not great and I had to look up at the screen. Movies were proceeded by Movietone News, cartoons, previews of coming attractions and sometimes serial shorts like Superman,

Blondie and Dagwood or some daring adventure series that always left you hanging until the next week for the next chapter. The next theater on Front Street was the Royal with a similar billing. The next theater, which was on the left, was known as the Bailey. It was the classiest theater in town and had ushers with flashlights to seat you and a balcony. Sometimes the weekend lines of people waiting to get in would stretch around the corner on Market Street almost to the Manor Theater which was on the corner of Market and Second Street. On the opposite side of Second and Market, diagonally across the street from the Manor, was another theater which never held my interest for some reason. I don't remember the name. When my cousin, Ray Walton, from Long Creek came for a visit we would attend every theater in town.

The Manor did have stage shows on occasion and I remember how disappointed I was after seeing the three stooges in person. The sound effects were lacking when they were on stage. On occasion, one of the cowboy heroes would be downtown on his horse to promote his films. Johnny Mack Brown was one I remembered seeing. They were always wearing a big white Stetson hat.

Things I remember about Front street: the Wilmington Hotel was located on the corner of Front and Red Cross Street. In the winter, the damp wind off the river would sweep up the hill to that corner and freeze you. On the north end of Front Street, just beyond the hotel, was the train station.

Going south, just down Front Street from the hotel on the right, was a barbershop manned by black men in white coats. The shop had mirrored walls, big padded chairs of scrolled metal, marble floors, a shoeshine booth manned by a black boy who could snap a tune while shining shoes.

A little further south down Front Street on the left was a Buster Brown Shoe Store that had a machine that allowed you to see your foot inside your shoe so you could tell whether it fit or not. On the same side of the street there was a Woolworth five and ten cent store, and provided my first introduction to air conditioning.

There was an Efird's Department Store with a moving overhead track system that allowed each cash register to send money and sales slips in a canister attached to the moving tracks to the overhead office for processing. It was quite a sight for a little boy from the country.

Also on Front Street was the tallest building I had ever seen, along with the first elevator. The elevator was operated by a black lady who sat on a stool. The elevator had to be stopped at each floor by her and adjusted to the level of the floor.

My first eye exam took place there while I was still living in Maple Hill, but I had many opportunities to go there for exams as the years passed and I found glasses to be a fixed part of my life.

I don't remember all of the stores on Front Street, but there was a parched peanut stand on the corner of Princess and Front Street operated by a blind black man. The peanuts were a nickel a pack and he could make change by the feel of the coins or bills. Very impressive to me.

Further down on the right in front of the Bailey Theater was another five and ten cent store. All of them had lunch counters and were very busy.

"Make do" must have been a holdover from Depression days because you could buy shoe repair kits that allowed you to glue a half sole on your shoe. Dry cleaners had booths to allow customers to take their pants off to be pressed while they waited.

Most everyone who went downtown would be dressed like they were going to church. Men wore suits, ties and hats. Every dry cleaners had a hat blocking service.

By 1943 I had a new brother, Asa James Walton, Jr. and we moved to a larger apartment located on Fifth Street. My Aunt Lorraine (mother's youngest sister) who moved to Wilmington first and worked at Saffo's Cafeteria had gotten married (Al Clure, a serviceman from Arizona) and rented a house on Fifth Street with an apartment which my parents rented.

We moved to Carolina Beach to take over a house that had been rented by Aunt Lucille, Dad's youngest sister. It was a cottage on pilings with a porch overlooking the highway and double garage below. Back of the garage was an enclosed area with a tub washing machine with a winger. I remember the winger well, because I got my fingers caught in the wringer and no one unplugged the machine until the wringer was halfway up my forearm. There was a safety device on the top of the wringer that you could hit with your fist to open the wringer but no one thought to do that due to panic.

Actually, we lived just south of Carolina Beach in an area known as Wilmington Beach (just north of Kure Beach).

Fort Fisher was an active military installation and had a lot of big gun emplacements for coastal and Cape Fear River protection (part of the Camp Davis Coastal Defense Army). Servicemen flooded Carolina Beach and it was loud and brash.

Britt's donut shop on the boardwalk was one of my favorite spots, along with the Wave Movie Theater.

In the spring of 1944, while we were living in the cottage at Wilmington Beach, my youngest brother Stanley was born.

My cousin, Ray Walton, came for a visit and we had a wonderful time in the water and on the boardwalk. We rode bumper cars, the Ferris wheel, and anything else that would interest us. We also enjoyed watching the Duck, a military vehicle based at the south end of the Carolina Beach and used for rescue whenever a swimmer got into trouble. The Duck, which had a boat hull and rode on huge rubber tires on land, could go through waves easily and turn into a boat with a propeller when it got into the water.

That fall, prior to school starting, the hurricane of 1944 hit. I was visiting my cousin, Ray Walton, on the family farm in Long Creek. We made a lot of reciprocal visits and I had a great time on the farm. My Aunt Lorraine, who was baby sitting my baby brothers while Mom and Dad were on a medical appointment for Mom in Wilmington, had to be evacuated by a big Army truck. No one else could get to her and my brothers because the ocean was coming over the sand dunes and flooding the streets. When I got back by bus to the beach everything was a mess. Most of the beach row of houses were gone or smashed. Every green bush and tree was brown from the blown salt water. But I had a great time playing in and with the debris on the beach.

My time at the beach was special, and I stayed in the water most of the time, when it was warm enough. Body surfing was my favorite water activity. I dug sand foxholes, played with a big chocolate lab with curly hair that showed up on a regular basis, dodged beach patrols in jeeps, looked at a torpedo from a German Sub that washed up on the beach, watched the P47 aircraft fly down the beach in the trough between the water and the dunes, so low you could see the pilots. I stared in awe as I watched them pull up to clear the fishing piers.

I made many trips to Wilmington by bus to go to the movies and remember passing a POW camp on the southeast corner of Carolina Beach Road and Shipyard Boulevard. I watched in awe the young men behind the wire in their POW uniforms.

I had heard that enemy subs were constantly trying to gain entry to the Cape Fear River in spite of the constant threat of guns and aircraft. Guns located at Fort Fisher were constantly firing. We never knew whether it was practice or the real thing. You rarely opened a cabinet in the kitchen without having to catch something that had worked its way to the edge of the shelf due to big guns firing. (I believe there were five inch, twenty millimeter and forty millimeter guns on the site.)

At Carolina Beach Elementary School at recess, you could hear the P47 fighters high overhead practicing, but you could not see them they were so high. We knew they were from the Wilmington Bluenthal Airfield (now ILM). Occasionally, a Piper Cub Grasshopper would land on a dirt road next to the school for practice. You could see patches in the fabric and it always created lots of excitement.

There was always something exciting to do at the beach. Our family went down to the rocks at Fort Fisher to picnic, fish and watch the huge ships come in the mouth of the river headed for Wilmington. My dad and a neighbor, Alvin Stiff, went to the fishing pier often. I got to fish with a drop line and often caught a skate or small shark.

For my eleventh birthday, in the summer of 1944, Mr. Stiff gave me a single shot .22 rifle he had gotten as a boy. I was thrilled beyond words. (It was a Truetest and was originally sold by Sears and Roebuck Catalogue.)

In the winter, the foam from a very rough ocean would blow along the beach whenever I walked it. It was very cold but wonderful. The walk to the Wave Theater at Carolina Beach was scary because it was so dark. There were no lights due to the blackout requirements.

The boardwalk had lots of beer drinkers and music. Soldiers were always playing the jukeboxes.

In 1945, after school was out, we moved back to Wilmington and I enrolled in the sixth grade at William Hooper School just down the street, north from where we lived. We lived in an apartment house at 1210 South Fourth Street. Dad had a small garden out back of the house (it was called a Victory Garden in those days). Meat was rationed, so we ate a lot of canned corn beef, canned sausage, canned salmon, and pork meat called fatback or streak of lean, streak of fat which was good for cooking vegetables. Margarine became available, but it was white, came in a plastic pack with a bubble of red coloring in the center that had to be pressed to break it so it could be mixed by squeezing until it became the color of butter. Seems it was a requirement of the dairy lobby that it not come mixed to look like butter back then.

We cooked on a gas stove and would light it with an old discarded welder's flint Dad brought home from the shipyard. His younger brother, Jerry, who was a supervisor helping build Liberty Ships, probably gave it to him since he had a lot of welders working for him. (It looked like a big safety pin with a little pan at one end which held the flint and striking plate. Pressing one side would cause the flint to move across the plate creating quite a shower of sparks.)

A boy across the street by the name of Eugene Peterson became a fast friend and we had great times building model aircraft, riding our bikes everywhere, making slingshots to use with green plums that were growing wild and plentiful, and trying our best to make gunpowder. We got sulfur, saltpeter, and charcoal from the corner drug store but were never able to make gunpowder to fire our little cannons we made from metal water pipe. We did manage to fire them using the heads from kitchen matches. We also found you could put a match head between two bolts using a nut to connect them and throw it on the pavement to create an explosion that sounded like a cap pistol.

We didn't live far from Greenfield Lake Park so we would ride our bicycles down there to dive and swim from the pier.

The war ended in 1945 and so did Dad's job. Working in Wilmington became a real challenge. We moved again, several blocks north, still on Fourth Street, to a house on a very tiny lot between a couple Dad knew from Maple Hill, Louis Gurganous, and a cousin of Dad's mother, Lee and Kate King, who had a small grocery store on the corner next door to us. Mother went to work briefly at a laundry and we acquired a live-in baby sitter named Mrs. Cushman. Dad struggled to find work as a carpenter in Wilmington, and was finally persuaded by a brother, Lou, to move to Alexandria, Virginia, which was enjoying a boom in construction.

In the meantime, I had graduated from William Hooper to Tileston to New Hanover High School. I was a freshman at New Hanover High in 1947 and as a member of the ROTC, participated in the first Wilmington Azalea Festival Parade. At New Hanover High I had three classes, shop, ROTC, and drafting, across the street from the High School in a building known as the Issac Bear building. In 1948 the drafting class I had in the Issac Bear building would often put me into class with community college students, if I ran late getting out of class. I loved drafting and often worked late in that class.

After school, I went to the YMCA, library, or work. I worked at a grocery store owned by a man from Long Creek. His name was Carl Powell and he often had me deliver groceries to tugboats tied up on the Cape Fear River. Keeping ice on the baskets of vegetables out in front of the store was a never ending task. One very pleasant memory from going to work was the delightful smell drifting from the Merita Bakery every time I rode my bike by there.

The community college eventually became UNC at Wilmington.

At the Christmas break in 1948, we moved to Virginia so Dad would not have to be a weekend commuter to be with the family.

My wartime memories of Wilmington as a youngster are all good.

Too Short for School
by
Mary Hodge of Southport

Mary Hodge was born in Chadburn in 1940 and grew up in Southport. Her story is loaded with memories of the good old days.

I can remember the man coming with a block of ice. Back then, we had an old icebox on the back porch and you kept ice in it. We had an ice pick that we broke the ice up with.

My daddy used to smoke our meat in the old pack house. He used to pack and salt fish in barrels.

The first outhouse I remember was in Fair Bluff, N.C. It sat out back of the house and you had to use the old Sears catalog or corncobs. I sure did hate to clean the outhouses out. Sometimes we just dug another hole and moved it to that spot.

Radio programs, what time we got to listen to it. All you heard was Amos and Andy or Hopalong Cassidy.

We had to do our homework by lamps and

Mary Hodge's family, Easter, 2007.

it wasn't easy to do it.

My mother and daddy had a big family. There were eight boys and six girls. I was the shortest one and when it was time for me to go to school, they wouldn't let me in school because I was so short. They thought I was too young. So I had to wait another year to begin school.

My dad did a lot of sharecropping. But there wasn't a day that went by he didn't have food on the tables. Because he had a garden and raised chickens and hogs.

I can remember killing chickens and hogs and even helping him clean fish. He would always tell me, "I wish you had been a boy."

We had an old windup record player and we played it over and over.

We had well water back then. We would have to keep buckets by the well to draw water up and down, and had the old dippers to drink water from as well. I can remember my aunt used to keep her milk down in the well to keep it cool.

We used to get the tin tubs out to take baths in. We placed it beside the heater and heated up the water during the winter, and on the porch during the summer.

We had to cut wood for the wood stove that my mom cooked on and made the best biscuits you ever tasted.

They used to have a spittoon in the corner where they would spit when dipping chewing tobacco and stuff back then.

We didn't have electric clocks back then. We had winding clocks back then you put beside the bed to wake you up.

Back then, you we had to work at corn shucking and tobacco tying and sometimes you did this right up to midnight. It was fun now that I think about it.

When I was in the first grade, my first book was Dick and Jane that we read over and over.

As far as remember, Grandma back then came and stayed with us.

Mary F. Hodge, age 66.

My grandmother on my mommy's side had a feather bed and used to feed one of us in the bed and made the other ones watch her do so.

My daddy could make the best scratch biscuits you ever could eat. You put a finger hole in it and poured syrup in it, or Jelly. It was delicious.

They wore bib overalls back then and still wear them now.

We would sometimes go to the field and break corn off and throw them at one another until Dad caught us and made us stop.

We went skinny dipping, my sisters and I.

We loved to go and visit with our grandmothers, but they stayed with us most of the time.

I always wore hand-me-downs and Mother used to make our clothes out of feed sacks we brought to feed the hogs.

Back then we had a lot of dirt roads and they had a lot of holes in them.

My neighbor and I used to make our toys out of clothespins. We made dolls out of

Mary's mother, daddy and all brothers and sisters except two at Southport Senior Citizen Building for 50th Anniversary.

them.

I can remember having a slop jar we put under the beds at night.

We lived in Tabor City for six years of my life. Then we started moving around. One was Fair Bluff and Green Sea, South Carolina. Then we moved to Southport and we lived at Supply and Midway and then moved on the Beach Road where my family lived when my baby sister got killed in a car wreck and my mom and dad adopted her two boys. I helped raise them.

My family and I still live in Southport to this day.

Green Worms with Red Horns
by
Esten (Jonnie) Johnson Gillis of Shallotte
From an interview by Karen Dolan

Karen Dolan had the following to say about her interview with Jonnie Gillis: "I know I thanked Jonnie for sharing her memories and pieces of her life with me, but I regret that I did not thank her for her patience with me, as I often repeated questions and misunderstood answers. I also regret not telling her how much I admire her for accepting the circumstances of her life with grace and for her nursing contributions. I know she will be reading this so I am grateful she will know what I neglected to tell her." We, too, are grateful to both Jonnie and Karen for their help with this book. We also thank Jonnie for reminding us of those pesky tobacco varmints with which so many of us are familiar.

I was born June 20, 1923 in Duplin County, about 12 or 15 mile from Wallace. I grew up on a farm about five miles from Harrells, North Carolina. There were six of us, my mother, father, and four children—two brothers and one sister. For market, we raised tobacco and strawberries. I worked on the farm and it didn't hurt me a bit. I never thought of it as work; it was just something we needed to do.

The thing that I disliked most was worming tobacco—pulling off all those tobacco worms. I hated it. Some people would put the worms in a bucket, but I never did; I couldn't stand that. I tore them in half and dropped them. There's a special worm for tobacco and they have a horn on their rear end that sticks up. If they looked too ferocious, we'd call my Papa to get them and he'd help us.

We planted tobacco in the spring and harvested in late summer as best I recall. Of course, there were plenty of chores besides that. We had a couple of cows that we milked from; my sister, Grace, milked one; I milked the other. We didn't do any plowing; the boys—the men folk—did the plowing. That was before we got tractors. The girls didn't do that, but the girls did a lot of other stuff like the housework. Momma did the cooking, but she also worked in the fields; we'd help her.

We didn't have electricity until I was a senior in high school. We had an outhouse and in the house we had what you call slop jars. They were chamber pots.

We had a wood stove for cooking and we had a wood stove in the living room for heat.

We had quiltings. It wasn't for the children; I was there, but I didn't participate. My mother and several of the neighbors would get together and they would quilt. They'd make quilts for the one where they had the quilting.

We had a wash house. It had a furnace and a big iron kettle; we'd put the soiled clothes in warm, sudsy water and we scrubbed 'em on the washboard. But we had a lady that helped do our laundry; in fact, she did most of our laundry, but she did it at our house.

Later on when they started putting fertilizer and stuff in printed fabrics, like calico, we used some of those for things, but not much—aprons and stuff like that. I never had a dress made out of it. We bought some of our clothes. Dad would buy our clothes and bring them home and they would always fit. I don't know why my mother didn't buy our clothes. My father was going to town all the time and she wasn't. He always bought at a store called Kramer's. The store is still there.

Dad was partial to Fords. He loved the Ford. We always had a car. We didn't have horses for recreation. We had mules for work.

We children would shoot marbles; that's one thing we would do and Dad would join us. I'm trying to think of what else we did 'cause I know we did other things. One Christmas, Santa Claus brought my older brother a football. It happened to snow that Christmas so we were all out in the yard in the snow playing football. I remember that, but I don't remember how old I was.

There was a lake that was not too far from us, within twenty miles, called White Lake. Papa would take us there in the summer. We didn't know how to swim, but we splashed around. They had public beaches around the lake. It was a big lake and very commercialized, but it's much more commercialized now.

It was a special treat. We didn't go every week, but we would go several times during the summer.

My mother's mother, my grandmother, lived about twice as far from us as Wallace and we would visit her every now and then. I loved my grandmother. She was real sweet, so like my mother. She loved us and we loved her. Just being around her was special. We would meet at her house Mother's Day and Thanksgiving Day.

We went to school by bus. It was five or six miles from us to Harrells. I had homework every night. My mother was a teacher before she married. She helped us if we had any problems. I never really had any school problems.

I went to James Walker Memorial (now New Hanover) Nursing School for three years to get my Registered Nurse degree and then I studied for six months at Margaret Hague Nursing School in Jersey City. I visited a classmate in Long Beach, California and liked it out there so I quit my job in Greensboro by telephone and stayed in California for a couple of years. I came back home when my parents became sick.

We were always active in church. We went to church in Harrells at the Methodist Church, which is still there. We had Sunday School every Sunday and preaching once a month when I was growing up. The church has always been very important to me.

The Blanket in the Field
by
Betty Lou Gurganious of Watha

Betty Lou Gurganious was born in Clarkton in 1949, grew up in Bladen County, and enjoys writing about her family. And this is what her story is about. Sadly, however, she chose not to reveal the last names of any member of her family in her story.

My story about home and family begins when my mom would take me to work with her and Dad.

I have a sister, Sarah, who was born before me, but she lived with Grandma, whose name is Sarah, too, and Grandpa because they loved her so much and they needed her with them. Mom and Dad also loved her. This was in the 1950s.

Betty Gurganious' mother; brother, Wilton; sisters, Sarah, Mary and Joyce and Betty.

I remember my mom (whose name is also Sarah) wearing a yellow shirt. It was like the sun. She also wore her blue jeans with the pant legs rolled up.

Mom would get up so early in the morning to prepare breakfast for Dad and me. We would wait for different people to come to the house to help Dad and Mom in the cotton fields. They would work together, every one of them. After we finished breakfast, Mom would take a big blanket, and me, to the field with her.

Mom would sing to me, "You are my sunshine, my only sunshine. You make me happy when skies are blue. You will never know, dear, how much I love you. Please do not take my sunshine away."

After she was through singing, she would lay me on that blanket. That's when I realized people were not the same color. My dad, Albert, had different people working and helping him. They would sing while everyone worked so hard out in the sun. The heat was so bad. They would sing about God and how good He is to everyone. Every day, the singing just got sweeter and sweeter, always singing about God.

Just being on that blanket next to that old field was so great to me. I enjoyed the singing so much. I would cry so hard when Mom took me home.

I also learned more about them and God.

My mom would sing also, "God holds the whole world in His hand." She would sing that a lot, even when she was tired.

You see, these dirt roads always carried me home. They always have many curves in them, also.

The dirt roads felt so good under your feet, running barefoot as a child, running home to Mom and Dad with your brother, Wilton, and sisters, Mary and Joyce, by your side.

I love my family and enjoy being with them. My mom was my best friend. She's not with us any more. I always want to write about her. She was a special mom.

My husband has been a good soul mate. He has been so good about helping me around the house so I can write. That really means a lot to me.

A Lover of Books
by
Mary Suchsland of Kure Beach

Mary Suchsland was born in 1928 in New Jersey and grew up there.

I am a seventy-eight-year-old happy, healthy widow. I am a mother of eight. I was one of seven children. We lived out in the country about three miles. Seemed much longer when you had to walk it. My father was a machinist. My mother never worked out of the home. We were poor but didn't know it.

I can remember the iceman deliveries. You had to tell him what size, ten cent or twenty-five were the usual. My siblings took turns emptying the melted ice from below the icebox. Of course sometimes someone would forget and that meant water all over the kitchen floor.

I recall the milkman making two AM deliveries. The milk was in glass containers. In the winter it would freeze and the cream would be pushed to the top of the bottle and this pushed the cardboard stopper out of the bottle.

My mom and dad were up early enough to get the furnace going and it would be warm when the children got up.

I remember the sheany man coming down the road on his cart drawn by a horse. He would call out, "Any rags and bones, any buttons." He would buy and sell almost anything.

We had an open well in our backyard. We had no hot water. All water was boiled on a coal stove. We had a tin tub in the basement for baths. Several used the same water. After bathing, you had to go outside to get back in the house.

In summer, we played in the woods around us and picked huckleberries for our mom to make pie. I remember the birch trees were our horses. They were very flexible.

We had a 1908 Edison Victrola that we played records on. My daughter now has that piece that still works.

When I was in sixth grade we moved to the next town. What a delight! We could walk to the store or ride a trolley car. Best of all, I could walk to the library. It was my first encounter with a library. I spent many hours there.

Sister Patricia, my teacher, would have someone in class read aloud a chapter or two from a library book. What a joy! I could hardly wait for the next chapter to be read. I think having a library card and using it is one of the greatest things that happened to me.

I went on to become a Registered Nurse. Joined the U.S. Navy during the Korean War. I met my husband-to-be there. We married in 1952. He died in 1997. I became the mother of eight children and I went to college.

I know I have passed on my love of reading to my children. One of them was on the board of literacy. Another reads to children several times a year. Another donates books to a class at Christmas time in my name. This makes me very proud.

It's not just books, I would be lost without the daily newspaper.

Drinking Cobie
by
Lois Hinson Hardison of Carolina Beach

Lois Hardison was born in Whiteville in 1927. She provides us with numerous memories of the good old days including duck riding and a 40 year career with the telephone company. And, as you will see, she enjoyed coffee at a tender age.

In my memories of the good old days, places, things, times and yes, even people, have changed. I grew up in the country in a Columbus County town, Whiteville, N.C., 50 miles from New Hanover County and

Lois and her husband, Al, in 1952.

Wilmington. New Hanover County had Hanover greens and we had collard greens, ha. As I am now a senior adult, having served as Mrs. Senior North Carolina Sweetheart Queen 2006, when I think of the good old days back then, people seemed happier and more content and could face difficulties a lot better and with less stress and confusion.

My parents, now deceased, taught my brothers and me to be honest. We worked out on the farm, picking strawberries, working in tobacco, chores of feeding the cows, horses and pigs, and getting in wood.

My mother made the best homemade biscuits. (Now, I never get any.) My granddaddy would give me coffee, as a toddler. I called it "cobie." My parents did not like for me to have coffee, but I loved it. They said it would make you old.

My grandmother had railroad snuff in a can and I had cocoa in a can, ha!

Lois and her daughter, Sabra, in 1957.

My granddaddy would pick grapes for me because the mosquitoes would really cover me and to this day, they still like to bite me.

I had a pet white duck and I tried to ride on her back. I was really very petite. Daddy said I weighed only four pounds when I was born.

We had a milkman and iceman who delivered to the door.

Mama and Daddy had an outhouse and we used the catalog for toilet paper.

Well water, later went to pump water. I would fill a tin washtub with water and let it set out in the sun for my bath.

I played games, like jump rope, jump board, marbles, jack rocks and hopscotch. I broke my arm jumping board.

When we started to grammar school, we walked to school and it was very, very cold or would catch the bus on muddy clay roads. For our lunch, Daddy would give us 10 cents and we would walk to a nearby store and get a Pepsi and a cinnamon bun. I studied and did my homework by a kerosene lamp, slept

Lois' grandsons, Joshua and Jeremiah Duncan.

Lois and her grandsons, Joshua and Jeremiah.

in a feather bed (bog down in it), had party line telephone service (long neck table telephone), about eight on the same line, but it was fun then.

At age 16, I graduated from high school with only 11 grades then in 1944. I came to Wilmington and started to work with a telephone company, then Southern Bell Telephone Company. I began as a long distance operator, where we would answer a signal by saying "Operator," had plugs and long cords to dial numbers and put in a call to New York, etc. for calls to relatives, boys in service and sweethearts (oh yes, sometimes we would listen in or monitor). I worked 40 years with the company, retiring in 1985.

I met my husband (now deceased), at the Moose Club at Third and Chestnut Sreet. He was a drummer and a tailor at a men's clothing store. We operators would go after work to the Moose to dance. Landmarks like the Moose Club, Bailey Theatre, USO Club, Carolina Beach Boardwalk, Lumina Pavilion, Wilmington College (Issac Bear Building), now UNC-Wilmington (I attended there).

I have one daughter, Sabra, and two grandsons, Joshua and Jeremiah, who grew up in the city and they don't know what the "good old days" were.

We moved to Carolina Beach, 15 miles from Wilmington, in the 70s and lots of changes have happened and landmarks have disappeared. High rises and condos are up. Our water pump house for Wilmington Beach, which I could tell people how to find my street, has been torn down and sometimes I even miss my street at night and go down to the next one. The boardwalk and parks have changed. But I like the beach and living here.

Lois Hardison, Azalea Festival.

Lois Hardison in 2006.

Ride the Bus...or Walk
by
Elizabeth (Betsy) Middleton Knight of Wilmington

Elizabeth Knight writes of a time when life was much simpler than today. She hints at celebrities and admits an early connection to rural life without electricity. However, perhaps without even intending it, she highlights the fact that few people, especially young people, had cars in those days. But city life provided an alternative to walking. Mrs. Knight was born in Wake County in 1924 and we think you'll enjoy her recollec-

tions.

My family moved to Wilmington from rural Wake County in July, 1935, when I was ten years old. When we first moved here we lived in a six-room house on Castle Hayne Road, across the road from Southern Oil Company, where Dad worked. I'm not totally sure, but I believe it is the same house that is now used by Godwin Oil Company.

About a month later, we moved to Audubon community, where we lived for approximately five years. We began attending church at Winter Park Baptist, and in the fall, we started school at Winter Park School, where Mrs. VanLandingham was my teacher in the sixth grade, and where I also attended seventh and eighth grades. In fact, the class I was in was the first to attend eighth grade in New Hanover County. Until then, as far as I can ascertain, when one completed seventh grade it was off to high school the next fall. So, I was glad to be able to stay at Winter Park School one more year because I was in no way ready for high school "in town."

My first year of high school we rode the streetcar to school daily, and, since we lived on Wrightsville Avenue, I walked down Audubon Boulevard to the Audubon station to board the streetcar.

We then moved to Winter Park to a house that was owned by a Mrs. Sweat who lived somewhere on Carolina Beach Road. We lived next door to the Miltons, and Billy Halyburton, for whom a local park is named to honor his war record, for which he was awarded posthumously, a medal of honor, came to live with his aunt, Mrs. Margaret Milton, there. From this house we moved to a house on the corner of McMillan and Wrightsville Avenues. Then we moved to a house next door to David Brinkley's mother and sister, though we never saw him, because he was away in service. This is where we lived when I graduated from New Hanover High School in 1942.

By then, Dad had quit driving for Southern Oil Company, and he went to work at the shipyard as a guard.

In 1943, Mom and Dad bought a house at the corner of 18th and Nun Streets in Wilmington. I was working in the County Agent's office in the Custom House (now the Federal Building) for County Agent R. W. Galphin.

The war was in full swing by this time in my life and I can't really tell you much, probably because we had no brothers in my family. I had some cousins who were in service, one captured by the Germans and held prisoner, but none of them were from Wilmington.

We were then members of Temple Baptist Church, and we met many servicemen from Camp Davis and Camp Lejeune through church activities. Except to go as a church group once in a while and serve refreshments to servicemen at the USO, we did not otherwise have much opportunity to meet them except at church because we did not dance. That is, my sisters and I did not dance.

A group of us girls did go to the movies a lot, though. Every time the venue changed at the Bailey, we went, two or three times a week. In fact, that is where we got most of our news concerning the war, as, of course, there was no television then. After my husband and I were married and television became a reality, we sometimes would walk downtown and watch it in a furniture store window for a few minutes at night.

We young people did not have cars back then, so we walked a lot to get where we wanted to go, or we rode the bus to work, to church, to the movies. It was either walk or ride the bus. And we felt safe doing it anytime.

Life was simpler in those days, and I guess I felt I had come a long way because I came from the country in Wake County where we did "enjoy" outhouses, chamber pots, no electricity or plumbing, taking baths in tin tubs, hog killings, mail delivered more than a mile from the house we lived in, biscuits from scratch (which I still make), feather beds, wind-up Victrola record players, dippers, cold water from the well, winding the clock.

Wilmington was simpler back then, too. Because I can remember when there was no College Road through Winter Park, and no Shipyard Boulevard, and only two high schools in the county, and no college, and certainly no shopping malls. Where did it all go? Progress! Or so they say…

The Garden Spot of the World
by
Gwendolyn C. West of Wilmington

Gwendolyn West writes about the place she loves best (and about her strange playmates).

I was born in Wilmington at James Walker Hospital in 1924 to Irma and Sterling Collins, and for the first twelve years of my life I lived on Carolina Beach Road near the last entrance to Greenfield Lake. We had an outside john and a pump on the back porch. I took my bath in a tin tub in the kitchen where we heated the water on the oil stove. I went to the school which is now the Shuffler Building and Mrs. Shuffler was principal. With no close neighbors, my playmates were cats, biddies, which my dad raised with an incubator, doodle bugs and minnows at the Lake.

Then a wonderful thing happened. We moved to Winter Park and my dad got me a horse. Betty Hall, who lived across the street, had a horse, too.

On Lake Avenue, John and Ada Garrett had a dairy with fifty black and white cows. They had a boy who took the cows out to graze each morning in the area where Roland

Gwendolyn West and Queen in the horse lot behind the house.

Grise School, Lincoln Forest and Pine Valley are now. At that time there were only woods. We would stay until noon and then bring the cows back to the dairy. Each weekend and all summer we would feel we were real cowgirls.

The only hard roads were Wrightsville Avenue and Oleander Drive, so we had plenty of places to ride.

We had no car, but the old beach car ran right in front of our house. I remember going on it with the Winter Park Baptist Church for the annual beach picnic. What fun it was to ride that car!

I love Winter Park and the most wonderful thing is that when I married, the Garretts sold the dairy lots to my husband, Frank Jamison and me. I now live on that property, and have since 1949. I hope I never have to leave it until it is time for me to leave this world. Winter Park is the garden spot of the world to me.

City Girl-Country Girl
by
Darlene Howe Drescher of Hampstead

Although Darlene Drescher isn't a local native, we can guarantee that you'll find her story compellingly and enjoyably interesting. Born in Dayton in 1934, she recalls her summers on an Ohio farm and provides a lovely tribute to a patriotic father. She suggested in a footnote that her stories may be boring. Far from it!

Growing up as I did in a big city (Dayton, Ohio), with the amenities of a big city, you can imagine how much I enjoyed the times I vacationed with my cousin, Louise, her parents, Aunt Molly and Uncle Rudy, and three brothers on "the farm." It was affectionately known as Uncle Rudy's farm, and it was about 25 miles from where I lived, namely New Burlington. It was a typical rural small "poke and plumb" town—if you didn't poke your head out of the window fast, you were plumb out of town.

Even though the farm consisted of only a few acres, to me it stood for those things city dwellers seldom enjoyed.

When I was probably 11 or 12, I had the opportunity a couple of summers to spend two weeks with them. Their farm critters included a milk cow named Ricka (short for Fredericka, my grandmother's name), a couple of dozen chickens plus a rooster, and various and sundry dogs and cats from time to time. They had a barn for hay, an apple orchard, a hen house for the chickens, the farmhouse, of course, and the outhouse complete with moon and Sears catalog. There was electricity in the house but no indoor plumbing. The furnace burned wood and the telephone was one of those wooden boxes mounted on the wall with a separate funnel shaped mouthpiece, ear piece on a cord, and a crank to summon the operator. They also were on a multi-party line of several neighbors, so someone was usually listening in on the conversations, including the operator. It was rather primitive compared to our house in the city.

Days began with the "alarm clock" in the form of the rooster, and continued with the "toilette" which meant a visit to the outhouse. (A "slop jar" filled in for nighttime trips.) Then into the kitchen to wash up with icy water from the cistern at the sink and a quick brushing of teeth with salt and soda instead of toothpaste. Breakfast was my favorite—Aunt Molly's all you could eat waffles smothered in her homemade butter. I had never tasted a waffle, and it was a big treat!

Speaking of butter, Ricka provided that as well. She was milked faithfully, twice a day. (Of course, sometimes she got into wild onions and the milk had a distinct oniony taste). I tried my hand at this glamorous chore, but I wasn't particularly successful. First of all, the three-legged stool wouldn't stay up on three legs for me, and her tail swishing flies likely as not hit me in the face as well. Apparently her udders didn't like my "touch" very well, either. About three squirts were the most I ever managed to collect and that rarely hit the bucket. She obviously was picky about who she was going to share with.

Then the milk was carried into the kitchen where Aunt Molly scalded it and strained it. Some of the cream that came to the surface was made into sweet butter in a churn—another chore I wasn't really successful doing because as it thickened, the cream became too heavy to churn all the way. The excess milk, when there was some, was sold in those large milk cans one finds nowadays in antique shops. Let me tell you, that was wonderful butter and milk!

Another fun thing was to gather the eggs from the nests in the hen house. Some of the hens were not exactly cooperative, either, and a few good pecks usually were doled out as we'd try to unseat them from their nests. But the fresh eggs collected couldn't be beat. There's no comparison with today's market eggs.

But that's not all the hens provided. The chickens were fed with chicken feed scattered in the barnyard; then Aunt Molly would select a particular hen that she said was ready for the stewpot because it wasn't performing up to par anymore. (And I guess somehow she knew which one firsthand.) Anyway, she'd set her sights on a particular hen in the barnyard and go after it. Now, Aunt Molly was not a particularly small woman, but she was fast! I can still see her chasing the doomed hen around, catching it, wringing its neck, and waiting for it to stop flopping around until it gave up the ghost. Then, into a large pot of boiling water it went to aid in defeathering it. That was something else! Louise and I would sit on the grass in the side yard and pick it clean. The good side of this was that we knew chicken and homemade noodles were coming for supper, so it was worth every minute of the feathers sticking to our bare legs and arms. Inside the kitchen, we'd find homemade noodles draped over every possible surface, drying, before going into the stewpot with the unfortunate chicken—Yum!

When we had time to just roam, we wandered into the apple orchard, climbed the trees and when the apples were ripe, enjoyed them. The extras were sold roadside. Also, sometimes we wandered into a neighboring woods to find the grapevine swings. Sometimes we'd just ride bikes down Cemetery Road, over the gravel, destination the cemetery itself.

On hot days if Uncle Rudy was around and could drive us, he'd take us to a deep creek with a swimming hole. What a treat to swing out from a tree into the middle of our private pond. Sometimes when we couldn't go to the creek, early in the morning we'd just fill up the washtub/bathtub with the icy water from the well outside and hope that by mid-afternoon we would be able to get into it to cool off. It was still usually pretty cold, but if it was hot enough outside we didn't mind.

During the week, Uncle Rudy worked in town so he was only around evenings and weekends. He'd dig garden for Aunt Molly's corn, potatoes, tomatoes, beans, etc. and her *gorgeous* flowers (her favorite word). These were undoubtedly enhanced by Ricka's leavings. We always enjoyed Aunt Molly's fresh vegetables, and didn't mind helping harvest and otherwise prepare them.

Uncle Rudy cut hay when it was ready and got it into the barn for the cow during the winter. He cut wood from the neighbor's land with hand tools and carried it home in a wheelbarrow to split, if necessary, and stacked it to burn for winter heat.

Every Saturday was bath day, and Uncle Rudy would draw and heat bathwater in the basement for baths. Because I was the guest, I got to go first (everyone went into the same tub—ugh!) so I was thrilled to be first. He'd make sure backs, ears and fingernails were scrupulously clean and trimmed. As I was beginning to "bud out," I rebelled, so he finally let me wash myself. He also cut the boys' hair when it needed it, in the front yard, in warm weather.

In addition to visiting for two weeks, in the fall, our family would go mushroom hunting in the neighbor's woods. We weren't looking for just any old mushrooms: we were looking for what they called hickory jacks. Mushroom connoisseurs say no such thing exists, but they were dinner-plate sized fungi and grew on fallen and dead hickory trees. When breaded and fried in butter, they tasted like chicken-fried steak.

There is just no way to describe how these times enriched my life. Now, some 60 years later, the house still stands. It was eventually plumbed and a modern furnace was installed. A bedroom upstairs became a bathroom and the livestock is long gone. The gravel road was paved and the creek and swimming hole dammed up to create a large recreational lake called Caesar's Creek. Even the cemetery is gone; having been relocated, and the whole "poke and plumb" town of New Burlington is underwater. But the memories prevail.

Patriotism and Immigration. I wonder how many out there remember the air raid wardens of World War II? Except for those summers on the farm, of course, I lived, as I mentioned earlier, in the large city of Dayton, Ohio, home of Wright Field, an Army Air Force base in approximately 1942. It was during the war years and civilians were asked to volunteer as air raid wardens during the war. My father, Henry Howe, an immigrant from Germany, was just such a man.

He was a very patriotic person who left his homeland at 19 years of age, having been thoroughly disenchanted with all that Germany was going through, to come to America to find a better life for himself. After settling in Dayton and becoming a naturalized citizen, he became probably one of the most dedicated Americans around. He simply loved the USA and all it stood for. He had found a life he loved, owned his own home and property, married and had three children, a job that fulfilled him, learned English, and was a model citizen.

When the call came out for wardens, he answered the call willingly and faithfully. It became his duty to patrol our street on nights when blackouts were ordered. In dark clothing, carrying only a flashlight to illuminate his way (street lights were extinguished) he'd walk up and down, watching for any lights in the houses that could attract the attention of enemy air traffic. We had blackout blinds so as not to be seen. And, at least once a week, he had to attend meetings where the men marched for an hour or so in a park about a mile away. We had no car so it was necessary to walk to and from. Inasmuch as he had a strenuous job laying brick and stone all day, this was quite a sacrifice, but he never complained.

Many are the times we huddled in our dark house as B-17 bombers rattled the windows on their approach to Wright Field (now called Wright-Patterson Air Force Base) but we felt safe because of his efforts and those of many others.

In spite of his dedication to his adopted country, there was a dark side to his being from Germany. Some referred to him as a Nazi and mistreated him as a result.

He took great pride in his yard—the front one especially—and spent hours manicuring it. One night during this time, someone, a suspected neighbor though we never knew who for sure, poured oil all over the grass and ignited it. Another time, a neighbor behind us apparently mistook his burying of household garbage in a compost pit for this "Nazi" burying German secrets and called the FBI who responded, made him uncover it all, only to learn this was only potato skins and other household refuse wrapped in newspapers.

In spite of these unfortunate situations, he remained dedicated to being the most loyal of Americans, saluting the flag and treating the *Star Spangled Banner* with hand over heart, and taught us kids to revere our flag. He eventually helped to bring over from the old country not only his whole family, but also a couple of close friends from childhood so that they could enjoy what America had to offer as well.

I have nothing but the greatest respect for my dad for his dedication to the homeland of his choice of which he was extremely proud.

Today, I've been married for 52 years, have three grown children and six grandchildren. I have lived in a four states: Ohio twice, Illinois twice, California, New Jersey, and Kentucky, and in Germany as I followed my husband, Carl, in his years in the Army, and as a sales manager for a large glass firm. We moved to North Carolina 10 years ago to escape Chicago's winter and love it here.

I have always loved writing—letters mostly. I am an avid reader of most anything, and feel I'm missing my right arm when I have no books to read when I finish an especially good one. I consider myself a fairly good cook and when I still could, loved gardening.

Twenty-eight Memories
by
John Russell of Wilmington

When we were soliciting material for this book, we published a list of things generally associated with the good old days. John Russell, who was born in Wilmington in 1933, confirmed that he remembered all these things and often remarked how they affected him.

1. Horsewagon iceman, cabbage head refrigerator.
2. Too cold to go to outhouse. We kept one or two chamber pots in the house.
3. Knickers: tight below knees; legs cold in winter.
4. Long walk to outhouse. We had a two-seater.
5. Remember Amos and Andy, Lone Ranger, Phantom and spooky shows (on the radio).
6. Had to wait long periods of time to use phone. Two and three party lines.
7. Used record player a lot. Your arm would get tired cranking up the player.
8. Trains: stand at track to wait for train to get there. Blew whistle. Used coal.
9. Diapers: had to wash out by hand but later washed in toilet.
10. Tin tub baths: had to fill up. Lucky to have hot water two or three times a week. Sometimes had to use leftover water.
11. Spittoons: used in house for tobacco chewing and for ash trays.
12. Getting flypaper stuck all over hand and face. Sometimes caught flies.
13. If you did not wind up Big Ben you would be late for school or work.
14. Corncob fights had corn silk all over you.
15. Mailman walking down dusty roads with dogs running after him.
16. Old book about see Jane run, see Dick run.
17. Remember going to bed and sinking down in feather bed and look up at stars.
18. Mama mixing flour for biscuits and rolling them out and cutting them out for pan.
19. Cords hanging down with hot light burning your hands and bumping your head.
20. Wearing bibs with side buttons not buttoned and strap loose.
21. After shucking corn we always had a corncob fight.
22. Old houses that were not lived in used to have a lot to plunder in and they were spooky.

John Russell.

23. Going to pond around your house or friend's house to cool off. Water hitting your body on a hot summer day.
24. My grandmother stayed with us so I never had to visit. No home back then for them.
25. I came from a large family, seven boys, so hand-me-downs were God sent.
26. Old dirt roads: when cars were on so much dust you could not see too far ahead. Stayed full of dust.
27. Old wagons make skate boards out of apple crates, kites out of newspaper.
28. Going to the well to get water. Line hard to pull up water bucket, heavy, scared I might fall in.

Patriotic Cattails
by
Sylvia Burnett Crippen of Wilmington

Sylvia Crippen, who was born in Burgaw in 1934 and grew up there and on Carolina Beach, has some exciting and enthusiastic memories of the good old days. You'll read about patriotic cattails, a ticklish iceman and even a German spy in this delightful story.

Charlie, the iceman, was a wonderful black man whom we all dearly loved. Every time we bought ice for the icebox, Charlie would give us a small piece "to cool you off in this heat." He loved children and was never gruff or unpleasant. Charlie was so very ticklish that he would squirm if a person was a block away and just pointed a finger at him.

The vegetable wagon was a favorite Tuesday and Friday happening. The vegetables were harvested locally, those mornings, and delivered to the cottages by a truck. The gardener would usually give us a little something to eat, perhaps a small tomato or string bean. We actually ate the raw string bean and liked it!

During the war, my brother Julian Burnett and our friend and constant playmate, Jimmy Westbrook, would dip cattails in individual buckets of red, white and blue paint, then sell them to the summer residents for five cents each. Too, we collected several things for the war effort, among them, tin foil on gum wrappers, which we rolled into balls, adding to them with each find. Collected also were toothpaste tubes which were made of lead, I guess.

I was one of eight children, so we bristled our way through quite a number of toothpaste tubes rather quickly. Ipana, I recall, and Pepsodent, were perhaps used mostly in our family. When at the end of the tube, we would place the tube on the counter or door frame, and starting at the bottom, scrape the tube with the handle of our toothbrush until reaching the cap. We were invariably surprised at the amount of toothpaste remaining in the tube! Our mother made all such patriotic responsibilities great fun for all of us.

There were blue light bulbs in all light sockets so the enemy couldn't see well from the ocean, though we had no idea the enemy was out there. We couldn't use flashlights on the beach at all, for the same reason. As a rule, we children used flashlights on moonless nights when playing Nyoka, Queen of the Jungle, or Arabian Nights, on the beach.

Julian and I went on a very dark beach one evening to play. Our sister Mary Elizabeth was sitting on the porch. I really don't recall where anyone else was at the time. However, we saw a flashlight blinking at the north end of the beach. This did not sit well with us because we weren't allowed to have one and didn't think it fair at all. We hurried into the cottage and with indignation, expressed our view on the situation. Our father came out to observe and within ten minutes a Military Policeman was there. We all sat on the front steps until the blinking was seen again. Both adults agreed that we were good citizens and said they would take care of it.

The incident was not mentioned again, though the next night, there was such a huge thunderstorm that the cottage shook violently. After the war was over in 1945, our father told us that the "flashlight" was a German spy in the attic of The Carolina Inn, which was owned by my father's cousin, Katie Hines, and he was signaling a German submarine right off the coast! The "thunderstorm" was the bombing of that submarine. My father knew we would tell everyone we knew about the incident, which would frighten all, so he kept mute.

In 1944, before hurricanes could be predicted and had no names, we were involved in a powerful one. Again, my brother Julian and I were on the front porch on a Saturday, enjoying our new windbreakers by unzipping them partially, holding them open and letting the wind balloon us across the porch. That entertained us for quite a while. The wind was getting fierce, thus we were told to come inside.

My mother had gone to Charlotte, taking my younger sister to a doctor there, and my father was with her on a business trip. That Saturday night my first born sister, Annetta, said she was so frightened by the sound of the wind that she prayed hard to let whatever was happening, happen in the daylight. Annetta taught school in Clinton, North Carolina and was home for the summer. Her prayer was answered. On Sunday, with fierce wind whipping his raincoat hither and yon, a policeman banged on our door loudly so as to be heard above the wind and rain, and told us we were in the midst of a hurricane and needed to evacuate immediately.

Because my brother and I had found a very young kitten the week before and brought it home, we were in a quandary as how to get him to safety. Annetta took care of that pronto. With five children as her responsibility, she suggested the kitten stay put. There was another sister, Ruth, who was to return to her job in Raleigh that day but obviously couldn't. Annetta was grateful she was there to help.

When we left the cottage, we were told to hold hands tightly and DO NOT LET GO under ANY circumstances. The whole area was a sea of water, which reached my waist, and with each wave breaking, rose higher. I recall looking back and seeing a one-story cottage disappear completely when a breaking wave flattened out.

Slogging to the bus station was a hazard, but being so young, I thought it quite exciting. Trailways bus line took everyone from the area to Wilmington.

We spent the night with a relative, Idabelle Abernathy. The next morning, she said we all deserved a cup of coffee after what we had been through. Boy, was I excited, but not for long. Young children weren't allowed coffee, period.

The older sisters went back to survey the area first, then sent for the rest of us to return. The bus dropped us off at the station and we, Mary Elizabeth, Julian and I, walked to the cottage.

The storm had left three feet of sand over the entire area. When we reached the Foster's cottage, just four houses from ours, a jeep was driving south as we were walking north. When we became parallel, the jeep ran over a hidden wire, which sprang taut, catching me chest high, flinging me into the air. I thought I was dead and so did my brother and sister. The soldiers rushed over, probably thinking the same as we. As it turned out, I was fine, just startled.

Returning, I was very pleased that the kitten was safe. A thought kept returning, however, and that was, if the house had been washed away, I could go back to Burgaw and play with my friends for the rest of the summer. Decisions, decisions.

Harry Merritt was the grandson of our neighbor, Mrs. Murrin. He was from South

Carolina and came to visit her every summer. There came a time when our sisters outgrew wanting to do the things which Julian and I did. When Harry came to the beach, it was a great joy for us because he would take us crabbing and fishing and complained not at all. We thought Harry was the best thing since sliced bread. Going to the Sound without a responsible person was not allowed. This was when the sound met the shore and there were no houses there. Just a small pier, black mud, a blanket of darting fiddler crabs which we loved trying to herd, oyster shells, and the best crabbing we ever experienced, using fish heads, given freely by the fish markets. (Today, my husband can't believe we were not charged for the shad roe if the fish we selected was laden with eggs).

In August, we would walk the shoreline and catch soft shell crabs.

My older brother, Gilbert, taught me many things. He was nine years older than I so he had a good audience. When he was taking a break from shoveling sand from the garage and I was four, he showed me how to store chewing gum, (which we were NOT allowed to chew), behind my ear. You can just imagine the result of that lesson.

Too, that same summer, he cut my hair, which resulted in my first trip to a salon and even they said "it would grow out." It bothered me not one bit. I absolutely adored him and went back for more.

He taught me how to cook an egg exactly as he liked it and how to wash his socks and rinse them until the water was perfectly clear. When he was in the Air Corps and came home on furlough, he brought an entire box of Heath bars, just for my own consumption. In a family of eight children, you can't imagine what a fabulous treat that was. He also gave my friend, Susie Ferrell, and me, a dime each. He took me flying in a small plane at the airstrip in Burgaw, which was one of the thrills of my young life.

Mother would have all of us lie on blankets on the beach on August 9th, 10th, and 11th in the evening and watch the stars fall. I truly wish we could see the stars now.
(Some portions of these stories were told by my sister Susie Burnett Jones in her book, *When The Moon Stood Still*, from the perspective of a 14-year-old. I was eight at the time).

A Quiet Hero
by
Obbie M. Blanton, Jr. of Wilmington

Mr. Blanton was a Wilmington police officer, and was followed into law enforcement by his children and many of his grandchildren. He tells his story with great humility and with touches of humor, and recalls many traditions that are no more. (We were impressed by his reminder of police call boxes, icons of the past that are now gone forever.) But shining through his recollections of the good old days is his pride in his uncle who

Obbie and his police car in the 1960s.

survived World War II.

I was born in 1935 to Obbie Melvin Blanton, Sr. and Jessie Madeline Woodcock Blanton. My father worked at the local shipyard during the war. I was raised in Wilmington but spent holidays and vacations during the summer at my grandparents' home in Atkinson, N.C. Their names were Virginia and Jesse Woodcock.

Back in the 1940s my grandparents lived in an old country wood frame house with a wood burning stove in the kitchen. Some great food came from that old stove. Grandma had what they called the safe where she kept fatback and sweet potatoes and cakes and pies when she cooked them. It was like an old china cabinet without glass, just wooden doors, a "food safe."

Their was also a wood burning laundry heater, they called it, or called a pot belly stove, in the living room to keep warm.

I remember my family talking about how my granddad's first wife had died very young. She was either doing laundry or making soap in a big cast iron pot with a fire underneath it. Her clothes caught fire and she burned to death. This was in the backyard of this same house. My grandmama went on to raise the two little children from that marriage along with her own four with Granddaddy.

On the back porch was a water pump. You would push the handle up and down several times until it was primed and then water would pour out the spout. They kept a pail of water by the pump with a long handled cup for drinking.

We used to make many a run, sometimes in the freez-

Four generations: Susan, Obbie's daughter; Obbie; Madeline, Obbie's mom and grandfather, Jesse.

ing cold, to the old outhouse out back. It was a two-seater. At first there were corncobs to use, and later I remember the Sears catalog. Now and then you might even spot a snake slithering away out the cracks.

We used to have family gatherings at my grandparents', especially for their birthdays. All the family would come and bring loads of good old country food: fried chicken, collards, chicken and pastry, cornbread, and biscuits so delicious they would melt in your mouth. There would be pies, cakes, etc. The adults would spread two sawhorses apart and put boards on them to make a table. After everyone was full, they would put a tablecloth over the food and leave it out from lunch until dinner. As far as I know, no one got sick. This is something you would never do today. We have learned so much about food contamination.

Obbie's grandparents, Jesse and Virginia Woodcock.

After the huge meal all the adults would sit on the back porch and chat, while we kids played tag and ball or just rested.

What a peaceful and wonderful life we thought it was. We kids didn't know the adults were talking about a terrible war, World War II. I remember my mother being notified that her brother, my Uncle Gurney Woodcock, had been taken prisoner of war. He later came home without injury, at least physically, and went on to live a quiet, peaceful life in that same old house he was raised in. He remodeled it into a beautiful place.

Despite all he had been through, Uncle Gurney loved a good joke and had a terrific sense of humor. Everyone loved to be in his company. He could keep you laughing.

Uncle Gurney went on to be mayor of Atkinson years later, but he never, as I can remember, discussed his ordeal as a prisoner of war. He was a quiet hero. He had a full military funeral in 2006.

My Uncle Gurney was the only Woodcock family member who served during that war. Our grandson, Adam Dillon, honored his great uncle by also serving in the Army and in the war in Iraq as a staff sergeant. He is now a police officer.

Uncle Gurner, his wife, Lois and daughter, Vivian.

Atkinson gathering.

I worked thirty years in law enforcement and started driving students on activity trips after I retired. I now drive for Cape Fear Academy.

My wife Mary and I have three children, fourteen grandchildren and two great grandchildren. My three children followed me into law enforcement as well as a son-in-law, two grandsons and one granddaughter-in-law.

I walked a police beat in downtown Wilmington back when they had call boxes on telephone poles to report to the station, so naturally I have stories to tell them about the difference in what I experienced in relation to their jobs now.

Those Days are Gone
by
Robert Goff of Castle Hayne

Robert Goff was born in Wilmington in 1934. He remembers party line phones, sparks down the light bulb wires during thunder storms and he knows what a haunted house is for: to get a kiss from your girlfriend!

Oh, yes, do I ever remember those days! Yes sir, I remember.

The iceman came around twice a week, Tuesday and Friday. A ten cent block was about two feet square. My brothers and I would take the broom with a string around the ice and carry it in and put it in the icebox.

Mama and Grandma had only one—in their bedroom. We found out what it was: a chamber pot.

Knickers: every small boy wore them to school and church.

There was an outhouse behind our house in town. Then Daddy put a bathroom in our house. Now we were something!

Radio programs were few, but most evenings we could hear the Lone Ranger and the Green Hornet. The Grand Ol Opry came home every Saturday night from seven to eight.

The party line phone was something. Get off the phone, I need to use it! Stop listening to my calls! I'm going to report you! Boy, they would get off quick.

We didn't have a windup record player but my friend did. Records were not very good and clear, but it was modern at this time.

There were two size tubs, number one and number two. The small tubs were for small children and the number two was for a much larger person and you heated the water in the fireplace by lamp light, the oil type.

Mama and Grandma used a spittoon every day. Railroad Mill snuff. I could not dip it at all. No sir, not me.

Flypaper was in everybody's house, in the kitchen and living room. Boy, was that a sight with all them flies and bugs stuck to it.

Grandma saved all the feathers from the young pullets (chickens) and made pillows and mattresses. They were all right at the time, but they wouldn't do nowdays.

We had no lights in our house on North 5th Street in the early 40s, but Daddy did get two put in later. But every time an electric rain storm came, boy the sparks would fly down those wires. I did not like that at all.

Bib overalls was the style at my time. Warm, durable, and you could go to church or work in them.

There were some haunted houses in town but most were out in the country. They were old farms where family members had died and the houses were left without any care at all. They were places to take your girlfriend to maybe get a hug or kiss.

We did a lot of skinny dipping in the summertime. We would find out where the girls were swimming and hope we could watch them swim.

It was fun visiting grandparents. We got to eat good then, country ham and eggs, corn on the cob and vegetables of all kinds. We would run the chickens and ducks, etc. And just seeing Grandma.

I didn't know there were any other paved roads but 17 and 117 that went into Wilmington. Streets in Wilmington were brick. Most all roads out of town were dirt or clay.

We made our own toys: rag dolls, wooden guns and trucks. They were crude, but we made do with them.

We had a hand pump in the backyard and there were public hand pumps on most city block corners but I could hardly make them work.

You could hunt squirrels, duck and deer eight blocks from Front Street, and catch perch in any ditch with water in it.

Yes, Wilmington has changed quite a bit. Most people don't remember, but Rocky Point had a little town in it. Dirt streets, wooden sidewalks, general store and a train depot for those traveling that way. Horses and mules were everywhere. Carts were the way you carried your produce to the depot, put it on the train and it was sent to New York or some other market.

In Wilmington we did have a Sears store downtown on Front Street, and Montgomery Ward and an A&P store. Fourth Street was the street to find most everything you would ever need. I could tell a long story but those days are gone now.

People have changed. You could walk anywhere you wanted to and feel safe. Not anymore. Too many rights are given to the public now, that affect your freedom. They lifted the law on ceiling prices and everything went sky high. You could do this, but you couldn't do that. You could sue at the drop of a hat. Yes, I remember the truth about the time I lived. God Bless America.

Going to Town
by
Janet Croom Nelson of Carolina Beach

Janet Nelson, who was born in Wallace in 1940 and grew up there, shares many memories of life in southeastern North Carolina.

My three sisters and I grew up in Wallace, N.C. I was the youngest, born in 1940.

Living in southeastern North Carolina during the 40s and 50s did not offer a lot of excitement. However, the excitement came about when we knew we were going to Wilmington, "town" as we called it in those days.

"Going to town" had a special meaning to us. It wasn't just shopping—it was the excitement of Efirds on Front Street. It wasn't going to the doctor—it was riding the elevator in the Mercusion Building. The elevator had a real live operator, handsome in her spotless uniform and her nails were always painted red.

Old Dr. Freeman took out my tonsils in the old Bullock Hospital on Front Street. This

James Walker Memorial Hospital in 1944 was demolished and apartments built in this location.

The grand opening of the Western Auto store in Wallace in 1948. At the microphone singing Dorothy Croom, Doris Teachey, Mary Ellen Brown, Ruby Danford, and Annie Helen Sholar. Dorothy, who worked at Western Auto, wrote the song they were singing which was broadcasted over WRRZ.

Robert Butler holding a box at the grand opening for his daughter, Cherita Butler, to draw a lucky name. In the foreground is Mr. Danford. Left to right: Doris Danford, Dorothy Croom, Ryby Danford, Annie Helen Sholar and Mrs. Robert Butler.

same Dr. Freeman also took my sister's tonsils out, right in his office, and then she was taken to James Walker Memorial Hospital. We both recovered nicely.

A younger doctor, Donald Anderson, came to work with Dr. Freeman in the 40s. Dr. Anderson did corrective surgery on both my eyes. My eyes were crossed, and after the surgery they were straight. My family and I will always be grateful for what Dr. Anderson did. I wore glasses after the surgery till recently, when Dr. Byron Stratas performed Lasik surgery and corrected my vision to 20/20.

We didn't always have an electric refrigerator. For many years, we had an icebox and the iceman knew how much ice we needed from a sign we hung on the front screen door. Hopefully, whatever the iceman brought and put in the icebox would last till he came again.

My dad worked in Wallace as an iceman. Later, he worked at Camp Davis in Holly Ridge and moved to the new Marine base, Camp Lejeune, when it was completed. When gas was rationed, my dad left on Monday morning, came back Wednesday evening, went back Thursday morning and came back Friday evening. My mom always had a hot meal on the table when he came home from work.

In the summertime, we ate a lot of butterbeans, okra, tomatoes, hot biscuits and cornbread. We grew a lot of our vegetables and canned or froze them to use in cold weather. We always had good food and lots of it.

The year my oldest sister, Dorothy, was to graduate, another [school] year was added,

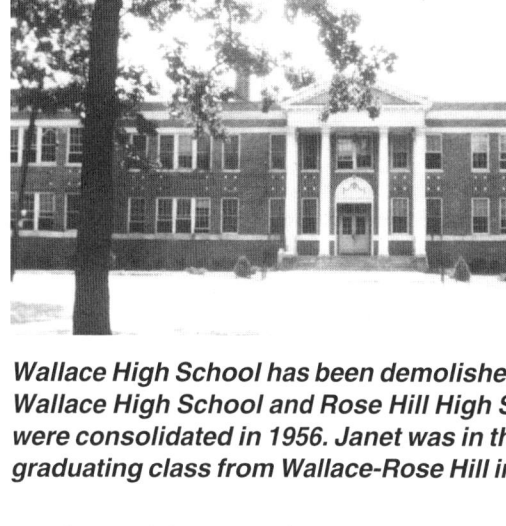

Wallace High School has been demolished. Wallace High School and Rose Hill High School were consolidated in 1956. Janet was in the third graduating class from Wallace-Rose Hill in 1959.

so she and the rest of us had to complete 12 years [of school] instead of 11. My other sisters, Betty and Virginia, and I did not like that one bit.

I can remember my first grade teacher, Kathleen Cook, put on a "Thom Thumb wedding." This was a production and hopefully she had a lot of help. I do believe folks paid to see it. I was a first grader and I can remember it was fun and I was part of it, along with lots of others who I later graduated with from Wallace-Rose Hill High School, to include: Janice Cottle, Marcell Cottle, John Teachey, Roy Cavenaugh, Jr., Jimmy Hundley, Judy Wells, Faye Southerland, Jeanette Turner, Delmar Minchew. The class members of 1959 still stay in touch.

Janet Croom Nelson with the bride doll Santa Claus brought in 1947.

Growing up in southeastern North Carolina was a good thing. We were taught values, to respect our elders and people of authority and most of us were in church on Sunday and Wednesday. If we didn't go to church, we didn't go anywhere else that day.

Robert Bryant, Ira Jackson, Virginia, Betty and Dorothy Croom in 1936.

None of us got into too much trouble that I can remember. Although Roy Cavenaugh, Jr. crashed his plane and walked away, only to die of a heart attack a few short years ago.

We all did all we could I'm sure, but we never hurt anybody, and as I tell people frequently, if I had known I was going to live this long, I would have taken better care of myself.

After retiring from DuPont in Richmond, Virginia, I'm doing what I've always wanted to do: live at the beach!

Boards of Education
by
W.C. (Bill) Annarino of Wilmington

Bill (AKA "Wild Bill") Annarino was born in 1933 in Norfolk, Virginia and grew up there. The title we assigned his story will come clear after you've read his list of memories of things that are no more. (We note, however, that just a few of these things seem to have persisted into present times.)

I remember the many forms of licorice candy, including the candy pipes and cigars. I also remember the candy "buttons," which were long strips of paper covered with candy buttons.

I built and flew stick-built model airplanes. Some were powered by rubber bands and others by gasoline engines or CO2 cartridges. I also built and flew gliders.

I listened to short wave world-wide radio broadcasts on transoceanic radios such as Halicrafters, Collins and Zenith.

Some of the games played were hopscotch, kick the can, hide and seek and "dinks." Dinks was a marble game where you tossed a handful of marbles in a hole in the ground. The most marbles "in" won all the marbles. We also played mumbly-peg, which involved flipping a small pocketknife from various hand positions, attempting to make the knife stick in the ground. The loser (optionally) pulled a peg out of the ground with his or her teeth.

I remember ammonia Cokes for headache relief, a product called Hadacol, which was an energy booster, and Geritol, an iron-poor blood enhancer. Paregoric was a tincture of opium to relieve pain like sore gums during children's teeth cutting periods.

I remember during World War II the air raid drills with their blackout shades, sirens and air raid wardens. There were Victory Stamps and war bonds, and the necessity of rationing things like nylons, butter, gasoline, tires and many foods. Many families grew Victory gardens, and I remember static chasers: radio operators.

Some of the personal items I remember are: tooth "powder"; pomade hair dressing; Wildroot hair dressing; Ipana toothpaste; Vitalis hair dressing; bobbie pins; garters and garter belts; nylon stockings with seams;

girdles and corsets; hooped skirts (Scarlett in *Gone with the Wind*).

There were foot-operated air pumps; lightning rods to diminish the destructive effect of same; and doctors who made house calls.

Reel-type lawn mowers (powerless mowers) were about all that were available in those days; fountain pens; school desk inkwells; Duz laundry soap; Daisy air rifles: BB guns were all readily available. Gillette promoted double-bladed razor blades.

Jodhpurs were riding breeches; pegged pants (tapered at the cuff area) were the rage; ducktail hairstyles (circa late 1940s); and winged tipped and white buck shoes went with them.

And finally, I remember switches: twigs or flexible rods used as "boards of education" for bad behavior.

Linda Jane Farris with her mom and dad, Nell and George.

Walking the Circle
by
Linda Jane Farris Register Baker of Wilmington

Some stories are timeless and this is one of them. Many of us conveniently forget our mischievous childhood escapades, but Linda Baker remembers...and entertains us wonderfully with this delightful tale about growing up near Lynchburg, Virginia where she was born in 1941, and later, in the Wilmington area. There's plenty of history along with the mischief. You won't want to miss this delightful tale.

When I was a little girl of five, my family moved to the country. In my family were my dad, George Farris, and mom, Nell Farris, my dog Frisky (an Eskimo spitz) and my Maltese cat, Blue. We had a nice two-story house and a small grocery store next door, with gas pumps.

It was the year 1946; we had electricity, but we did not have running water in our house. We had a hand pump off the kitchen where my mother got the water to prepare our meals, and for taking baths. In back of the house down a small path was our outhouse. My mom planted pretty flowers by the path, but it was always scary to me. I hated to go to the outhouse. I was always afraid something was going to snatch me right down in that hole. I'm pretty sure I didn't go alone, that my mother went with me.

In our bedrooms we had chamber pots, white porcelain with black trim. I remember using it, but don't remember my mom cleaning them, which I'm sure she did each morning.

My dad had a job in construction, so my mom ran the store and had to take care of me. One day I got bored, so I took down a box of Ex-lax. It smelled just like chocolate. I tasted it, and it tasted just like chocolate. So I ate a couple of pieces. It was so good I ate a few more. Then my dog Frisky came in and I fed the rest of the box to him. You can imagine what happened to me and Frisky! My mom said I could have killed him, but he survived and lived for a ling time. And me? I never want another piece of Ex-lax as long as I live.

Another time that I remember, we had dried beans stored in barrels in front of the counter in our store, so I mixed them all up good: pintos, black eye peas, northern, and limas. My mom was pretty upset with me about that, so I never did that again.

Summer had finally come, and I could play outside in the warm sun. I loved to lay in the green grass and watch the clouds go by and make pictures from the clouds. Sometimes I would lie at the top of the hill and roll down to the bottom and get up and do it again till I was real tired and then take a nap in the sun. I still love to lie in the sun and take a nap.

When my mom washed her clothes she would boil the white clothes in a large black pot. Then she had a large pole she dipped them out with and put them in large galvanized wash tub in cold water to rinse them. Then she wrung them out and hung them on the clothesline. When she starched her curtains, she would put them on stretchers in the sun to dry and whiten them.

Linda Jane's dog, Frisky.

In the summer when it was warm weather, my mom would fill the wash tub in the early morning, and by afternoon it would be nice and warm and I would have my bath on the back porch. In the winter I had my bath water heated in the kitchen.

One time I remember sassing my mom and she washed my mouth out with Octagon soap. That was awful; I did not do that again.

I loved making believe and pretending, so one day I took the two Adirondacks chairs and the double and turned them upside down. At each end I took two large brooms, and put the broom side down and put them at each end. Then I got one of my mom's sheets and tied an end on the poles for a sail. Then I took two pillows and I sat up the pillows and pretended to sail away to another land. Sometimes I would put the sheet over the chairs and have a tent, and put my teddy bears in it and pretend we were far away.

Sometimes I would watch the convoys going down the street. We were close to military bases, and we were also close to an airport. One day when I was out watching the airplanes take off and land, I decided to go visit a neighbor, a friend of my mom's. I went up on the porch and her door was open, so I looked in the screen door. On her table were four large meringue pies. Oh how I loved meringue, so I opened the door and I called out, but nobody answered. I thought just one little taste won't hurt, but needless to say, I did not take one taste. I ate the meringue off all the pies. Then I started for home. When I saw the neighbor coming, I told her someone went in her house and ate the meringue off all her pies. She did not let on that I had

Linda Jane's house in Lynchburg, Va. is still standing but moved back from the road.

meringue all over my face. She said when she told my mom, she thought it was funny, but my mom did not think so. She went to the hedge and broke off a long thin switch, and stripped the leaves off and she whipped me till blood ran down my legs. I didn't get many whippings, but I have to say that was a really bad one.

In the summer when it was really hot, I would go to the well and let down the wood bucket till I heard the splash. Then I would pull up the coldest, clearest water and take the copper dipper and dip into the cold water and it was so good, the best water I have ever had. (I have two antique dippers hanging in my kitchen now, a stainless and copper, remembering the good old days.)

In the late summer we would get our pails and go blackberry picking. There was a small mountain behind our house, and just at the edge of the mountain was a railroad track. We had to cross the track to go up on the mountain. We also had to watch out for black bears—they liked blackberries too. We would pick and eat at the same time. The berries were so big and juicy and sweet, and when we got home we would have juice all over us. Then Mom would bake those big cobblers, and we would eat them with mounds of vanilla ice cream.

I used to like to see the big steam engines pulling all those cars and the little red caboose in the back. The flagman was on the platform and he always waved at us.

In the fall, the Gypsies would have a gathering. They would put up tents and have palm readings and fortune telling. I really liked to go there they had such colorful clothes. The ladies, with their big earrings, would dance in their full skirts and peasant blouses, and the men had sashes and turbans on their heads. At night they would gather around a bonfire and play instruments and sing songs. It was so exciting to a small girl.

Also about this time, the circus came with

Linda Jane's dad's store is still there but the gas pumps are gone.

their big tents, animals, clowns, and the girls on the trapeze. There was also the food, candy apples, cotton candy, peanuts and popcorn. It was so good.

But all too soon, winter came with the snow. I was living in Virginia at the time and we had deep snows. I hated wearing shoes, so more than one time my mom caught me running out in the snow with no shoes on. I loved making snow cream. It was so good.

But on those bad days I had my playroom upstairs to play in. I had my teddy bears, porcelain dolls and Raggedy Ann and Andy. We did tea parties, had a hospital, and reading time.

I loved books. I had a bookshelf with a lot of books, and my parents read to me most every night. So I would read the story by the pictures. My dad worked long hours, but at night he was never too tired to read me a story, or make up a story, or sing me a song. He played by ear and could play the banjo, mandolin and harmonica. My favorite books were *Little Black Sambo*, *Ugly Duckling*, *Uncle Remus*, and *Bible Stories*. I always liked music and two songs I remember I liked were *Little Slow Poke* and *Buttons and Bows*.

In the summer of 1947, my dad decided to sell the house and store and bought a silver trailer so we could go with him on his jobs. The trailer was the top of the line at that time. We had running water and electricity, a small bathroom, and a very large bedroom in the back with lots of storage over and under the bed. It had a nice living room. The sofa converted into a bed, the table was in the wall, and a small lever would release it out of the wall for mealtime.

The ironing board was also in the wall in the kitchen. Also in the kitchen we had an icebox, and the iceman came and brought big blocks of ice. Sometimes in the summer, the iceman would cut large slivers and we would sit in the shade and eat it till it melted. That was so good.

For three years we lived in that trailer and traveled all over North Carolina. But soon my mom said she wanted to live in a house again, so we sold the trailer and moved into a house in Mount Olive, North Carolina. And from there we came to Wilmington, where I grew up.

I was eleven years old when we moved to Wilmington in the Sunset Park area. I was in the 5th grade and I had to walk to school because my mother did not drive. I really hated walking by myself because at that time I had not made friends. Some days it was really scary. But soon I made friends and then it was fun.

After school we played jacks, the game with marbles and a small ball. I was very good at it and won most of the time. The other games were hopscotch and double Dutch jumping rope. Sometimes I would gather up the small children and tell them stories.

My mom made goodies for snack time, like gingerbread, bread pudding with lots of raisins, cookies, and popcorn, with Koolaid.

When I was twelve, we moved to the Wrightsboro area. We lived in a wooded area, no close neighbors. I loved living there. We had a small garden, which was my duty to water and weed.

My dad and I used to go rabbit hunting. He made the traps, and we would go and see if we caught anything. I never saw my dad kill or skin them, but I used to have a whole drawer full of tails. I thought they would bring good luck. Then my dad would cook them up golden brown, with brown gravy and mashed potatoes, and from scratch, the biggest, fluffiest biscuits. What a meal!

Then my dad had a bright idea: he would make some rabbit cages and we would raise our own rabbits. So he made the cages and got four rabbits, and those rabbits started multiplying and we had to build more cages. I started naming them and no way was I going to eat any pet rabbit, so we gave them to the old folks' home. I'm sure they didn't have a problem eating them.

While we were living there, I joined the 4-H Club. That was when I first started to sew. I made a full skirt from Indian head fabric. I sewed it all by hand, even put in a zipper, button, button hole. My dad was so impressed he bought me my first sewing machine in a cherry cabinet, which I still have. I made a lot of clothes on that sewing machine, and ended up sewing for the rest of my life.

One day my brother, who was five at the time, and I went for a walk down a dirt road, singing and skipping along. All of a sudden I looked behind me and there was this snake lying in the road all coiled up. Nothing I hated worse than a snake, so I grabbed

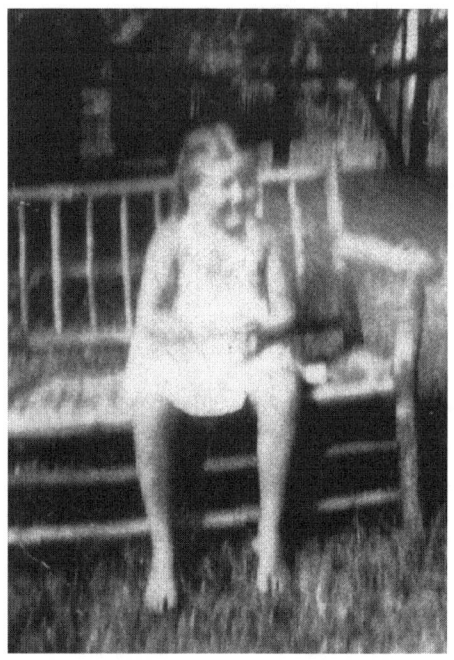

Linda Jane Farris in 1949.

up my brother and started screaming and ran back through the woods to the house. My legs were all scratched, and I thought my heart would jump right out of my body. Next time we went walking I was careful to keep my eyes open and not run into any more snakes.

We lived way up on a hill, so I had to walk down the hill to catch the school bus. I was the first stop in the morning about 6:30, and I was the last stop in the afternoon. I got home about five. I usually had most of my homework done when I got home, but if not, I started it right away.

GA Coronation. Linda Jane Farris below arrow.

My dad usually got home around 6:30 and sometimes in the summer I would go down to meet him and catch a ride on the running board of his truck up to our house. That was so much fun.

We moved again to a neighborhood which had a lot of the kids I went to school with. Sometimes in the early evening in the summer, we would walk the circle and sing songs, like *Three Coins in the Fountain* or the Everly Brothers. Sometimes we would sit on the porch and listen to stories on the radio. One of my favorites was Sergeant Preston of the Yukon. It was about this time we got our first TV. We didn't get a lot of programs, but it was really neat. We bought this color cellophane paper and put on the front of the TV, and called it color TV. We watched the Creaking Door, and a Millionaire giving away money.

After dark in the summer, a group of us would walk the circle. Down around the curve was an old slave graveyard. A lot of stories were told about it, and sometimes the boys would sneak down there, and when we came by, they would make noises or jump out at us. We would run screaming, and then we would start to laughing because they got us again. Those were fun and scary days.

Out back of our house was a large grape arbor, and those grapes were so big and delicious and the leaves were so big and green. We would get up under them to feel the cool breeze, and munch on the grapes.

It was about this time I wanted to be a blond, so I put a whole bottle of peroxide on my hair. Well, I got blond hair all right, but I really got a scolding from my mom. It took quite a while for it to grow out. My mom said, "Don't be surprised if all your hair falls out." But I was lucky, it turned out okay.

It was also about this time that Elvis appeared on the Ed Sullivan Show. They wouldn't show him below his waist. My mom said he would never last. Boy, was she wrong! I sent away for Elvis portraits, and put them in frames by my bed and nightstand. My dad bought me a record player in its own case that played 45s. I bought all Elvis's 45s and put them in a record case to match my player.

When I was fourteen, I was going to Wrightsboro Baptist Church. We had a girls' group that was called the GAs. In this group we learned missions, helping others, and learning the Bible. We learned Scriptures and recited them to members of the church to make our steps. There were five of us that became queen that year: Betty Jo Matthews, Barbara Crumpler, Helen Burton, Rowena Porter and me.

We had the first GA coronation. It was so beautiful, and afterwards the church gave us a social. What a great night. Afterwards, several of my friends went home with me to spend the night. Needless to say, we didn't get much sleep that night.

That summer wasn't as much fun. Mom said we were growing up and needed to be more responsible. That meant more chores, and that just wasn't what I had in mind to do all summer. So I got a job working on the bookmobile. I loved books anyway, and it was only two days a week. Then I got a job at Mays Five and Ten, working on Friday nights and all day Saturdays.

When school took back in, my dad said no more working during the school year. So off to high school we went. What an experience, but soon it was nothing changing classes and meeting friends in the hallways, and going to lunch at a hangout near school, eating cream filled donuts and Pepsis for lunch and listening to the juke box.

We were very serious about school and we worked hard and made good grades.

On Sundays after church and lunch, my dad would take me and my friends to the Biltmore Dairy bar and buy us our favorite ice cream treat. Sometimes we would go to the Bailey for a movie, or sometime we just walked and window shopped. Back then stores were not open on Sundays. Sometimes we just stayed at my house and lounged out in the swing on the porch and had lemonade and cookies, and dreamed about what we would do when were all grown up. Those were the days.

I had a wonderful childhood, and great parents, and as I look back, they truly were the good old days.

A Toddle House Romance
by
Cody D. Smith of Tabor City

This isn't really a romance story, but it ends that way, very happily. And the rest of Cody Smith's story is happy, too. We think you'll find it interestingly enjoyable.

I was born at home on September 3rd, 1937 in a little community called Flint Ridge, a few miles out of Heath Springs, South Carolina, located In Lancaster County.

I remember my mom used to cook all our meals on an old wood stove. We never lived in a house that had electricity until I was about 12 years of age. We did not have an Inside bathroom or inside plumbing. We got our water out of a well where you would drop a bucket on a rope down into the well and pull the bucket of water out. So you could say instead of having six rooms and a bath, we had four rooms and a path that led out to the outhouse.

My dad worked at a sawmill where he cut timber for a lumber company. The name of the company was Hutton and Bourbonnais out of Hickory, N.C. I have a W-2 form from his employer there in 1950. His total earnings that year were $1141.85.

I got my first drivers license at age 14. I drove the family car, a 1939 Chevy, on the road test. It did not have turn signals or windshield wipers. I still have a copy of my license from 1953.

We moved to Charlotte, N.C. when I was 15 years old. I went to work in a supermarket that year at a store called Park-N-Shop located on Wilkinson Boulevard. The store building is still there. My starting pay was 35 cents an hour. You could buy a Pepsi or Coke out of a vending machine for five cents.

In 1955 I went to see a country music show at the Carolina Theater on North Tryon

Street. The main attraction was a singer and his name was Elvis Presley. That was the only time i ever saw him in person.

In 1964 I took a second job driving a Yellow Cab at night. I wanted to learn all the streets in Charlotte. I would stop in at a little all night diner called the Toddle House on South Boulevard to buy coffee. I met a pretty young lady who was working there. Her name was Wanda. I asked her for a date. On our first date we went to a drive-in theater in my 1956 Chevy convertible. Two weeks later we got married. That was on December 22nd 1966. We just celebrated forty years of marriage this past December, 2006.

I am 69 years of age and I still work full time in a supermarket. Boy, I sure wish I still had that 1956 Chevy convertible!

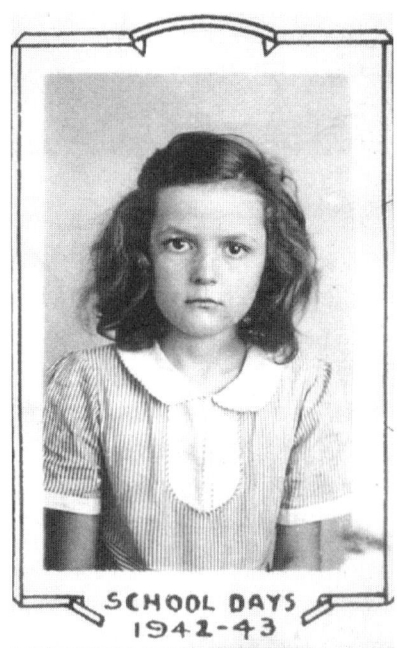
Elsie Packer Smiley.

Salty Water and Trolley Rails
by
Elsie Packer Smiley of Wilmington

There have been times in the past when something we all take for granted these days—water—wasn't quite so certain. Elsie Smiley has some interesting memories about that precious commodity.

I have lived in Wilmington most of my 73 years. I have seen lots of changes. I'm not sure that a lot of them are for the best.

I remember once when the city water turned salty. I'm not sure of the year—I think maybe 40 or 41—but we had to get water for drinking and cooking wherever we could.

There used to be beautiful ornate water hand pumps on different street corners. We children had to go pump water in huge pails to use at home. This was *our job.*

There was also an overflow at Spofford Mills on Wrightsville Avenue. My parents worked in the mill. The water flowed from a large pipe in the ground and dumped into a large ditch that ran along the side of the mill and under Wrightsville Avenue. The water was very cold, clear and really good. We would collect that in pails and take it home for drinking. We children were very happy with our job.

At this same time we lived close to the mill. The old trolley line rails were in front of our house and I remember beautiful wild pink roses growing along the rails. We loved picking those for my mom.

The trolley line once went to Wrightsville Beach.

Beautiful memories of a childhood past.

Freedom from Knickers
by
Richard Cushman of Southport

Dick Cushman was born in Brockton, Massachusetts in 1931 and grew up in Randolph, Massachusetts. We assume his delightful memories are about his boyhood there. Except for the geography, it's obvious that boys are boys, no matter where they were raised. Here's a story that will take you back.

Around 1940, all the kids in our neighborhood got out of school, went home, changed clothes and went out to play until the street lights came on. We played all kinds of games, sports and built huts in the woods.

However, when a plane flew over (mostly a piper cub) all activities stopped while we watched the plane.

While shopping downtown, I ran into a large crowd on the sidewalk gazing at a store window. When I got to the crowd, I saw what they were looking at: a TV! My first sight of a TV.

Every Saturday afternoon my neighbor took all the kids on his truck to the movies. The movies had two features, comedy shorts, *The Eyes and the Ears of the World* news and previews. The ticket cost ten cents. The price of the tickets went up to eleven coins and my mother couldn't afford eleven cents and ended my Saturday afternoon at the movies.

As a young boy I had to wear knickers. I hated them! The corduroy made noise when you walked and the stockings would not stay up. You were constantly pulling them up, even while running. Finally, the age of manhood came and freed me from knickers. A big event.

Azalea Queens and Air Shows
by
Karen Jarrell Edwards of Hampstead

Don't let the title fool you. Karen Edwards' story covers far more than this, including a "green bean snake," the pleasures in downtown Wilmington and an adventurous father who was high in the hierarchy of the sheriff's department. This collection of family memories will entertain and inform you. Mrs. Edwards was born in Wilmington in 1958.

I am the youngest of six children. We all grew up in Wilmington, including my mama and daddy. My parents, who are now deceased, are Rudolph and Hazel Jarrell. My daddy was born in 1914 and died in 1999. My mother was born in 1913 and died in 2006. My family consisted of love, God, family, church and friends.

My daddy was a people person and sometimes he would invite people over to make homemade ice cream. Of course it wasn't an electric machine. It had to be churned by hand. The anticipation was a thrill and it was the best ice cream I've ever eaten.

One of my many memories is of a hot summer day in our garden in the bottom field. We were picking green beans and suddenly my niece started screaming and jumping around. She had picked a small green snake! We still laugh about that today.

Another fond memory is of going shopping downtown with my mother. That was where most of the stores were then. We would go to Belk's and Penny's and Kresses, etc. When I was a little girl my mama and I would walk into the drugstore. I can still remember the smell of food. We would shop and then go to the food counter and sit on those stools that go round and round. We would get a sandwich and a Coke and sometimes I could talk my mama into getting some of those warm cashews. Then we would go to Penny's.

Penny's had an elevator that to a child looked like a big black cage. I was thrilled and afraid at the same time to ride it. The elevator sounded like it was going to fall apart and did not feel very stable.

I can remember Monkey Junction. It was only woods and fields back then. My daddy had a tractor and he would go and cut down the weeds.

My daddy was the Chief Deputy of the Sheriff's Department. He had many different duties. He was involved with many of the Azalea Festivals. One year, and this is in the best of my family memories, Daddy escorted one of our Azalea Queens. He walked along beside the float she was on.

On the day of the Azalea Festival parade, we would go into the old courthouse and go upstairs and watch the parade out of those large courthouse windows.

I remember going to many air shows. Daddy would be working and he would come and have lunch with us. Mama would pull out fried chicken, potato salad, etc. It was a feast for the eyes and for the stomach. When I was three or four years old, my sister and her family were with us at the air show. I don't remember the year. That day, my daddy was working at the air show. He had been asked to fly on the airplane that was bringing the paratroopers in. He declined, saying he didn't like to fly, which was fortunate because the airplane crashed and there were some fatalities.

When the battleship was brought up the river to its berth place, my daddy rode on the tugboat that pulled it.

My mother told me that when they moved to Masonboro Sound there were very few homes. Mama told me that you could drive to town and never see another car coming or going. She also told me that the only way on or off Wrightsville Beach was to ride the trolley car. Mama said everyone walked or rode a bicycle or a horse to get around. She told me that very few people back then could afford a car. She said no one back then locked their doors.

Karen Sue Jarrell, age five, in 1963.

The home my parents raised us all in was first my mother's uncle's house. She told me she would visit in the summer and played there when she was just a little girl. We recently found out that their house is 167 years old.

When my parents moved into the house, there were no modern conveniences. They had an outhouse, a wood stove to heat and cook on. They pumped water outside. My parents had chickens and a cow named Penny. My mother would catch a chicken, kill it, clean it, pluck it and cook it. Wow!

Mama once told me that she only started gaining weight because she would milk the cow and let the milk sit and take the cream off the top and drink it. She said it was delicious. She also churned her own butter.

I once asked my mother what she did for fun when she was a young girl. She told me that friends would get together, borrow a truck and then drive into the woods, which is now South College Road. They would park, cut the radio up and use the bed of the truck as a dance platform. They would dance the night away.

Daddy told me that his grandfather lived in Southport. To visit him, they would take a one car ferry across the river. It would be muddy and wet. Back then the old cars had very thin tires and they would get stuck many times before they got to his grandfather's home.

I hope you have enjoyed some of my family memories. Thanks for the opportunity to share these precious memories with you.

The Yo-yo Champ and Streaked Butter
by
Nancy Oakley of Wilmington

Life north of the Mason-Dixon Line may have been different back in the good old days, but in many, many ways, it was the same. These memories from Nancy Oakley, who was born in New York State in 1937, will strike a familiar chord for almost all of us who are from her generation.

I lived in Syracuse New York when I was a child and here are some of the things I remember from those days.

I remember standing on a street corner in my neighborhood with a bunch of kids playing with our yo-yos. Duncan Yo-yo used to have contests back then on who could do different tricks or who could keep their yo-yo going the longest. I remember winning the latter and received a badge and a brand new yo-yo. I was thrilled and wore the badge proudly.

I used to play for hours under the dining room table with my paper dolls. I used Kleenex for beds and made little boxes for other things. You had to cut out your dolls and clothes, and that was part of the fun.

Entertainment then was playing kick the can, red light green light and hide and seek. We didn't sit in front of a TV or play video games.

Since I was a thumb sucker, I remember Mom putting me to bed with these horrible leather braces, one for each elbow, so I could not bend my arm. They were itchy and hot to wear and I usually found a way to get them off. Mom finally gave up.

One of my favorite things to do was sit in the kitchen with Mom while she fixed dinner. It was my task to knead the color into the oleo. Back then, oleo was white and came with a little packet of yellow coloring. If you didn't like the white color you could knead the yellow into it so that it looked more like butter. If it was not kneaded thoroughly, you had streaks through it. It sure didn't taste like butter.

One of the things I hated most was when Mom decided I needed a permanent. She would take me to the beauty parlor and there I would have to sit for hours with this thing on my head. They put some kind of wires in my hair, then turned on the electricity to make the hair curl. I usually looked a sight but Mom thought it was beautiful.

On the way to school there was a little grocery store that sold penny candies. We used to stop there with our lunch money and get a little bag full of candies. Buttons were a favorite, also little wax bottles with flavored juice in them.

I remember my grand parents' farm with the outhouse in the back. They had a pump in the kitchen for water and a wind-up Victrola where you played the old 78 records such as the "The Black Crows." The refrigerator was cooled by big chunks of ice and if you wanted an ice cube, you had to use an ice pick to get a chunk off the block.

These are some of the things I remember the most. Of course there were the usual, five cent drinks and the 25 cent movies. Most of all, there was more family life than there is now, and some of those times are remembered fondly.

Woods That Are No More
by
Stanley Harold Harts of Rocky Point

Growth and change are themes that are repeated throughout this book. However, the term metamorphose might be more applicable in this particular story. Mr. Harts elegantly combines the qualities of poignancy and acceptance in describing the region where he has spent his life. He was born 1952 in Burgaw.

I have had the opportunity to see the decline and rebirth of both a community and a home in my 54 years.

On June 23, 1952, I became one of the first newborn infants to arrive at the newly-completed Pender Memorial Hospital. The hospital was, needless to say, much smaller then than it is now.

My parents were William Frank Harts and Mary Joy Hancock Harts. I was brought into this world by the late, great Dr. Nathan Carl Wolfe, whom I believe to this day to have been the finest physician I ever encountered.

When I was two years old, my parents bought and moved into a two-story clapboard house on N.C. Highway 210 in Rocky Point. This house had a colorful history long before that date (1954). It was built about 1898 by Dr. Elisha Porter for some of his family. At that time, the house had no electricity or indoor plumbing, but it was wisely built on high ground, and has withstood every hurricane from then to now.

Our home is said to be haunted, and in truth, some dark deeds have been associated with it, in its long past. In the year 1917, a cousin of my grandfather's, Lula Futch Hale, lived there with her husband, John Thomas Hale. One May day, John T. Hale was shot to death back of the lot, in what was then a strawberry field. (It is now part of the grounds of the new Trask School.)

Although the victim's brother, David L. Hale, was tried and sentenced to prison for the crime, suspicion has always existed that he was covering for someone else. He died in prison the next year, and Lula Hale the same year of tetanus.

William Frank Harts and his son, Roger, in front of the Harts' home at Rocky Point in 1985.

The house then passed to Lula's sister, Lonnie Futch Reaves, and her husband Ivey Reaves, who reared their children there. When Lonnie died in 1947, her casket lay in state in what is now our living room. My grandmother, Amanda Watkins Harts, would never sleep there for that reason.

When my father bought the house, Highway 210 had only been paved a few years earlier. The home had electricity, but was deficient in wall outlets. Water came from a hand pump outside, and a bucket and dipper always rested on a side table in the kitchen.

It was about 1956 or 1957 that the outside hand pump was replaced with an electric one, and the water bucket in the kitchen replaced with an indoor sink. The dipper continued to be used by my father until it literally fell apart some 20 years later.

However, hot water and an indoor bathroom did not arrive until about 1964. Our telephone was installed in 1966. The Wilmington phone directory, which I still have, was about a quarter of its present size.

The barns and outbuildings that originally came with the house are gone now, replaced with newer ones. But in what was once a blacksmith shop, my siblings and I used to play house with an old wood burning stove and wooden wagon wheels. A wooden leg from a previous owner also reposed in the barn for years.

The community of Rocky Point has, itself, changed as much as my home. When I was a child, the railroad was still the hub of the neighborhood. In addition to the rail depot and loading dock, five stores and the post office once clustered along the two streets that ran parallel to the tracks. One of the stores belonged to my father's brother, James Harts, and is now the only one still standing.

Passenger train service in Pender County ended in 1960; the station was closed in 1962 and removed in 1973. I had always wanted to ride that train, but never got to. The last railroad tracks were taken down in 1986, when even freight service ended. There has been talk of restoring the main rail line to Pender County (there were once three lines), but at present it remains only talk.

One after another, the stores and shops clustered around the railroad closed down. The Rocky Point Elementary School closed in 1963; it was reopened in the 1970s as a private school, but closed again. The Trask School has opened in its place, directly behind my home, and a water tower now dominates the eastern skyline. I have left an acre of woods growing as a buffer zone on my land.

The old post office has seen two moves; first to Highway 117 south of the crossroads, and then to a larger building to the north. The original building lacked an indoor bathroom!

Today, the new nucleus of Rocky Point lays claim to its own supermarket and a host of shops and filling stations. Pender County has become one of the fastest growing counties in the state, as it takes in the overflow from its parent county, New Hanover. Amazingly enough, Pender's population stayed around 18,000 for thirty years until after 1970, when people began to pour in. Now it is past 40,000 (2000 census).

I will admit, personally, that all of this growth is exciting to watch, and provides a lot of conveniences. But, looking back through time, I miss the days when, as a child, I picked huckleberries, plums, and wild cherries, without interference, in woods that are now no more.

Charlie and the War Injuries
by
James Carmer Davis of Wilmington

We never cease to be amazed by the diversity of adventures we receive about life in the good old days. James Davis, born in Wilmington in 1931, certainly didn't disappoint us. Here's a tale about airplanes, ice trucks and an (almost) practical joke.

When I was a boy, my parents, Myrtle and Norman Davis, had a cottage on the north end of Carolina Beach. We would spend a part of every summer there.

The Pennington brothers (Mr. Warren and Mr. Jimmy "Skinny" Pennington) had a Ford tri-motor aircraft which held about 15-20 passengers. During the summer before World War II (1939-41) they would take passengers up for sightseeing tours over the coast from Carolina Beach to Wrightsville Beach, Masonboro Inlet, Fort Caswell/Long Beach area and back to Carolina Beach, about a 20 minute trip.

My friend, Owen Bessilieu, and I used to hang around the landing strip near Kelly's Kupboard on the north end of the beach. Occasionally, we would help Mr. Pennington clean out the plane when a passenger got airsick. Mr. Pennington would take us up for a flight when his plane wasn't full. We probably went up with him eight or ten times during the summer—a wonderful, exciting experience for two growing boys. Our parents never knew we were doing this until later in life.

During those summers on Carolina

Beach we also often rode on the back of the ice truck with Charlie, the Iceman. We would eat the small slivers of ice off the floor of the truck to cool off.

On one occasion, while Charlie was delivering ice to a home, we took an ice pick and chipped off some ice from a large block. Charlie caught us and said, "Man, don't do that! That's my profit!"

I grew up in the neighborhood around 17th and Ann Streets. As a young teen, I spent a lot of time at the old YMCA at 3rd and Market. One day we were horsing around in the YMCA swimming pool and I fell and hit my head on the edge of the pool, cutting a gash on the back of my head. They took me to the doctor and he put a big bandage around my head and sent me home.

One of my friends who lived down the street from me had fallen off his bicycle and broken his shoulder, and was in a cast which covered his shoulder and his arm. He and I were sitting on his front porch playing checkers—me with my head bandaged and him in a cast. A neighborhood lady walked by on the sidewalk and asked, "Were you poor boys injured in the war?" (This was during World War II.) We had a good laugh at her expense.

Overflowing Beds
by
Florence Simmons of Wilmington

We were very impressed with Mrs. Simmons' story of life on the Foy Plantation, and we could feel the joy she described when her family moved to a larger house where the beds weren't "overflowing with children." She writes of the time during World War II when soldiers waved from train windows, when life was filled with a lot of walking and meals were lots of beans. Mrs. Simmons was born in 1935 in Wilmington

Florence Simmons inside her church in 2006.

and grew up in New Hanover County.

Our family [family name not given] lived in Pender County until I was five years old. We lived and worked on Foy's Plantation. There were milk cows, horses and pigs. There were plenty of pear trees and fig bushes.

My family also ate wild animals such as deer, squirrels, raccoons and birds. They fished, crabbed and dug oysters and clams.

We lived in a two-bedroom house with two beds in each room. There were nine of us in those two rooms and fireplaces in both rooms. The kitchen set away from the house. It housed an old wood stove, two wooden homemade chairs and cabinet. We ate a lot of beans.

After moving into New Hanover, about two blocks from the Pender line, it was a blessing. We had much more room. The house had six rooms—oh, what a relief!

We did a lot of walking from New Hanover to Pender County. The only grocery store and post office were in Pender. We didn't mind—

The family reunion in 1992.

we were used to walking everywhere, even to church, which was two miles both ways.

Our grocery store owners were Mr. and Mrs. Goldie. Mr. Goldie was a very nice man. He would sometimes give us kids candy. Our postmaster was different. Her office opened at one o'clock and if you weren't there by two o'clock to pick up your mail, you missed until the next day or whenever you could get there. She wasn't a friendly person.

I loved the house in New Hanover. We had more room and a kitchen in the same building. We used a wood heater in that house and no beds overflowing with children.

Everyone continued to work in the fields, planting peanuts which were planted by hand. I can hear the overseers saying, "Put the peanuts in checks."

We also picked beans, corn and grapes in their seasons. When our backs gave out picking beans, we crawled on our knees. They used land plaster on peanuts to kill bugs.

We loved living near the highway which was narrow at that time. We even lived near the railroad tracks. Oh, what a joy! We could wave at the soldiers going through on the train and they hung over the windows waving and smiling at us. Oh, what a joy to see people, both black and white, waving and smiling at us. We loved it, so amazing.

We walked to school in New Hanover two miles back and forth. My teacher, Mrs. Sharpless Hansley, was a sweet person, but stern in her classroom. The schoolhouse had two rooms, divided. On one side was Mrs. Hansley and Mrs. Johnson taught on the other side. Excellent teachers.

Later, when I was in fourth grade, our school closed and we were transported to three different schools and teachers. It was good and we fitted in. The teachers in our new schools were nice and caring.

We didn't have much, but those were the best days. Now, everything is very upsetting, especially when all things are changing so fast.

Cheap Swings and Crank Phones
by
Name withheld at contributor's request

The major purpose of our books is to memorialize the people who experienced history. We do not necessarily celebrate them. Rather, their identities provide a personal reference point in time for contemporary readers and a genealogical reference point for future readers.

A secondary purpose is to memorialize occurrences, places and things, as this story does, that don't normally appear in the standard history books.

In the over forty books we've compiled about various North Carolina communities, we have recorded memories of over 6,000 individuals. This is only the third request we've had for anonymity, and only the first of those three that we've accepted.

That said, we apologize to those of our many readers who probably would have readily recognized this contributor who, we believe, was a Wilmington schoolteacher, and who was born in 1929.

I moved to Wilmington in 1964, shortly after the Coastline Railway moved away. "Hi Buddy" Wade was the mayor.

We rented a house for $85.00 a month. There was a grocery store one block to the right. Jarmon's Drug Store was two blocks to the left (on 17th Street). Chestnut Street School was two blocks away. I taught there and could walk to school. I really didn't need a car, which was a good thing because we had only one: a Volkswagen Beetle.

We bought a swing, including chain, for our front porch for six dollars.

Port Authority headquarters was a small office on College Road. UNCW was one building across from New Hanover High. Belks was downtown where the main library is. Efird's Department Store was on Front Street.

There was a post office on Castle Street where the Girls Club is. Also on Castle Street was a small appliance store. The owner could fix anything.

At the corner of College and Oleander there was a horse pasture where Toys R Us, etc., is now.

I grew up in Laurinburg where we had a wooden crank phone on the wall. When you cranked it up, you reached the operator and you told her the number you wanted. The phone always went out in a storm.

Driver's Education was nonexistent. My mother taught me to drive on back roads. "Go faster," she always admonished me.

We've counted our blessings for having lived in Wilmington for 43 years. We do wish that the powers that be would forget the convention center, leave downtown alone, and use that money to fix the sewer system.

A Successful Career
by
Virginia Judy Wiard Kelley of North Topsail Beach

Only a few can begin a life's work in childhood and continue doing what we love. Judy Kelley, who was born in Washington, D.C. in 1937, has apparently succeeded in doing just that.

My mother, Mary Margaret Barber, was born and raised in Wilmington. She went to Winter Park School where she skipped 2nd and 8th grades. She graduated from New Hanover High School at the age of 16 in 1925, the first class to go four years at NHHS. Her brother, David Dennis Barber, Jr., gradu-

Judy Kelley.

Judy Kelley, age 17.

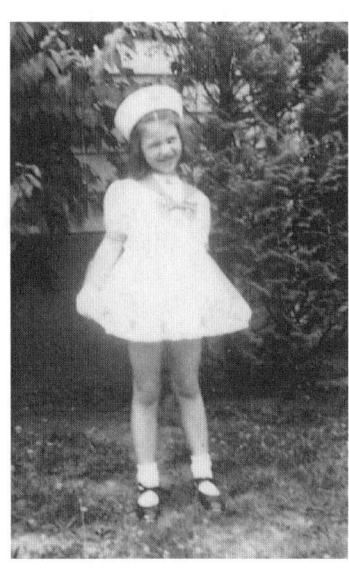
Judy Kelley, age 7.

Judy Kelley, teacher, age 55.

ated in 1922, in the first class to ever graduate from NHHS.

My mother went to Washington, D.C. to work for the federal government and meet my dad, David Kyle Wiard, who was from Illinois. Dad was on the boxing team at the University of Florida at Gainsville and at Georgetown University in D.C. He was working as a capital policeman when he met my mother. They were married at my grandparents' home on Wrightsville Avenue in Wilmington on July 2, 1930.

When I was born, my parents were living in Arlington, Virginia. At the age of six, I started taking tap and ballet lessons. In 1947 we moved to Pleasantville, New Jersey where I started taking dance lessons from Tony Grant who had his own "STARS OF TOMORROW" show on the Steele Pier in Atlantic City. We performed as fill-ins on his show in the summers and in the Miss America Pageants at the Convention Center.

In 1953 we moved back to Wilmington where I continued my dance training and began teaching with Betty Cress, a former Rockette. Ms. Cress became my mentor. She took me to New York to try out for the Rockettes in 1956. I wasn't tall enough so we came back to Wilmington and she started her own line of girls and called us the Cressettes. We were discovered by Ronney Bartley, leader of the Ronney Bartley Orchestra. He booked us on an eight-week tour including ten states where we performed at officers' and NCO clubs on various military bases.

After graduating from NHHS in 1957, I went to Washington, D.C. to work for the Bureau of Engraving and Printing. I met my husband, Skip Kelley, a week later and we were married at St Mary's Catholic Church in Wilmington on my parents' 30th wedding anniversary. We had five children: three girls and two boys. Our middle daughter died after the third brain operation in 1965.

When the children were a little older, I became a dance teacher at a local dance studio. Skip was a journeyman electrician.

We retired in 1999 and moved

Judy Kelley, age 67.

to Wilmington. I became involved in the North Carolina Senior America Pageants and was selected to represent North Carolina at the National Pageant in Reno, Nevada in the year 2000. I became State Director and had my own pageants for the next four years. In 2005 I was a judge in both North Carolina and New Hampshire. Presently I am teaching tap at the Senior Center in Wilmington and co-director of the North Carolina Senior America Pageant along with Beverly Wetherbie of Aberdeen, North Carolina.

Cornbread and Milk
by
Ruth Yale Agee of Shallotte
From an interview by Karen Dolan

Thanks to Karen Dolan, here's another great story about the good old days. We were especially impressed by Ruth Agee's anecdote about crossing the swinging bridge to catch the school bus.

I was born January 1, 1933 in Hillsville, Virginia. I grew up in Virginia with three brothers and two sisters. One sister and one brother died at birth and one sister died at age 12. I later moved back to North Carolina, where my parents were originally from and where my children were born.

My daddy did odd jobs—a lot of odd jobs. He stayed busy, but he didn't have a permanent job. But he did a lot of stuff for a lot of people.

We didn't have a telephone; we didn't have television. We had dippers and tin bathtubs, spittoons, fly paper, winding the clock, corn shucking. Radio drama programs—we didn't have that; party line phones, we didn't have; wind up record players we didn't have; steam locomotives we didn't have either. We had tin bathtubs though.

We took our baths in a big round wash tub in the kitchen in the wintertime and in the summertime we'd put it out in the backyard.

We played ball with a piece of wood that we used for a bat and I think we had a roll of yarn that we'd put on the bat and we played with that. We didn't have hardly anything. Back then, you didn't have stuff.

We had a cow. We had milk and butter. We had chickens. Momma made our dresses out of feed sacks and the boys' shirts out of feed sacks. Once in awhile, we'd luck out and she'd get a solid color piece of feed sack. And she'd make pants for the boys. The kids at school used to call me "Feed Sacks." They knew...like they were wearing them too. Well, they weren't all wearing them. Some of them didn't wear them, but they would pick on the kids that they knew was.

My name, nobody knows it, but I'll tell you, was Lena Ruth and they called me "Lean Meat." I'd cry and Momma and Daddy finally got so they would call me Ruth. I remember it was horrible. I think then kids picked on children a lot more than they do now. Well, I wouldn't answer. It got so bad I wouldn't answer unless they called me Ruth. I know that was hard on Momma and Daddy.

My mother, when she was seven years old, she had infantile paralysis that left her with a short leg and a deformed hand. She could do things though; she raised all of us and cooked and sewed and everything. She'd do things I can't do. She's been gone a long time, but I think about how she worked. She had a wash tub and a scrub board, you know, to wash stuff. She'd wash and iron and cook and can. We didn't freeze 'cause we didn't have a freezer. My momma was quite a woman. She was. Young people today wouldn't tolerate it.

Our house was on a little bank up the hill and we had to walk down past the neighbor's house and go across the river to get on the school bus. They had a swinging bridge [across the river], but when they had a flood, it washed it out. Some of the people took their children across on a boat. They had a little paddle boat. Momma and Daddy wouldn't let us ride on the paddle boat. They was afraid we'd get drownded. So we didn't go to school until after they put the bridge back in that was washed away. They come down there to see Momma and Daddy—the people from the school wanted to know why we weren't in school. Daddy told them, "When you get that bridge fixed so that my children can get across the river on the bridge instead of riding in a little paddle boat across the river, they'll go back to school." And we did. But it took them a long time to get that bridge in. I missed a bunch of school.

Then Daddy got sick when I was in the seventh grade and I had to quit school. I didn't go to school after that, but I went to work. I worked as a housekeeper for a family named Cashion.

Editor's note: the following text was added to Mrs. Agee's story. We believe it was probably written by her daughter although there was no indication to that probability. Therefore, we can not be certain whether it is a continuation of Mrs. Agee's first person narrative or a third person account of events from her daughter's viewpoint. We therefore include it as a quote: "Mama started working Highlandes-Sewing Plant 1967—worked until 1980. She worked at Jones starting in 1980 to 1995—fifteen years. She did not start when they opened."

That was a long time ago. I don't know if it was a year or not. I worked there until they got Jones Department Store built. For every hour I worked, they paid me a dividend.

When I was a child, we had an outhouse and we had a well. That's where we got our water. We had a wood stove for cooking and a wood stove in the living room for heating. The beds had quilts 'cause we didn't have any heat except in the kitchen and in the living room where we had the wood stove.

My sister died when I was about twelve years old. She had rickets. Back then, they didn't have medicine for a lot of stuff. We had a doctor that come when mother was pregnant and he'd deliver the baby. If someone was real sick, Daddy would go after him and he'd come to the house. I don't think you could get a doctor to come to the house today.

In the summertime I ran barefoot and I worked in the garden. We had a creek near our house we would wade in. We didn't go swimming 'cause we didn't know how to swim. The creek was cold, but we'd get in it and play anyway.

The neighbors had a big apple orchard on the hill above our house. We got half the apples and Momma would peel and dry the apples for winter and make apple pies and cobblers. We always had apples. Momma canned vegetables. We had beans, corn, potatoes, sweet potatoes, cabbage, lettuce, tomatoes, and pickled green tomatoes. We kept turnips and rutabagas in the basement. The kids would bring in the firewood, feed the chickens, and bring in the eggs. Daddy milked the cow; Momma strained the milk and put jugs of milk by the artesian well that bubbled up. In the summertime, we got ice for the box by the well to keep the milk cold. Momma baked cornbread in a cast iron pan in the stove and corn fritters on top of the stove. I wish I could have a slice of her Momma's corn bread with a cold glass of milk.

Castle Street Memories
by
Odessa Parker Koen of Wellsburg, New York

Absence does make the heart grow fonder. In the case of Odessa Koen, who was born in Wilmington in 1934 and grew up there, it obviously also heightens the memory. Mrs. Koen paints a beautiful picture in words, not only of her Castle Street home, but of all of Wilmington and the surrounding area. Among a host of other memories, she recalls a frightening bout with diphtheria, smooching in the back of the movie theater and meeting her husband at a drugstore soda fountain. If you're a Wilmington native, you'll want to read this one.

Odessa Parker Koen.

Wilmington, North Carolina is my heritage and holds so many memories for me. The Cape Fear River, the mansions, some of the churches, and even the cemeteries in Wilmington have some interesting stories.

I was born in 1934 in Wilmington. My first memories are of events that took place on Castle Street close to Front Street. I remember the streetcar tracks on Castle Street and of course the brick streets. I clearly remember waking up from a nap. I heard a noise outside, so I looked out the window. The circus people with animals were parading up Castle to go to 17th Street to pitch the Big Top tent. The monkeys were funny, the elephants were overwhelming to see, but the lions were just plain scary. They were in cages, of course, but growled with mouths wide open.

We moved from Castle Street to 6th Street. But since we lived two blocks from Castle, I still found that street fascinating.

I remember Mr. Wheeler's shoe repair shop—at least I think that was the name he went by. I do know he was very talented in repairing old shoes. After a five or ten cent sole, my shoes felt like new again. Then the bottom of the shoe outlasted the top. It sure was better than walking on the cardboard or newspaper that was cut to fit in your "holey" shoes.

Castle Street was also exciting when, maybe once a year, Gypsies came by and settled down there for several weeks. I was afraid of them. They were very colorful with scarves tied around their heads and their jewelry colorful and there was lots of it.

I remember Mr. Craig's grocery store. Baskets of peanuts, sweet potatoes, mixed nuts, etc. were placed around in the store. My favorite part of the store were the glass cases the candy was placed in. If my grandma ordered groceries from Mr. Craig, they were put on credit and delivered by bike.

Simon's Department Store was my favorite after the candy store. I got to go there once a year to buy a store-bought dress. I remember a yellow taffeta one that made a noise when you walked. Of course, a pair of shiny black patent shoes completed my outfit. I felt so good with them on. I usually had feed sack dresses made by my grandma.

My grandparents had chickens and several turkeys. Feed for them was in cloth feed sacks. Lots of these sacks came in very pretty prints.

At 5th and Castle was the popular Hall's Drugstore. You could buy enything there, from cold medicine, Lydia Pinkem to "3-6s." In the back of the store it was like a doctor's office. Dr. Hall could take care of your minor cuts, sore throats or fever. Or he could prescribe some kinds of medication.

During the good old days, food, milk and ice deliveries were popular. A man came by with a horse-drawn wagon. The wagon had plenty of veggies, including my favorites— cantaloupes and watermelons—and there were lots of corn, collards, cukes, green beans, tomatoes, butterbeans and beets.

Since we didn't have a refrigerator, we had ice deliveries. We used to like to get up in the truck when no one was looking. The ice shavings cooled us off on a very hot day.

We had a milkman, too. The milk had lots of cream on top. Grandma would carefully skim it off and use it for other things.

The telephones back then were annoying. They had party lines. Private lines were hard to get and probably cost more. If you had a party line, you were on a line with several people. This meant you couldn't use the phone all the time when you really wanted it. People listened in on your conversations.

We had no TV. We had a windup record player and a radio. Everyone had to gather around the radio to follow the Amos and Andy, Lone Ranger, boxing and the war news. We listened to that twangy country music. I like country music, but not that old stuff.

In the winter we liked to roller skate. The city would block off a street so we could have some fun skating. I got some skinned knees and I lost some of those skate keys.

Wash days had to be sunny and preferably on Monday. The wash was first put in a black wash pot filled with hot water. There was a fire underneath the pot to keep it hot. We used a stick to jab the clothes. Then the clothes were put in a tub with a washboard and then it was rub-a-dub.

There were usually two rinse tubs. No rinses like Final Touch or Downy. But for the washboard tub there was plenty of homemade soap or Octagon soap.

After the clothes were wrung out by hand they were hung on a clothesline, which was held up by long sticks.

The houses were heated with wood or coal. I will never forget the big blaze when kerosene was added on top of the wood. Our fireplace was in the living room and used only for special occasions.

We couldn't go into a room and switch on the light. Our lights were a long electric wire with a light bulb attached. Sometimes there was a chain or string on it so we could turn it off or on. Lots of times the string would break and you'd find yourself in the dark. I did not like the dark.

"Pepsi Cola hits the spot. Twelve full ounces; that's a lot. Twice as much for a nickel, too. Pepsi Cola is the drink for you." It was good if you had the money to buy it. So was Orange Crush, R.C. Cola or a chocolate drink. You could get a bag of candy for five cents, too.

Breakfast tables always had biscuits. Cornbread was for dinner and supper. Sundays we had fried chicken, potato salad, a vegetable, fried fatback and a sumptuous pound cake with chocolate icing or carmel icing. The chicken and cake were always prepared on Saturday. The chicken was killed and dressed then, but fried after church on Sunday.

We kids usually spent Saturday afternoons in the movies. I had two older brothers who really weren't happy when their two younger sisters had to tag along with them on Saturdays. My sister and I had to run to keep up when we *walked* to the movies. I always liked to sit in the back of the theater. We had to sit close to the front.

The Bijou, Royal, Carolina, Manor and Bailey Theaters were in downtown Wilmington. I was especially fond of the Bailey when I was in my teen years. I got in for nine cents (for children under twelve) for a while longer than I should. And I sat close to the back so I could smooch.

The City Market on Front Street was popular on Saturdays, too. People would bring veggies, fish, crafts and rummage things to sell. It was interesting to walk around and hear all the bargaining going on. It was even more fun if you had things to sell. The fish smell was not too pleasant, though.

Some of the downtown stores that stand out in my mind are Belk's, Efird's,

Woolworth's, McClenands, Kress dime store, Sally Frocks, Diana Dress Shop, Saunders Drugstore, Saffo's, Murchison Building snack bar, the H & W Cafeteria on Princess Street. But most of all I remember Futrelle's Drugstore. The fountain at Futrelle's is where I met my husband.

Way back in olden days when you went downtown, you could never miss the blind man selling peanuts. The aroma of the roasting peanuts filled the air. The man never missed giving you your correct change.

I really hated to see the visiting nurses and health officer come around. They were always walking up the sidewalk to your house when you least expected them. The nurse always wanted you to say "Ah" and she had lots of questions she'd ask. I had lots of contagious diseases while I was young. I had scarlet fever, two different kinds of measles and whooping cough. They all kept me confined to the house for a while.

We were quarantined with childhood diseases. A yellow sign was put on the house to prohibit visitors other than the family. I remember when I had chickenpox. After a few days I felt pretty good so I decided to go to a neighbor's house. The kids were all on the front porch, so why couldn't I go? Well, probably the health officer was called and he told me why.

At about the age of eight or nine I contracted diphtheria. I know my parents and grandparents thought I was going to die. They were crying. I was put in a little building back of James Walker Memorial. There were only four of us in this building. We *never* saw each other. It was really boring. My family could not come in the building. They had to stand outside and look through a window, which was down, of course. Everything I had come into contact with before and while I was in the hospital had to be burned.

Greenfield Lake is one of my memories of Wilmington. The beautiful peacocks, flowers and bushes, the magnificent cypress trees with the hanging moss and the really scary alligators are etched in my memory. Also, it was five miles around the lake. I loved to walk there with some of my friends.

The shipyard days were really memorable, too. The news of Pearl Harbor was really a nightmare for a child. Every time the sirens sounded and we'd have an air raid drill I was so fearful. We had to pull our dark shades down and turn off all lights. I just knew we'd be bombed, too.

We had shortages of many items. Gas, sugar, shoes, stockings, bananas, etc., were hard to come by. We almost had a fight in the grocery store when the clerk came out of the back room with a cart with bananas. We had ration stamps for several items.

We had savings stamps. We'd buy them at school on different days. We could fill a book of stamps, which amounted to $18.75. Then we could buy a savings bond.

The Atlantic Coast Line Railroad was a popular way to travel. I didn't travel too much but I remember the rides at Christmas time. We rode to Castle Hayne, picked up Santa Claus and soon went back to Front and Red Cross to the station.

Odessa Parker Koen.

I only went to three schools. Since there were practically no pre-schools then, I entered the first grade at Tileston School. I remember the principal, Mr. Grise, Miss Meta Legrande and Miss Kelly.

The fifth grade was exciting and I was a little afraid. I went to the second built Sunset Park School. I remember being a cheerleader and drawing in

Mrs. Murphy's class. She was a strict teacher but I found out later a very good one.

Last but not least, I went to New Hanover High. We had to cross Market Street to go to our classes at the Isaac Bear Building. Even though I had no reason to go to the ROTC building, it was across the street from the main building, too.

If you passed the high school at lunchtime, you could usually see Dale K. Spencer, the principal. He would be walking the sidewalk with a big smile on his face and sometimes with an ice cream cone in his hand. He was really a nice man.

Growing up in Wilmington, I attended Immanuel Presbyterian Church. I remember the sound of the bell that rang every Sunday morning. I remember the children's choir. I didn't know my future husband at the time, but we walked side by side to the front of the church to sing, especially at Easter and Christmas. We went there while the bells rang to pray after the war ended. This church held many happy and sad memories.

Wilmington was, is, and evermore will be close to my heart. I am so proud to call Wilmington home. I've lived in the North for over 40 years, but I am so thankful for my Southern heritage.

Grandpa's Smoking Jacket
by
June Stannus of Southport

June Stannus was born in Newark, New Jersey in 1924. She grew up in Sag Harbor, New York, the location we believe she is describing in her story. These wonderful memories of a bygone time come from the other side of the Mason-Dixon line. We think you'll enjoy them.

Grandpa raised me until his death. We had a big, old coal stove which took up half the kitchen. We cooked on it and it also heated the house.

Grandpa was quite the gentleman, never coming to the table in his shirtsleeves. He always wore his pale gray smoking jacket.

I remember the iceman who came every few days to carry in blocks of ice with metal tongs. There was always a sign in our window, and the number showing on it was the amount of ice we needed. We had a wooden icebox and he would place the ice in a metal lined space on top which then closed with a wooden lid. There was an orange tray on bottom, and my job was to empty it or I had a floor to mop!

After dinner, we retired to the parlor and I would wind the Victrola and play the beautiful Straus waltzes, while Grandpa rocked in his chair, smoking his meerschaum pipe and clapping his hands while I danced.

Came summer, Grandpa would send me to the saloon down the road with a tin bucket to get it filled with beer. And, yes, I remember the shiny brass spittoons.

We'd sit on the wisteria covered porch, singing old songs and playing with our dog.

Now, even at my age, after all the time that I've lived, all the things that I've done, all the places I've been, nothing can even compare to the happiness I knew back then.

The Greek Blessing
by
Gaynelle Grantham Hinson of Wilmington

Deposited there on the brink of our nation's greatest war, Gaynelle Hinson viewed Wilmington with awe and trepidation. Her story, peppered with charming anecdotes, reveals how she came to love the city during its transition from sleepy port to wartime preparedness. Mrs. Hinson was born in Sumpter, South Carolina in 1922.

AWESOME! That was the only word to describe my Wilmington in 1941. It was so BIG! I fell in love with it instantly. BUT…

I had lived all of my nineteen years in country areas of South Carolina and the largest town I'd been in was Mullins, which would probably have fitted into two blocks of Wilmington at that time. I'd been married almost a year, was pregnant with my first child, away from home area for the first time, and I was just plain terrified.

My husband, Lewis Hinson, however, was walking on air. He knew the city and often visited his favorite brother who lived here. He brought me for a short visit, went out on the second day just to "look around," and when he came back a few hours later, he had a job with Hughes Brothers. He had also found and rented us an apartment. I had no idea what "an apartment" was. I only knew houses.

It's gone now—that wonderful old Princess Building. Our apartment there consisted of a large bedroom/sitting room and a much smaller kitchen/dining room. The toilet facility was outside the apartment near the fire escape. The kitchen had an oversize window above a large sink: my first running water. Also my first gas stove—a monster I was scared to death of, with good reason. The thing hated me.

My husband left Hughes Brothers to work the lunch counter at a stag bar almost beneath our building, and often ran up the stairs with my lunch. On his breaks and after work, he took me for walks. Doctor's orders. I was not brave enough to venture out alone.

I'll never forget that first walk. He'd told me there was a river at the foot of Princess, and I loved rivers. I visualized sitting beneath the trees on the bank with my husband and a cane pole. I was glad I hadn't told him my

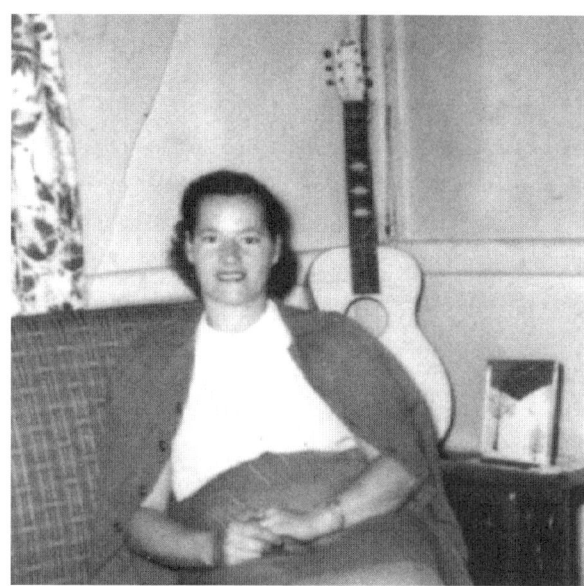

Gaynelle Hinson in the 50s.

thoughts. There certainly was a river, but it had no trees, no actual bank like I was used to. What it had was a shaky wooden platform, on which sat three men and a woman, all blacks, all poorly dressed. Each held a cane pole, and they were catching fish, huge catfish. Excitedly, I looked questionably at my husband. We both liked to catch and eat catfish. He shook his head slightly, led me over to one side, and pointed to a large iron pipe jutting about two feet out into the river. Out of it spewed globs of indescribable mess. "Sewage," he whispered.

At the end of the hall outside our apartment was a large window that overlooked Princess Street. I liked to sit on its large seat and watch the people scurrying about below, most of them soldiers and Marines, since war hung like a dark cloud over us all. My husband and his brother had both tried to enlist in the Navy, before receiving their draft cards, not telling their wives, of course, who were elated when both were rejected because of bad eyesight. This window had no screen, and sometimes I liked to lean out so that I could see down the street. When my husband saw me doing this, he yelled at me—loudly.

One of those who heard him and came to see what was happening was Paul Ambrosiano, owner of the building, the guy we rented from. He and his brother, George, had a tailoring shop at the head of the stairs. My husband explained, Paul nodded, and went back into his shop without saying a word. George, however, shook his head, smiled at me, and said, "Is a no-no. Scare me, too, little mama." When I came from the hospital with my baby a few weeks later, George was the first one to come in to see her. He put a coin in her hand, closed her fingers around it, and mumbled some Greek words I couldn't understand. "Is blessing," he explained.

A lot seemed to happen all at once. My brother—my best friend—came to say goodbye. Drafted. He'd felt unable to join because it meant our father would have to give up his small farm.

My brother, and the friend he'd brought with him, decided to go to a movie, and chose the Bailey Theatre. He came back exclaiming about "…carpet so deep your toes would get lost if you were barefoot." He and I walked around the corner to Woolworths, and I bought him a small metal-covered Testament for his shirt pocket, to protect him. I'd read about one deflecting a bullet for someone else. This actually worked for my brother, also.

Going out for walks was no longer a problem, since the baby needed fresh air. Being stopped every few feet for one of the military "to see the babe" made my heart ache, but there was no way I would not do this. I will never forget the only time I ever let one of the guys hold her. A young soldier, looking about sixteen, stood still on the walk a few feet away. He took a few steps toward me, stopped again. I hesitated, feeling uneasy, then moved to pass him. "Please, please," he said, and I could hear tears in his voice. I stopped, of course. "Could I just see her little feet?" His tears overflowed. I turned back the blanket, slipped off a bootee. "I've got a baby at home," he told me, really crying now. "I've never seen her. I'll probably *never* see her. I'd give anything to just hold her." Without hesitation, I handed her over to him. He moved over beside a building and held her, gently caressing her little fingers and toes. Perhaps five minutes passed and then, grinning broadly, he handed her back to me. My eyes still teary, I turned and went back to my apartment.

Later, remembering, I realized he probably meant that he wanted to hold his own baby, but I never regretting doing this.

We moved down the hall to a three room apt because I was pregnant again. My husband went to work at the shipyard. Since he already knew how to weld, he taught others. Our windows all now had blackout shades and I had to use a flashlight, with weakened batteries, to check on the baby.

Soon after our second child was born, an enemy craft was said to have been seen offshore, and my husband quickly moved us to his hometown of Fair Bluff. Several of his friends from there were working at the shipyard, driving back and forth. He bought a van so they could all ride with him. When he felt it was safe again, he moved us back.

Maffet Village, we were told, was especially for shipyard workers. We were there only a few months and I hated every minute of it. If you opened window or door to try to cool the place, it was filled instantly with children, some even in diapers. The small fan we had probably saved our lives. My youngest was learning to walk and the cement floors made her ankles swell. Her doctor frowned, told me she was the third child he'd seen with that problem, and gave us a permit to move to Riverside Apartments.

Wow! What a difference! Gates already attached at top and bottom of stairs, *two* window fans, carpet, drapes, *plus* wonderful neighbors. This couple had no children and fell in love with mine. What more could I ask for?

When he was no longer needed, my husband left the shipyard. As time passed, we left and returned to this city several times. Then, now, and always, it remains MY WILMINGTON.

Hanging Out on the Corner
by
H. Mike Dolan of Bolivia

Most of us have observed the construction of what we term super highways. How'd you like to find out your kids, or your grandchildren, were playing around the construction site? That's just a hint of what you'll read in Mike Dolan's tale of growing up in Jersey City, where Mike was born in 1942. You'll enjoy this one.

It's been more than three score years ago that I walked the streets of downtown Jersey City. Upon riding through on a recent trip, I marveled at the changes. The cobblestone streets that the horse-drawn milk wagons clippety clopped over are long gone. The tenement homes not far from the Holland Tunnel have been replaced with new townhouses. The price of one of these townhouses exceeds the price of all the tenements that existed. My grammar school was four blocks from the Holland Tunnel and some of the kids crossed the streets daily without any incident. Today, crossing the street leading to the Holland Tunnel would be a daring feat.

Many of the schools in Jersey City were private Catholic Schools and my alma mater, St. Michael's, was one of them. Our school dues were ten cents a week. All six children in my family attended the school and having the sixty cents each week for the six of us wasn't always in the budget. It was really embarrassing to be reminded that I was two weeks behind for my school dues of ten cents. In retrospect, I would have to say my parents got a pretty good bargain for ten cents a week.

One of my vivid memories is of the building of the New Jersey Turnpike. One of the spurs came in from Newark Airport and through our neighborhood on to the Holland Tunnel. The construction workers dug huge pilings that were 20 feet deep. The site was near the old Erie Railroad, which was a playground of sorts for us. The train tracks had coal that fell out of the hopper cars which we could bring home for our coal burning stoves. There was a tunnel not far away and the train would slow down and we could jump on and ride it up to the tunnel. To us, it was like an amusement park ride. Since this was our playground, the pits for the pilings dug by the construction workers became an adjunct to the playground. After the workers left, we would climb down the ladders into the pits and play tag, king of the mountain, and a few invented games.

The construction workers introduced us to pocket money. In the morning, they would send us for coffee and give us a nickel or dime for going. For lunch, it was a similar chore and we were happy to have some money in our pockets. Later on, they let us take out nails from the wood used for scaffolding and paid us a penny for each board we finished. Whenever I come near the New Jersey Turnpike, I tell people that I helped build it.

Any kid raised in Jersey City during the 40s, 50s and 60s will remember the movie theaters at Journal Square. There were three: the Stanley, the State and the Loewes. Every week would be a new feature and somehow we would find a way to come up with a quarter to see a first-run movie, the cartoons, the newsreel, and a serial. They were all fine theaters, but the Loewes was majestic. To a young imagination, it seemed to be the Taj

Mahal. It was inconceivable that anything could be grander.

One of our pastimes in the city was hanging out on the corner. We would play games like kick the can, hock-a-bocka-bean-stalk (hiding something and giving directions to those looking for it), Red Rover, Johnny Jump the Pony and many others.

As we became mature teenagers, cars were our main thought and we created a game called cars. Each person hanging out on the corner was given a number. As a car came by it was yours if it was your turn, and we would see who could get the best car. So if your number was four, every fourth car was yours. We would hope that a Cadillac Eldorado with the big fins was in the area and would come by for our number.

It was a rough neighborhood, but we didn't know it. We were poor, but we didn't know it. We had a great childhood, and now we know it. Those were the days.

Old Joe's Bottom
by
Ann Montgomery of Wilmington

As children, most of us can recall a forbidden area, one we naturally came to know intimately despite, or perhaps because of, the "Don't go there" admonishments. Ann Montgomery describes just such a place in enchanting detail. (We assure you, however, that the special place is geographical, not anatomical.) Miss Montgomery, who was born in Wilmington in 1926, further entertains (yes, entertains) us by recounting her memories of a funeral plagued by disaster. Read on...you'll enjoy this one.

As we get older, memories make up a huge part of our thoughts, particularly when we get together with friends. My niece, Becky Rivenbark Gregory, is turning 65 this year. We still laugh and remind her of a time when my family was enjoying a Sunday dinner, and all the grownups were sharing stories of things we remembered in our pasts. Becky started crying. "Everybody else has memories," she sniffled, "but I don't have *any at all*!"

We assured her that the time would come when she would have plenty of memories to share, but that was little consolation to a six- or seven-year-old. Believe me, no one enjoys sharing stories of her past more than she does now, and I hope she will send some to you. *Editor's note: we did receive a charming tale from Becky Gregory.*

Perhaps you could use a story or two from my childhood memory bank.

I spent my first twelve years growing up in the Dry Pond area at 909 South 5th Street, a house that still stands today. I was pleased to see that a scenic byway has been designated for downtown Wilmington, and runs from the Isabel Holmes Bridge through the historic district and on to Castle Street and down 5th Avenue to Greenfield Lake. It passes right by the house I lived in and the area called Dry Pond—a very scenic route.

Many of my happiest days were spent in what we called "Old Joe's Bottom," which was a sunken area on the west side of 5th Avenue between Dawson and Wooster Streets. (As you can see, we were not used to saying 5th Avenue so I still say 5th Street.) Of course, this area was considered dangerous and "off limits" to us. However, in those carefree days, no one knew exactly where we were during the daylight hours; and as long as we appeared for meals and were in the house by dark, we were considered safe and accounted for.

We had great times in the Bottom. Of course, every now and then some meddling grownup would come to investigate our paradise and cut down the rope we had strung between trees—one on high ground and down to a low tree at the bottom. It was great fun to catch hold of the pipe [on the rope] at the top after we hand climbed the tree, and to slide down for a great ride. As far as I remember, no one ended up with broken bones. But it could have happened and the grownups felt duty bound to protect us—and thereby spoil our fun.

There was also a pond and a natural spring that flowed through the Bottom. We had fun building dams, catching tadpoles and jumping across the water, usually ending up soaked.

Another fortunate possession of mine and other kids in the area was an old tire. You could roll it for blocks or you could crawl inside and let someone roll you over and over until you finally fell out—laughing all the way.

I was lucky enough in our depressed neighborhood to have a bike, but it took a real beating, because all the less fortunate kids had to learn to ride on my bike and the only way they could stop was by running into a fence or tree. And that was hard on the bike.

We were fortunate to have a sidewalk in front of our house and on down the block so that made for good skating. Also, the steep driveway offered a challenge to the better skaters. I would usually ask for a new pair of Union Hardware skates every Christmas, but inevitably I would leave them outside after the newness wore off. They would be confiscated by some industrious boy as wheels for a gocart or to make a skate board. I never learned to be much of a skater anyway, because it was no fun to skate alone, and I would use one skate and let a friend use the other. We became quite proficient at skating on one skate, however.

My friend Vernell and I once undertook a special project. Someone—I don't remember who—had tied a string on a June bug's leg. We would hold the string while the bug buzzed around and around. But, alas! The

Ann Montgomery in 1995.

bug finally died. Vernell and I felt obligated to give it a decent burial and funeral service.

We found a matchbox, lined it with cotton and put our dear departed insect friend inside. Then we covered the box with material from a torn sheet (or dish towel), dug a hole and buried him. Now all that was needed was a tombstone.

From an old storage house on the back of our property we found some wall plaster that had fallen. Great! I borrowed a hatchet from the woodpile and Vernell held the piece of plaster on a rock while I undertook to shape it like a tombstone with the hatchet. The only problem was that Vernell's finger got in the way of the hatchet and that was the end of the funeral service.

My dad was home, and after washing Vernell's finger off, he gave her his handkerchief to wrap it in and whisked her off to the doctor for stitches. What was remembered and repeated most, however, was that Vernell, sweet little always neat Vernell, was actually "dirty" from our playing in the dirt (we didn't have grass in our yards then). Her parents were so embarrassed that Mr. Montgomery had had to take their dirty daughter to the doctor for stitches. Her mom had her bring my dad a brand new handkerchief. And several days later, my older brother Cameron, who Vernell idolized, went down and carried her a present: a June bug all packaged up as a gift.

Until this day—some seventy-five years later—the famous "June bug funeral" is always mentioned when we are reminiscing, whether it be in person or by phone.

We moved from 5th Street when I was in the fifth grade at William Hooper School. I had some great times at that school, on the playground at recess. Hopscotch, dodge ball, catch and other pickup games were played. But my favorite was a ball game called "roly poly." Does anyone else remember that or did we just make it up?

These are just some of the wonderful childhood days that I remember when I was living in Dry Pond.

Spooks, Elephants and Alligators
by
William Small of Wilmington

These are exactly the kinds of stories we like to publish in our books, and we thank William Small, who was born in Wilmington in 1923, for telling them. We think you'll enjoy them very much.

My parents, the Small family, rented a two-story house at 9th and Market and the first night after moving in they heard someone walking up the stairs, and a door opening and closing. My father investigated and found Mother in her nightgown shutting a door that was open. They talked to the neighbors who informed them there was a ghost in the house. They moved out the next day.

In 1927 when I was four the circus came to town and after the evening show an elephant got loose and traveled down the streets between the houses. The space between the houses wasn't wide enough and the elephant pushed some of them off their foundations, scaring the people inside.

When I was fourteen years old, my father went fishing and brought me home two baby alligators. We lived at that time on Metts Avenue. I built a cage for them and thought I would make pets out of them. They grew rapidly and were about two feet long in a couple of months.

One day I came home from school and one of the alligators was missing. I looked all over for him but couldn't find him.

About a month later I came home from school and my mother told me a lady in Forest Hill wanted to talk to me. When I went to her house she asked me if I had an alligator. Old dumb me said, "Yes, but he got away." She said, "Well, I know where he is. He's in my fish pond in my back yard."

She had had these beautiful fan-tailed golden fish in her pond. And when we looked, there sat my alligator, fat as a butterball. He had eaten all of the fish. The lady said I would have to pay for them at six dollars each. My dad said I would have to pay and I didn't have the money. So she said I could mow her grass. For this she reduced my debt by one fish each Saturday. And that was done by the old type rotary lawn mower.

I didn't want anything to happen to the other alligator so I decided to give him to the zoo at Greenfield Lake. He was about three feet long by then. So I taped his mouth shut and got on my bike, and enroute a car stopped suddenly and threw me on the door. Fortunately, the window was down so I just draped over the door. The driver was astounded to see this boy on a bike with an alligator under his arm. Anyway I got off the door and I don't want any more alligators.

Black Dog Woman
by
Mary Shipman Blanton of Wilmington

This is an extremely impressive story of humility and humanity. It centers around a mid-century Mom and Pop Wilmington grocery store, but reaches out to all the world as an example of ideal human relations. You'll enjoy it, from the nickel pickles to the moonshine jars. Perhaps you, or your parents, ran an account with Shipman's Grocery. Mary Blanton was born in Wilmington in 1936 and grew up there.

It was around the year 1939 that two brothers, Alvie C. Shipman (my dad) and his brother Marson Shipman, both of whom had moved from Bladen County with their parents, Rosa Turner Shipman and Marson Smith Shipman, opened a grocery store as partners at 819 Grace Street. The store was right on the corner, looking down about a block away at James Walker Hospital.

The Shipman family also included their two sisters, Estelle and Anniebelle.

My dad, Alvie, and my mom, Doshie Thompson Shipman, and I lived in a two room apartment back of the store. The apartment had a large kitchen, living area and one bedroom. In the middle of the kitchen was a potbellied stove. Mom would get up early on cold mornings to start a fire so my brother, Alvie, Jr. (called Sonny, who came along when I was five and a half) could wake up to a warm apartment.

There was a door leading from our apartment into the grocery store. Dad would go into the store and start a fire in a potbellied stove in the middle of the store so his customers, who were both black and white (because we lived in a mostly black neighborhood) could keep warm.

Some of these customers were street people. I remember they called some of them winos. All were welcome. They would sit around the fire and talk, as I remember, mostly politics because World War II was starting.

My Uncle Marson and his family lived upstairs in two rooms. My grandfather, whom I called Paw Paw, lived in one big room across the hall from them. Just outside his room was the only bathroom in the building. This totaled five rooms plus the store.

Paw Paw would spend a lot of time with my brother and me. He took us everywhere with him. I had a doll carriage which was fairly big, and my brother was an infant in 1941, so Paw Paw would put him in the doll carriage and take me by the hand. Off we'd go down to the railroad to watch the trains come in. I remember a railroad man holding a lantern to guide the trains.

Mary Blanton.

My Paw Paw had worked for the railroad until he had to retire, and he loved to talk to the guys working. After he could no longer work, he picked up jars and sold them to moonshiners for a little pocket money.

One Christmas, Paw Paw was on his way to the bank to get our Christmas gift which was always a shiny silver dollar. It was a few days after a big snow and the walks were slippery. Paw Paw fell and was taken, with pneumonia, to my Aunt Estelle's house. While he was delirious, my cousin Rosaline Rouse Barnes has told me, he was still worried about me and my brother getting hurt. He would say, "Mary, get out of the street," and was calling my brother's name, "Sonny, Sonny."

Doshie and Alvie Shipman, owners of Shipman's Grocery, in 1965.

He was always there for us and was a wonderful grandfather to all his grandchildren, even until the end, as he died of the pneumonia. I still miss him. I can still feel his loving care and concern for us.

Paw Paw loved sweet potato pie, but hated milk. When my mom baked the pies, he would ask, "Doshie, did you put milk in the pies?" My mom didn't lie. She just asked, "Paw Paw, why would I put milk in a sweet potato pie?" This made him happy to eat a lot of pie.

My dad's grocery store was as I said in a mostly black neighborhood with a few white families. We grew up respecting both races. We all took care of each other. Mom had a very dear black friend named Sarah. Sarah would babysit me, often at her house next door. She had such a warm, inviting home. I can still taste her good cooking. Oh! Me! Oh! My! Soul food! And sure enough, it was good for my soul.

Later on, my dad bought out my Uncle Marson's share of the store and then Mom worked with Dad. It became a Mom and Pop store and my uncle went on to work for a dry cleaner.

Around this time we all had moved from the area. My uncle moved to 11th Street between Grace and Chestnut and we moved to 205 North 12th Street between Grace and Chestnut.

The way Mom and Dad operated the store was like this: she would cook breakfast and lunch and would go for each meal and relieve him so he could go home for awhile. Most often they would both walk back and forth. Then in the afternoon, she was home when we got home from school. They both closed the store as we got older and she could leave us.

I never remember my parents being apart for one night. They never took a vacation. They were together for 46 years until my dad passed away in 1974. Mom lived to be 93 and passed away in 2003.

If someone needed groceries, my dad would give them credit if they couldn't pay. He kept ledgers. My dad only had a grammar school education, but was excellent in math. He could add quickly in his head. He had trouble spelling, though. So in his ledger, he might write "black dog woman" if she had a black dog. If it was her mother, he would write "black dog woman's mother." He would associate something with a person and write that as their name because he couldn't spell the name. I think he did well to run a business for over 30 years with little education.

Dad would also let his customers pawn things with him for groceries. I remember one being a watch and another an iron. When they paid him they got it back. He always made sure they were taken care of.

Dad had a big oil drum in the store with a pump at the top. The customers would bring their oil cans in and he would pump oil in them. He also sold what he called kindling wood so people could start their fires, then they most often used coal.

He had a big round hoop of cheese on the counter and a huge jar of dill pickles. I remember the pickles were a nickel. And of course I loved the candy case full of penny and nickel candy. He also sold loose cigarettes for a nickel apiece.

People would come from James Walker Hospital at lunch and grab some crackers and Vienna sausage or potted meat along with a soda. Some would buy Johnny cakes and put a slice of the hoop cheese between them.

Some of the prices in his ledger were like six eggs for 25 cents, two sticks of butter for 20 cents. Box of Tide, 35 cents, and sodas were a nickel.

And, yes, we had an ice box with the contents on top and blocks of ice on the bottom. I chased that ice truck many a time for pieces of ice.

Dad's store was also a popular stopping place to pick up a snack for police officers when they were in the neighborhood. I guess they must have kept a good eye out because I don't remember much crime back then, just them chasing moonshiners and the moonshiners rushing to flush their stuff down the toilet.

My dad would lock up at night with just an ordinary padlock that anyone could have easily broken. But black and white looked out for him and rthe store because he looked out for them.

Back then, as I got older, I could walk from 12th Street to Front Street by myself and feel safe. I worked when I was 16 years old at S.H. Kress Company on Front Street, and would walk to work and back, even at night, safely. Black and white looking out for all of us.

I tell my story about those days because we all got along, black and white. We helped each other. We didn't need much to make us happy. We had one another. We had what I thought was a wonderful life.

At age 18, I went on at the New Hanover Public Library driving the county bookmobile. When Hurricane Hazel hit, we had been driving to deliver books at Wrightsville Beach and Carolina Beach. My husband and I had been married just a few days when Hazel struck. He was called in by his National Guard unit and actually guarded the beaches. It was quite a sight when we were allowed to drive the bookmobile back to the beaches. Total devastation. Our patrons who had been coming before started coming back.

In the Winter Park area, one of my patrons was David Brinkley's (the newscaster) mother. Often, his brother Jesse came with her. I remember one Christmas she talked about David coming home and she wanted to make his favorite white fruitcake. I couldn't imagine a white fruitcake, but as I got older, I realized she meant a light fruitcake as compared to the dark kind.

I also was a school crossing guard at 13th and Meares Street, where it was mostly a black neighborhood. The people were wonderful to me. They became my friends and looked out for me for approximately 27 years. This was parttime, so in between the morning and afternoon, I would go work as a cashier in the lunchroom at nearby Williston Middle School. I also worked later on as a bus monitor on the New Hanover County Central Bus Division. After over 30 years with the schools, I retired due to poor health.

Mary's dad: Alvie Shipman, outside of Shipman's Grocery, holding his dog, Weepy.

Our six grandchildren adopted by Brian and Loi Pettus, a retired Wilmington police officer.

I loved all the children I came in contact with, and tried to help them grow into caring adults. I still see some of them out working, and I remember them and they remember me. I miss working with kids. They were the light of my day.

I married Obbie Blanton in 1954 and he retired from law enforcement in 1985 after 30 years in that field. We had three children, all of whom went into law enforcement. We have 14 grandchildren, six of whom are adopted and are multi-racial. We have two great grands.

I point out the race issue because I pray that we all can be accepting and live in harmony.

A Good Place to Croak
by
Houston Hendrix of Wrightsville Beach

Houston Hendrix admits he's a coastal transplant, but he makes it clear that the Wilmington area is where he intends to spend his final days. His story is short but full of energy...and love for his adopted home.

I was born in Wesley Long Hospital in Greensboro, N.C. on June 17, 1947. I grew up in Reidsville where my family owned and operated the walk-in and drive-in theaters.

My aunt and uncle (also my godparents), Sydney and Janie Bluhm, bought an oceanfront house on Charlotte Street at Wrightsville Beach the year I was born. I spent a lot of time there growing up and ended up buying my own house on South Lumina Avenue in 1989. When I croak, it will be there.

My fondest memories at the beach are of playing under the house. Back then the tide would come right under the house and wash us away.

Other fun was when my mother would take me crabbing near the bridge. Maybe because I was much younger, but the crabs seemed so much bigger then. Anyway, it was fun and I always enjoyed it.

Even today at age 60, I still love to surf fish and I always keep a crab pot in Banks Channel.

A Generation of Heroes
by
William G. Pepe of Hampstead

Rather than occasions and incidents, this story is more about values and attitudes. Bill Pepe, born in 1921, is a child of the Great Depression. We respectfully submit that his views are far closer to reality and truth than today's expressions of political correctness and liberal...well, enough said. If you're an old-timer, you'll appreciate this story.

My name is Bill Pepe and I live in Hampstead, N.C. with my wife of 60 years. We have two living daughters; our son was killed in Viet Nam.

I was born in Chelsea, Massachusetts and lived most of my young life in Paterson, New Jersey. With the advent of World War II, I enlisted in the Army and became a veteran of the landings on Omaha Beach on D Day. For this action, I was awarded the Presidential

Unit Citation, the French Croix de Guerre, Avec Palme and the Belgian Croix de Guerre. More recently, I was awarded the French Medal of Honor with investiture into the Legion of Honor, with the title of "Chevalier." I am now retired and living the life of comparative ease, spending most days on the golf course pursuing the elusive par.

We have a wonderful brood of grandchildren and great grandchildren and except for the untimely death of our heroic son, life could not have been more rewarding.

There was a time when I was a child that life was simple. We had nothing, but then, we expected nothing. We were poor but we didn't know that because everyone I knew was living under the same conditions. Those that had shared with the less fortunate and there was no shame in receiving. It was a true communal existence where neighbors looked out for each other. We may have been economically disadvantaged, but we were happy in our ignorance and life was good.

My introduction to formal education came with my enrollment at P.S. 17, a primary school, where Mrs. Noonan, the principal, was more of a mother than an educator. She was kind and compassionate and had an uncanny eye for a troubled child. It was a small school and she knew each of us by our given names and approached us as a friend. When a child needed hugging, she was there with an empathetic touch, but when we were disciplined, we knew exactly why.

We started each day with an assembly period as Mrs. Noonan would read a passage from the Bible, the 23rd Psalm being my favorite; perhaps because it's the one I could most readily identify with. We would then pledge allegiance to the flag, sing the national anthem and segue into an old favorite by Steven Foster.

We were not at all concerned that what we were doing was politically incorrect, nor were our parents. We were happy children.

The ACLU was not hovering over our heads, dictating cultural and curricular ideology. We had no liberal, political extremists polluting our susceptive brains. We had no far out radical groups pushing their own private agenda into the impressionable minds of unsuspecting children. Mad Madilyn O'Hair was still a devout Roman Catholic and we had teachers who were more like elderly aunts who really believed in what they taught. We were there to learn the three "Rs" and we did so in an intimate, friendly atmosphere.

Our clothing may have been patched but it was clean and the respect we had for our teachers was not born of fear but of admiration.

I can still remember, with remarkable clarity, old Mrs. Crowshaw reciting the "Ballad of Barbara Fritche" with tears streaming down her ancient face. It was she who first put me in touch with myself and taught me to not be afraid. I had a small talent for drawing and she would keep me after school to draw historical scenes on the blackboard. Now, most folks would look upon this as detention but I would look forward to these sessions alone with this remarkable woman. She was like the grandmother I never had.

She also gave me my first present that I did not have to share with my siblings. It was a Waterman fountain pen with a transparent ink reservoir. I treasured that pen, not so much for it's intrinsic value, but because she thought enough of me to trust me with it. I carried that pen with me from that day forward until I lost it on the beach in France.

It was Mrs. Rosenberg who taught me that good music need not have a beat accompanied by lyrics. Each Friday afternoon, we would spend an hour listening to Walter Damrosch and the NBC Symphony Orchestra play excerpts from light opera to Ferdie Groffe's *Grand Canyon Suite*.

Mr. Micelli, the janitor, whose job it was to distribute those little bottles of milk during

W. G. Pepe preparing to attack the front nine in 2007.

recess, always made sure every child got one whether or not they had the five cents cost.

At war's end, I returned to old P.S. 17 to visit with Mrs. Crowshaw but found that this dear old woman who abhorred killing at any level or in any form had died during the worst killing spree ever visited upon mankind.

Over all, I do not think our generation turned out too badly. As a matter of fact, Tom Brokaw thought so highly of this period in time that he honored us in print. Unfortunately, I think this recording fell way short of its mark. He had an excellent opportunity to write a landmark testimony to an outstanding generation of people. Instead, his effort was nothing more than a soporific compilation of superficial characters of fringe elements of a core society.

I remember when November 11 was still known as Armistice Day and Mrs. Noonan would invite two World War I veterans to speak to us. How grand these men were, resplendent in their neatly pressed uniforms with highly polished flying boots and colorful campaign ribbons adorning their manly chests. I was in total awe of these giants among men who flew airplanes and shot down the evil enemy. Each year, I looked forward to their visit with the eager anticipation of a child, and as the time approached, I was beside myself with escalating excitement.

These two men epitomized the manifestation of the heroes of "Dawn Patrol" and "Wings."

In those days, with so little to call our own, everybody had an idol or hero and a dream world into which he could escape. These two men were my conduit out of reality to a place where no one else could visit.

Then one year, they did not come and Mrs. Noonan had the sad task of informing us that one of these young men had died from wounds suffered in the war. I was crushed. How could he have died? He was a legend, he was bigger than life, he was my hero, he was immortal. It was my first experience with the fallibility and mortality of life. I felt cheated and deprived, my heroes had feet of clay. These men remained in my memory and I would imagine myself flying those ancient Sopwith Camels and spads. I always regretted having been born a generation too late.

When World War II broke out, I quite naturally applied to join the Air Force but was turned down because of my third degree flat feet. With this condition, no branch of the service would have me, so I signed a waiver freeing the military of any responsibility for my flat feet. I still have difficulty rationalizing why the Air Force, the military branch that does most of it's fighting in a seated position, rejected me, while the Army, the branch that does most of it's fighting in an upright position, accepted me. Can you imagine anyone signing a waiver to get INTO the army?

Penny Candy and the Cold War
by
Karen Dolan of Bolivia

Karen Dolan, born in New York City in 1947, was concerned that her story might not fit in because she grew up in New Jersey. On the contrary, it fits perfectly in this book of memories. Here are some delight-

ful memories of the good old days with which anyone who recalls the fifties and sixties will identify. We should also mention that, besides her own story, Mrs. Dolan interviewed a number of residents at the Autumn Care facility in Shallotte and wrote their stories for them. We are immensely grateful for her "beyond the call of duty" assistance in helping to preserve memories from the past. You'll find these stories scattered throughout these pages under her byline as interviewer.

Although I grew up a post World War II baby boomer in New Jersey, I imagine that many of my childhood experiences might be similar to many others who grew up in suburban communities in the fifties. On summer evenings, boys and girls of all ages would play kickball in the street or hide 'n seek in neighborhood yards. The older kids didn't seem to mind if the younger ones joined them for these games, but spud and stoop ball were strictly for the older kids. We didn't stop playing until it was too dark to see the ball or each other. At school recess, boys and girls also played kickball together, the girls hiking up their skirts far enough to be able to kick the ball. Dodgeball, prisoners (also played with a dodge ball), red rover, and red light, green light were also popular schoolyard games. On the street, there was no parental supervision. At school, our regular teacher took us outside for recess. Rainy days meant playing 7 Up or duck, duck, goose at our desks.

The girls also played jump rope, hop scotch, and jacks, and occasionally boys would join us in a game of "statutes" or Mother may I?" We girls would sometimes enlist the boys on our street to join us for a fantasy game of "Robin Hood" played on the banks of a stream in the woods behind my house. Of course, the boys preferred playing "soldiers" with us girls as the nurses. The boys refused to join us for the garage shows we put on, but we managed to corral them for our audience and made them pay a penny to watch our shows. I remember playing the part of the then-popular Grace Kelly in my pink bathing suit in one of our shows and thinking I was quite something. I also recall dressing up as a gypsy to be the fortune teller in the summer carnival five of us neighborhood girls put together and naming the carnival the "Ansurucife" Carnival, using the first two letters of all of our last names. My older brother and his friends wouldn't have been caught dead coming to our shows, plus they were busy playing baseball, mowing lawns, and devising a miniature golf game in my backyard. I can't recall if they played solely for their own amusement or if they charged the younger kids to play.

I do know that all of us kids of all ages relied on our imagination to find creative ways to spend our free time. I'm sure there were times when we were bored and I'm equally sure our parents didn't feel sorry for us if we dared to complain. They also didn't buy us Halloween costumes. We were left to our own devises to come up with a costume, so quite often we used old clothes to dress up as a gypsy or a tramp. I still have a picture of me and my best friend, Barbara, wearing our mother's (mothers') old clothes and lipstick for Halloween. In the sixth grade, I became more creative and made a top hat to go with the black jacket I wore as part of my circus ringmaster costume. I was probably tired of dressing in old clothes!

Summers also meant lazy afternoons coloring pictures or writing poetry on a blanket spread out in someone's backyard, or soaking in the small pools that were popular in the fifties, or running through the sprinklers used to water lawns. The sound of the ice-cream truck bell meant rushing home to beg our mothers for money to buy an ice cream cone or popsicle (Popsicle). Some days, my mom said no.

I'm not sure exactly how old I was when I was allowed to walk into town to go to the candy store, but I do remember the variety of "penny" candy found there—candy cigarettes, dots on a sheet, chewable lips, and plastic bottles containing sickeningly sweet syrup. It didn't matter. We loved all the candy varieties and had a hard time deciding what to spend our pennies on. In middle school and high school, we'd go to one of the two candy stores with a soda fountain and order a ten-cent coke (Coke) and a nickel stick pretzel. When the first pizza shop came to town, we teenagers were thrilled to hang out there eating pizza (a quarter for a slice) and playing the juke box. For two summers, we even had a trampoline center right in the middle of town. What fun! I also have fond memories of square dances held in the parking lot of the town's very first supermarket, a Girl Scout trip to Washington, DC, ice skating on the town pond, class trips where the girls wore their Sunday-best coats, hats and gloves, school dances and CYO dances where most everyone danced to their favorite rock 'n roll tunes, and taking the bus to local movie theatres. In high school, large groups of girls would ride the bus to NYC to go to Radio City Music Hall to see the Christmas show and a movie. We'd stand in line for hours in the cold, but we didn't mind.

Probably the scariest part of growing up in the sixties was the Cold War threat and the Civil Defense air raid drills where we kids had to cover our heads at our desks. Most likely there were times when friends hurt my feelings and times when I hurt theirs. Most likey (likely) there were times when the older kids weren't nice to the younger kids or to each other. Probably our parents worried about all kinds of things and scolded us at times. Probably we kids sometimes talked back and sometimes got in trouble. But, somehow, time has dimmed these memories. The more enduring memories are ones of a happy childhood blessed with many friends and many good times.

Green Stamps, Tobacco and Hogs
by
Sue Creech of Wilmington

It's interesting that the concepts Sue Creech writes about still exist today, but progress has changed them into something entirely different. You'll enjoy this story. Mrs. Creech was born in Brunswick County in 1929.

Back in the l950s and 1960s, saving Green Stamps was really exciting. We would pick up the stamp book and catalog from the grocery store. There were dishes, glasses, pots, pans, linens and lots of other things to use in the home. ! still have a red aluminum pitcher with six tumblers in different colors to match and they are still pretty today as if they were new. My grandchildren love to drink out of them.

S and H Green Stamps really paid off back then. For every dollar we spent we received free Green Stamps. With all the new gadgets and modern appliances, we don't have time to waste and save stamps.

I read in the newspaper some time ago, you can buy from some merchants and earn points for different items. As for myself, I look for, and cut, every coupon I can and get a few cents off my grocery bill.

When I was about nine years old I learned to hand tobacco. My older sister, brother and I helped our aunt and her family put in tobacco. I wasn't tall enough, so was given a box to stand on and hand two tobacco leaves at a time to whoever was stringing it on a long stick to hang in the barn to cure. We helped her two or three summers and within a few years I was handing tobacco nearly every day of the week.

We would get paid when the tobacco was sold in Whiteville at the market in August and September. Our money was used to buy our school clothes in the fall.

All of we children worked every summer in tobacco for different families. We didn't have a farrn, only a large garden. We had lots of fun but we worked hard and steady.

Neighbors helped neighbors when hog killing time came. This happened in the cold winter so the meat wouldn't spoil until it got salted down or smoked.

Early in the morning, the vats were filled with water and a fire built under them to scald the hogs in. While the water was heating up, the men went to get the hogs. They generally shot the hogs between the eyes.

By this time, the water was hot enough to scald them. Two chains or heavy straps were put across the vat. The hog was laid on the chains and two men on each side would turn the hog over from side to side until the hair would pull off easy. Then it was put on a large pile of pine straw and all the hair was pulled off.

The hog was hung by its hind feet by a gamble on a tall scaffold. A gamble was a piece of round oak wood about fourteen inches long and four inches thick with each end whittled off to about two and a half inches. Each end of the gamble was inserted in the heels and hung up to be washed and drain. Then the hog's insides was cleaned out.

When I was a little girl, it was real hard to watch. As I grew up, I got more used to it.

Later, the hog was cut up into pieces that could be salted down and some also smoked. There was lard and sausage to be made and also cracklins.

Everyone had a good time at hog killings. All the neighbors that came and helped went home with fresh pork for dinner. Then after a few days went by, another neighbor would kill his hogs and everyone went to help him.

Remembering back, it was so great to see families helping each other.

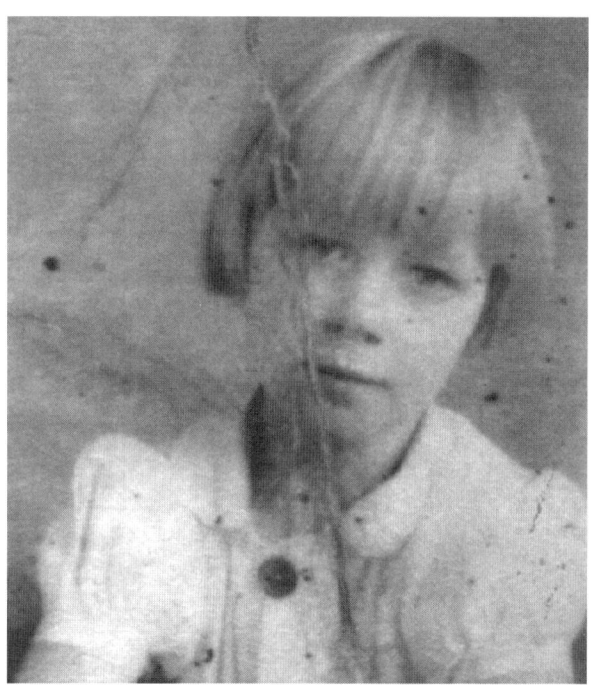
Sue Creech's second grade picture.

Comic Book Sundays
by
Mary Swain of Wilmington

Remember those Sunday afternoons? Ice cream, perhaps, or swimming? Or maybe just visiting on the porch. Mary Swain's father provided a very special Sunday treat. We think you'll enjoy reading about it. Mrs. Swain was born in Wilmington in 1937.

Most every Sunday, we drove both cars to church, because afterward, Dad took my sister and me to Wolff's Newsstand on Princess Street for comic books. He turned us loose in there, to choose any ones we wanted, and since most of them were one nickel each, the three of us wound up with a sizable stack.

Mom drove her car home to prepare lunch while Dad, Sister and I tended to our usual

Sunday business, and she always exclaimed, "Oh no. It's obvious what will be going on around here the rest of the day!" as we piled our reading pleasure on the floor by Dad's chair.

Immediately following lunch, the three of us attacked the comic book tower, while Mom busied herself with crochet—wadding string, Dad called it.

We girls preferred to lie upon the floor by Mom's and Dad's chairs to read. The silence was broken only by our occasional giggles, or Dad's chuckle.

Comic-book-Sunday afternoons were delightful family times, and those little books were not put aside until five o'clock—time for "The Shadow."

But that's another story.

A Variety of Pumps
by
Mona P. Scott of Wilmington

Mona Scott, who was born in Wilmington in 1932, tells of all the pumps she has seen in the Wilmington area. She also provides an excellent description of her relatives' homes in the Mount Misery Road area.

After the terrorist attacks in 2001, and threats to pollute our water supply, my husband and I purchased a new lift hand pump and planned to install it in our backyard. The

Father, mother, brother, and Mona in 1947 or 1949.

Mona's parents at Goshen Baptist Church.

bright red pump reminded me of ones I'd seen in my childhood.

As a child, my parents, brother and I lived on Fifth Street in Wilmington. We had city water, but there were still large pumps on certain streets throughout the city. One close to my parents' home was located on the brick laid road on Wright Street between Fourth and Fifth Streets. These pumps were for the use of the public.

Every Sunday, we attended my parents' church, Goshen Baptist on Mt. Misery Road in Leland. There was an old rusty pump at the side entrance of the church, but it was no longer used.

After worship service on Sunday, our relatives would always invite us to have dinner at their homes. They all lived close to the church.

One of my uncles and aunts lived on Mt. Misery Road also. Visiting their home was always pleasant and fun for me as I had two cousins my own age to play with.

Their driveway circled their home and my dad would always drive to the back entrance and park. As we went up the steps to the door, we entered the screened in back porch. The kitchen was to the left, and as you walked in, the big cast iron wood stove was to your left in the corner of the room. A sink and a lift hand pump was in an extended alcove connected to the kitchen.

Another pump was located on the side yard and used for farm duties. Grapevines and small utility buildings and a barn lined the circular driveway. A field was on each side of the home. The field to the left was for horses to graze, and back of the field was a pond of water for them to drink.

The pond was also used for baptismal services for the church when the horses were fenced in. Rural churches didn't have installed baptismal pools then.

The field to the right was for growing vegetables, etc.

Oil lamps were still used at night as electricity hadn't been extended to that area.

Other relatives' homes were located on Blue Banks Loop Road. You would turn to your right off of Mt. Misery Road. The All Soul's Episcopal Church was located at this little crossroad.

Several miles down this dirt road my widowed aunt and her family lived in a yellow colored painted home. When we visited there, their pump and sink were located in a corner of the kitchen. It had a step up to the triangle arrangement.

Elsie, age six years, six months and Mona Peterson, age six years, eight months; and Evelyn Evans Hull, age six years, three months.

L. R. Hobbs, grandfather; Blanche Hilburn Hobbs, grandmother and Aunt Maggie Hobbs Wilson clearing a lot.

Two other homes down that road, where two other uncles and their families lived, was a natural wood home, and another painted green. Their pumps were located on the open back porch.

Now, the thing about these pumps, they had to be primed. A container was always full of water, and reserved for that purpose. The water was poured into the top part as you picked up the handle to start the pump. Most times, the steel handle would "clang" against the lower part. Then, as you began to pump with all the strength and muscle power in

Mona P. Scott and brother, L. W. Peterson.

your arm, you held the other hand over the mouth, and heard gusts of air and squeaking noise as the water from the pipe in the well would come bursting forth, cold and clear.

With Homeland Security set up after 9/11, my husband and I never had to install the new pump.

My husband, Marvin Eugene, and I have been married 54 years. We have a son and two daughters and their spouses. We have six grandchildren. We always lived in Wilmington.

A Lot of Dreaming
by
Audrey F. Teachey of Wilmington

Throughout this book, you'll encounter laments that today's children are unfortunate to have missed the kind of life we old-timers lived during the good old days. Audrey Teachey reinforces that lament by describing her idyllic childhood and teen years in Rose Hill. Her delightful memories include toad frog houses (how great to be reminded!), a reference to "garden houses" (read on and you'll understand) and of course dreaming with friends on the porch.

My hometown, Rose Hill, Duplin County (which was New Hanover until 1750 AD) North Carolina, was a very small place when I was born March 23, 1920. The streets were not paved and were scraped once a week. Along the edge of the street where the sand banked up was a wonderful place to make toad frog houses.

I lived in a thirteen-room house my grandfather had built in 1913, and my grandmother lived with us. The house was wired when it was built. All the wires were on the ceiling with a long drop cord in the middle of the room. Each month, Homer Stanley read our meter. Mother cooked on a wood stove with a hot water reservoir. She made biscuits from scratch three times a day. There was a fireplace in each room, Daddy cut the wood to fit the cook stove and the fireplaces.

Our water came from a deep well in the yard and a hand pump was on the side porch. There was a tin, long handled dipper that hung by the pump and the water was always cold. We did not have a public water system, so there was an outhouse for a toilet, my grandmothers called "Garden Houses," because they were back of the Garden. China chambers with lids were under each bed. That was a chore to empty all of them each morning. There was a pitcher and wash basin in each bedroom for bathing. In the summer we had our baths in a tin wash tub, that was real fun.

We always had a flytrap hanging beside each outside door. Also, in the summer we bought ice from the iceman every Saturday. A fifty pound block would last a week in our wooden ice box. We had feather beds on top of our mattress and springs in the winter, because they kept us warm.

We had a telephone on the wall in the front hall, with a stool under it so we children could reach it. There was one central operator. When we called we picked up the receiver and said, "Hello Fanny" (we all knew her name) "please ring Aunt Alma for me" (and Fanny knew each one of us). Later, we could ring up each other. Our ring was one long and two shorts. Still later we had a party line with four houses on the same line. When you went to use it and someone else was on the line, you had to wait until they finished before you could use it.

When electric appliances came out we had to have our house rewired. The first radio we had was a Philco, and the only station we could get was Cincinnati, Ohio. I think their call letters were WKEM. We could get Amos and Andy and Lum and Abner, who owned the "Jot-em-down Store." Later, when Raleigh had a station, WPTF, we could get more programs. WPTF meant "We Protect The Family." It was owned by the Durham Life Insurance Company. "Singing Sam" was my favorite program. It was sponsored by the Coca Cola Company. Our first washing machine was an EASY wringer washer, made by the Tide Water Power Company.

When I started school, my birthday came one month before the school year ended. So, Mother took me to the first grade, then to the second grade. The first and second grade teachers lived next door to us. They were Misses McGlowhorn and Granger. They told

Mother they had already taught me everything you learn in the first and second grades. They decided to let me start the last month of the second grade. From then on, everyone in our class was two or three years older than me.

When I was nine years old, Mother decided it was time for me to take piano lessons. I played for church service the first time when I was eleven years old. I went by train each Saturday to Goldsboro for my music lessons at Goldsboro School of Music until I received a Teacher's Diploma at fourteen years old. My teacher's name was Dr. K.F. Hurst, a German. I played piano or organ in church for fifty-two years. I then had to stop because I had arthritis in my hands.

We had a wind-up record player, a Victrola, that played records the size of a 33 1/3. My grandparents in the county had an Edison that played a round record like a paper roll. They also had a wind-up clock made in 1875. My grandfather bought it the year they were married, 1888. It has two faces: the top one has the hour, the minute and the second hands on it. The lower face has the day, date and month on it. I am still winding that clock. It has never stopped, unless I forget to wind it.

When we went to the movies, we had to go to the next town because we did not have a theater. The movies were silent, the words were written across the black and white screen. Someone had to read it for me. There was music in the background, and it sounded like an organ.

My cousins that were boys wore knickerbocker pants until they were twelve. Then they could put on long pants. We girls looked forward to getting hand-me-downs from the older ones. There were about three girls that gave to me. Then I passed them on to the next one.

One of my friend's grandmother lived on the street where the train came through town. We sat and watched it many times. They were steam locomotive trains with vamp wheels. The train that came through at 8:00 AM and went back at 12:00 noon was called the Shoofly, and the train that came through at 11:00 AM and went back at 8:00 PM was called the Mail. These trains traveled from Wilmington to Rocky Mount and back each day.

There were sixteen of us first cousins who lived within one and one-half blocks. What one of us couldn't think of, another one could. We were always busy and did not have time to get in trouble. We knew if we did, someone would tell on us: our mothers were all sisters.

This was before radio and television and we had to create our own entertainment. We girls all had homemade toys. Our paper dolls and their clothes were cut out of magazines and catalogs. We made our doll clothes from scraps left over from our dresses. I even made my first dress for my sister when I was five years old, under mother's supervision. Our doll furniture was made from pasteboard boxes and our doll cribs we made from round oatmeal boxes and spools from thread were our wheels. We used wooden blocks from my uncle's factory to make our stools and chairs for our playhouse, which was one of the sheds behind our house.

In this same place, when we were a little older, we would make up plays, with singing and dancing. Our curtains were made out of old sheets. When we did this, every child in the neighborhood would be there. All of us knew how to play some kind of musical instrument, from a piano to a violin, or from a Jews harp to a comb and we all knew how to sing.

On New Years Eve, we made a big bonfire with all our Christmas trees. It was bad luck to have a tree up on New Years Day. The fire would be in the middle of the street. When the fire died down we would roast marshmallows.

There was an empty lot beside our house that belonged to us. This is where we all learned to play baseball and touch football. One of my chores was to cut the grass on this lot with a push lawn mower.

There was a place just outside of town that was covered with pine trees. We called it The Piney Woods. In the spring, we would go out there and have an Easter egg hunt, which we all enjoyed. This place is gone and covered with houses now.

We had an annual event at White Lake, which was near us. Our whole Sunday School would go and have "Dinner on the Grounds" and spend the day. We would all come home sunburned and tired, but we never complained we had such a wonderful time.

On a hot summer day, Mother would say, "You children put on your bathing suits, we are going to the river and cool off." She would take as many as our Ford touring car would hold. Gas was 10 cents per gallon then. We never thought of asking to stop for a drink or a hot dog. We took it all with us from home.

Every summer, Daddy would rent a cottage at the beach for us for two weeks. We would invite our aunts, uncles and cousins to come and stay a few days. The house was full all the time. Those were very happy days.

In high school, we made our poodle skirts and wore black and white saddle oxfords shoes. Some of our dresses were made out of feed sacks. After I was married and had a daughter, I went to some of the farmers who raised chickens and purchased feed sacks to make her dresses. You could starch them and they looked like linen.

In our teens, we would gather on the front porch at our house (it was the largest porch in the neighborhood) and tell all kinds of stories, sing, and plan our futures. There was a lot of dreaming going on and we all enjoyed it.

My childhood days in my hometown are gone but certainly not forgotten. Those were surely the "Good Old Days."

Upgrading from an Outhouse
by
Marie Whitman of Wilmington

Marie Whitman, a lifelong Wilmington native, was born in 1941. Here are some of her delightful memories of the good old days, including some radio programs recognizable by most old-timers. Marie's parents were Creasy A Swann and Exie Evans Swann Blackburn.

I was born in Wilmington, the youngest of five children, at the old James Walker Hospital. We lived in a house off Carolina Beach Road, equipped with an outhouse. Mama washed on a washboard, we bathed in tin tubs set in the sun to warm the water. When I was five or six years old, we "upgraded" to a house about a mile down the road which had indoor plumbing.

My Poppa raised cattle and ran a meat market with my dad. We were always warned not to go in the pasture when the bull was out.

Inside the barn was an old wind-up record player with thick records we'd crank up and play.

Silver Lake was crystal clear and a delightful place to swim. There weren't any houses around, just a dirt road leading to the lake, white sand dunes surrounded it.

Echo Farms really was a dairy farm. Trucks loaded up with glass bottle milk to go on their routes.

Landfall was all woods with a broken down mansion that we liked to think was haunted.

One of my favorite places was the train station downtown. I'd board a train each summer and head to Washington, D.C. to spend

Marie's mother's grandparents' home in Freeman was still there ten years ago. Fourth from left is Marie's grandmother, Callie Alford Evans. Seated next to her are her parents. Picture taken in 1900.

a couple of weeks with my sister.

We all had "party line" phones with different rings for different homes (two short, one long, etc). It was fun listening to the other calls unless you got caught.

On the radio played, "The Shadow Knows," "Cisco Kid," "The Lone Ranger," "The Fat Man" and such.

Dick and Jane (see Spot run, run Spot run - sound familiar) was first reading books. Actually, I saw one at WalMart recently and bought it for the memories!

Memory Minders
by
Christina (Mickie) Annarino of Wilmington

Christina Annarino was born in 1935 and grew up in Detroit, Michigan. She provided a list of memorable products, items, traditions and "stuff" related to the past. These things may appear cryptic except to contemporaries of Mrs. Annarino.

Household and related items: aluminum Christmas trees; bed headboard reading lamps; Big Ben windup alarm clocks (would love to have another).

Comics, etc.: Katzenjammer Kids; Gravel Gertie; The Schmoo; Kilroy.

Candies: Teaberry gum; Black Jack gum; "Slo-Poke" all day suckers; Jujubes (hard candy which could be hard on teeth but great.

Miscellaneous items: movie newsreels; Pete Smith specials (movie shorts); poultices (medical uses); Cushman motor scooters; Whizzer motorbikes. The above mentioned items sure bring back those great moments/memories experienced during our growing up times.

Clothes and related: leggings; spats; zoot suits; string bean neckties (very narrow).

Automotive: steering wheel "spinners," AKA suicide knobs; leopard skin seat covers (cool in the 50s, do you remember?); curb feelers (spring loaded rods to alert drivers of curb closeness to prevent scuffing whitewall tires—they worked for us); chrome plated hubcaps called "props" due to their similarity to airplane propellers; vacuum controlled windshield wipers. They were terrible and hardly ever worked.

Ration Stamps and Wind-up Victrolas
by
Virginia K. Wallace of Wilmington

Virginia Wallace was born in Wilmington in 1926 and grew up there. Her memories hark back to pre-electricity days, and then on to World War II. If you're a member of her generation, you'll enjoy, and identify with, her story.

In my 80 plus years, I have seen and remember so many changes of which I will name a few.

Starting with the 1920s, my father was in the grocery business at Sneads Ferry in Onslow County. My oldest brother, Lenwood

King, was born there in 1913.

In the early 1930s, my parents and brother moved to Wilmington. In 1925, my youngest brother, A. L. King, Jr., was born and I was born in 1926.

My grandparents had a Victrola—the kind that you had to manually wind up. Their lighting came from kerosene lamps and the cooking was done on a wood stove. When my grandfather passed away in 1944, they still did not have electricity.

During the 1940s, while I was in high school, we were suddenly forced into World War II. Immediately everyone was introduced to and issued ration stamps and tokens. In addition to paying for our meats, canned good, etc., we had to use our red and blue tokens that were issued to buy most food products. Blue tokens were used for canned goods, drinks, etc., and red tokens were used for meats. Back then, most groceries were delivered to your house. I still have a small bag of red tokens.

We also were given stamps with which to buy shoes. The best I can remember is that you could get a pair of shoes every six months. Gasoline was also rationed and we were issued stamps to purchase gas. Yards were cut with push mowers because of the gas rationing.

Virginia King Wallace, age five, and brother, A. L. King, Jr., age six, in 1931.

My mother used a washboard to wash our clothes and then later we had a wringer washing machine. Clothes were hung out to dry on clotheslines because there were no dryers. At our home we used an oil stove for cooking.

When I moved away from home into an apartment, I'll never forget our method of getting ice. We didn't have a refrigerator, but instead had an icebox. Every day the iceman would come around delivering ice. We were given cardboard signs with 5,10,15, etc. pounds of ice that we would need. These signs were placed in a window where the iceman could see it and he would deliver the amount of ice listed on our sign.

Remembering World War II, my mother would have two or three servicemen at our house for dinner on Sunday and she would feed them a hearty meal. My youngest brother was in the service and he assured us that those boys looked forward to their Sunday dinner and appreciated all of the attention they were getting. This made us feel really good that we could help them in some small way.

It was a sad day in 1945 when we heard over the radio that President Franklin D. Roosevelt had died. Most of us still remember where we were and what we were doing that day when we heard the news.

During the time of World War II we had many blackouts—air raid sirens would go off

Virginia King Wallace, age five, and brother, A. L. King, Jr., age six.

and if it was nighttime we turned off all the lights and covered all the windows so our house would be good and dark. I spent a week at Carolina Beach with a friend of mine and we were located on the ocean side. All the lights on the front of the house had to be out so we could not be seen from the ocean.

These were times at our young age that we would remember for the rest of our lives. Fortunately, all of our blackouts were only for practice.

The day that we received word that the war was over, some of my friends and I walked down town to celebrate with many people, especially our friends. Everyone was so happy and we laughed and cried with tears of joy because our emotions were so high.

The other day a friend and I were reminiscing about our younger days, and I thought of the Lumina Pavilion at Wrightsville Beach.

In 1903 the Tidewater Power Company purchased an oceanfront lot for ten dollars, and upon the lot was built Lumina. It got its name from its glowing lights. It even served as a navigational landmark for ships at sea. Lumina, constructed of heart pine, opened on June 3, 1905.

Lumina was usually accessed by "Beach Car," an electric trolley that ran from downtown Wilmington, and operated by Tidewater Power Company. I've been told that it cost about 35 cents for the 35-minute ride, and the trolley carried about 68 people. The trolley made its final run in 1940 after an automobile route was developed.

Lumina offered bowling lanes, restaurants, movies and an elegant dance hall where the big dance bands of the ear performed.

Ed and Virginia Wallace at their grandson's wedding in 1997.

As times changed, Lumina changed too. By the 1970s the once elegant ballroom stood darkly deserted, and in 1973, the Lumina Pavilion was demolished.

The name Lumina still lives on in our hearts and memories.

I probably could go on and on, but I'll give someone else the chance to express their feelings. These were hard times, but they definitely were the "Good Ole Days." I look back now and have the utmost appreciation for them.

Two Sips at Grandma's House
by
Barbara Marshall Guy of Wilmington

Regrettably, Barbara Guy chose not to reveal the name of her grandmother in this delightfully presented account of long ago visits. She does, however, describe with wry humor such contemporary details as sweeping behind the yard chickens, the buzzing outhouse and the solitary corncob. Mrs. Guy was born in Wilmington in 1926. You'll enjoy her tale, even though Grandma is anonymous.

Some of my fondest childhood memories are of Sunday afternoons when my mother, daddy, and I loaded up the 1936 Chevy for a trip to Duplin County to visit my grandmother She was raised, along with ten or eleven siblings, in the Buckner Hill Plantation House. Incidentally, this is the big white house where many scenes in the movie *Divine Secrets of the Ya-Ya Sisterhood* were filmed.

After my grandmother became a widow and raised three daughters, she moved into a little unpainted two-room frame structure not far from where she had grown up. It had front and back doors but was very dark inside. I don't remember any windows. There were oil lanterns.

Her front yard was always neatly swept with a corn straw broom because she kept free-roaming chickens. In front of the house was a huge gardenia bush which gave off a heavenly scent. Out back were two enormous grapevines, one with black grapes and the other, green. The juice was very sweet, but lyou had to get rid of the skin, pulp and seeds. My grandmother made her own wine, and I was allowed about two sips each visit.

In order to get a drink of water, I had to have help. I was not to be near the well, which was surrounded by a wooden build-up. There was a bucket secured by a rope. When one of the adults brought up a bucket of water, some would be poured into a gourd from which I could drink.

The bathroom was an outhouse down a long path. There was an unforgettable odor in there and great buzzing noises. I'm sure my grandmother treated with lime at regular intervals. For toilet paper, there was a thick Sears Roebuck catalog. I always wondered about a dried corncob hanging in there. This was my least favorite place on the visits.

When I had stayed overnight once, I remember going to Sunday school in Faison, riding in the back of a wagon with wooden spoke wheels with several cousins who lived nearby. This wagon was pulled by a mule under the control of my Uncle Ben.

To this day a family graveyard is located through a field from the Buckner Hill House. Dr. Hill, my grandmother, grandfather and several children who died young are buried there.

The Vanished Communities
by
Silas Sneeden of Wilmington

Silas Sneeden was born in 1921 at Sea Gate, and as he says in his story, he has seen a lot. You'll find this to be very true as you read, and we can promise you that you will learn a lot.

In 1950, I moved from Sea Gate, N.C. to Nonester. My plan was to take a year of my life to do the things I wished to do. I wanted to live on Catfish Creek for a year. I wanted to hunt and fish for one year before I had to go back to working and raising a family. But things happened that changed my life forever.

We were laying brick on the top section of Belk-Berry at 2nd and Chestnut when the scaffold gave way and three of us fell about 75 feet. James Lowe died and I went into a coma for seven days. Frank Richards had a double fractured pelvis and a broken foot. I had a split pelvis that went into my bladder. Frank was in the hospital for 47 days in I was in there 52 days. It took two years to get back

Silas Sneeden in 1958 with the bear he shot.

to normal. I had to sell my home at Sea Gate to survive. I had to start all over again. With five children it wasn't easy.

Frank Richards, my brother-in-law, had a small tract of land about 300 yards from the old post office site of Nonester. He let me have a small part of it to build my house on. I was living in a house that Roy Hobbs built from houses town down in Wilmington. The house was built for a man to live in and take care of his hogs. I bought the house and garage for $500.00. The house had to go to make room for Sutton Electric Plant. I built a house of one large room. I worked a lttle at a time to enlarge it and I was raising five children. I was able to go back to work after two years.

About this time they were laying out for 421 Highway and building the Sutton Electric plant.

When Mr. Fleming bought the other half of the property, there were about 12 squatters on the land. Mr. Fleming never told them to leave. He had Mr Schull to arrange the houses so as to give them deeds where they lived. There were two families living at Nonester.

Nonester was a small place of a post office and train stop. It was Number 2 train stop on the Fayetteville line. The next was Number 3 and it was Richard Switch. It had a post office and loading platform with two two-story buildings. Blanch Stanley, my cousin, said when she was a child, she lived in one of the houses.

At one time, there were six houses in this area:

Silas Sneeden in 1976 with his pet ferrets.

Thornberry, Rat Island, Fisher Creek, Mount Misery and Nonester. All of these homes just vanished. I believe a large forest fire swept through there, because at all sites there are only brick pillars standing—not even any old timber left.

Silas Sneeden in 1958 with the fish he caught in Cat Fish Creek, now Sutton Lake.

Some folks still wonder how Pocomoke got its name. There was a large Indian tribe named Pocomoke, close by. One of the fertilizer plants that was built in the 30s was named Pocomoke. During World War II, the Pocomoke site was used to build dry docks for the Navy.

New Hanover County made their landfill at Pocomoke, which is now Flemington. I think the county is building soccer fields on this site.

For many years all the land was turpentine. When I moved to Nonester there still were remains of the camps the workers that collected the rosin lived in.

Silas Sneeden in 2006.

The camps were at Nonester and Pocomoke.

When I was about five years old, we lived on Old 74 and Navasa Road. At that time there was the ferryboat and a train running to Southport. My father had a little business there and he was a cook of Southern fried chicken. I have never seen any cooked his way. He would roll the chicken in thick batter and fry it in deep fat.

When the train to Southport stopped there, my father would push me up into the cab and the trainman would let me ring the bell and blow the whistle, and he would run the train a little ways and then bring me back.

When we went to Wilmington it was like a picnic. Me and my siblings loved the ferryboat. There was a fence law at that time. When there was a rain, the water would rise and the hogs and pigs would get on the roadbed and you had to pick your way through.

The ferryboat ended when they built the bridges. They built them about 1928. I went to the dedication. A barge with fireworks was at the Cape Fear Bridge. A friend of mine who was about 16 years old was on the barge when a blast happened and he lost an arm. He was known as Nubb Savage the rest of his life.

These are a few of the things I have seen in my lifetime. Believe me, I have seen a lot. I am 85 years old.

A Snowy New England Romance
by
Colo Hayes of Wilmington

This delightful story takes place far from Wilmington, and we're sure you'll enjoy it. Although it's a love story, it's primarily about farm life in New England. In it, you'll find some major differences, very interesting ones, from farms here in North Carolina.

My father, Colo E. Hayes, was born in New Durham, New Hampshire in 1892, and my mother, Bertha MacCorlie Hayes, was born in Providence, Rhode Island in 1894. This is a story about how they met and got married.

My mother's father, whose family owned a wooling (woolen?) mill in Maine, worked for the government checking wool coming in to the United States. She had three other siblings, two brothers and one sister. The oldest brother was a "G man" before the FBI was founded.

While my mother was going to secretary school, her father came down with tuberculosis. She stopped going to school and stayed home to help take care of him. Sadly, in a few months he died. Shortly after, my mother became sick and the doctor said she had also contracted tuberculosis. My mother was seventeen at the time.

In those days, if you were young, they would send you up to a cold climate to try and cure you. There was a place where they sent people in Canada, so she went to Boston and took a train to Canada. The train got as far as New Durham, N.H. and was stopped by a heavy snowstorm. Back then, the engineers had to stop the train until the tracks were clear of snow, and they would go in to the towns and ask the locals for boarding. My mother was taken in by my grandmother.

My grandfather owned a dairy farm. He

and his brothers had owned the Hayes Knife Factory, but during World War I, they could no longer get the German steel that they would only use. They sold out and he bought this farm.

My grandfather had seven boys and three girls. The farm was packed with horses, cows, chickens and hogs. My mother stayed with them for several weeks while the snow was cleared on the tracks.

By the time my mother was to go to Canada, my father was already falling in love with her. He told her about a cabin he and his brothers owned on top of a mountain, and explained that it was just as cold there as it would be in Canada. He asked her to marry him and said they would spend the winter up in the cabin, where she could get well.

At the cabin, there was a deep hole dug into the ground where they kept salt pork, bacon, smoked ham, beans, flour and potatoes. He figured whatever meat they needed other than that, my father would hunt for. If he could see it, he could shoot it.

They were taken up to the cabin by one of my uncles using a horse and sled to the mountain, and then they had to snowshoe to the cabin. My mother and father stayed until late spring 1911.

After seeing a doctor, she found out that she had scarring on her lungs but other then that seemed to be in good health. They moved in to the town of New Durham and my father went to work at a wood factory. There, he turned out table legs and handles during the winter months, and in the spring he would play baseball.

Factories back then used to own baseball teams and tour all over New England. My father would be gone for weeks playing in Vermont, Maine and New Hampshire. He realized that my mother did not like him being gone for so tong, and he quit the factory and opened up his own garage in town. He got a town contract, and took care of the town truck and tractors, along with people's cars.

After my three sisters and I were born, they moved to Massachusetts, where he found work in a large garage until the Depression hit. Unable to find work, my father and our family moved back to the family's farm in New Hampshire.

Even though we didn't have any money, living on a farm, you never went hungry. I was five and remember watching them feed all the animals and how his dog would bring the cows to the barn, where my father and his brothers would milk them by hand.

In the winter they would cut a hole in the pond, and cut ice and put it in the ice house, where it would be covered in layers of sawdust. My grandfather had a smoke house where they would smoke the pork.

After a few months we moved to Maine where they bought a house and my father opened another garage. The house was hit by tightening, and burned to the ground.

My family moved back to New Hampshire where he bought a gas station and a garage.

My grandfather's farm had a large field that was fenced in so the cows and horses could not get in to eat the grass. In the fall, the grass was thick and tall. They would cut it and let it lay out in the sun to dry. Then they would hand rack it into piles. They would fill a large wagon, pulled by two horses, with the hay, by hand with pitchforks. It then was hauled to the barn an on the second floor there were two large doors with an iron railing running the whole length of the barn and going outside about three feet. A large hayfork with four arms and hooks on the end would ride along this rail. Outside, it was lowered down onto the hay and the arms were wide open. A rope was hooked to this and a horse would pull it up to the rail where it would lock onto a pulley. Two of my uncles would then pull it inside and let the hay fall to the floor. It took three trips to unload the hay wagon. While it was going back to the field, the two would move the hay to each side of the barn. This would take about three days to do, hoping it would not rain because the hay had to be dry to put there.

In the center of the barn's second floor was a trap door where they would put the hay to fall down on the first floor. Then, by hand, it would be put into bins along the side the cows were on and the other side where the horses were.

The cow side was more than half of the first floor. At the end of the cow's side, there were stalls where the cows would be put to milk. The milk would go into large pails and when the pails were full, the milk would be poured into large, tall copper tanks. These had a handle on each side, and when full, a tight cover would be put on and two brothers would carry them into the icehouse. Then they would fill up quart glass bottles and a cardboard cap would be put on. This was raw milk. It was not pasteurized and cream would come to the top.

My grandfather had two one-horse carriages where ice was put and the milk bottles were put on top of the ice. Eggs were put into baskets with hay in them—there were no egg boxes then. Early every morning, the milk and eggs would be delivered to different houses in town. Milk was five cents a quart. The customers would leave out the empty bottles and they were taken back to the farm and washed. Don't remember what the eggs cost. Customers would just pick out as many as they wanted.

Out by the cabin we lived in when we had to come back to the farm was a building built over a large hole dug into the ground. There was no first floor, just steps going down into the hole. It was called a dirt cellar, and along both sides there were bins where in the fall, vegetables were put. Paper would be put down on the floor, and tomato plants would be pulled out of the ground with the roots and dirt still on them. They would put these on top of the paper and you would have fresh tomatoes till December.

There was always a lot of food. Breakfast was early and you had eggs, bacon and corn meal or pancakes with maple syrup, made there on the farm, and sausages. They got up at four A.M. to milk the cows, and then came in for breakfast. My grandfather always said, "You have to have a good breakfast to do a day's work."

Their lunch was different. They drank milk and had hot apple pies and meat pies made from deer meat, and fruits. Dinner was large: meat, potatoes and vegetables.

In the kitchen was a large icebox where food was kept. There was a large metal container on the floor beneath the icebox that caught the melt water.

To get electricity to the farm, my grandfather had to buy five poles to string the wire to the house. Only on the first floor did they have light bulbs hanging down in the center of the room, with a pull chain to turn them on and off. There were only oil lamps on the second floor.

Outside, they had six outhouses. They were out by the barn, three for the men and three for women. They had two large wells for water. Water for the animals was taken from the pond.

My father died in February 1970. If he had lived one more week they would have been married sixty years. My mother died in August of 1977.

I have two sisters living, one is 93 and they other 87. I am 83 years old and have two sons and two daughters. My oldest daughter is retired and lives on Bald Head Island, N.C. My oldest son lives in Maine, where he works for Federal Express. My younger son owns his own computer consulting company and lives in Cross River, New York. My youngest daughter is a high school special education teacher, and lives in Scottsdale, Arizona. I have two beautiful granddaughters and two handsome grandsons.

I worked for 35 years in advertising in New York City, where I raised my family. I now live in Wilmington, NC. and am very proud of my family history.

The Rooster and the Eyeglasses
by
Betty G. Duncan of Wilmington

Some of the best stories we've ever gotten are about, of all things, roosters and outhouses. Betty Duncan, who was born in Clinton, N.C. in 1944 and raised in Wilmington, has a story that has both of these topics. It may just surprise you.

I can go back to when I was seven years old.

My brother could not go outside if our rooster was out. The rooster would jump on Dan's head and go to pecking. Mama didn't know why, and Grandma said it was because

Betty's mom and dad, William and Mae Bell, in 1950.

Dan wore glasses. So one day, Mama took his glasses and he went outside and that rooster did not come near him.

We lived so far back in the woods if you walked to the mailbox you had to pack a lunch. Most times, Mama took the horse and wagon.

My cousin would come and stay with us come summertime. My sister Frances was crippled, and Joyce took tobacco sticks and made Frances some braces to walk on.

We did not have a bathroom, so we went to the outhouse. Mama would go with us, but one morning she would not go. So I went by myself and I fell in that big hole. Mama heard me scream and came running. I was crying and Mama just stood and laughed at me. I told her to please get me out. She was laughing so hard she dropped me back in that big hole. She got me out and put me by the well and washed me clean. I will never forget that day.

My good old days are my memories. They were the best.

Brother, Dan; sister, Frances and Betty in 1950.

When the Railroad Left Wilmington
by
Shirley King of Wilmington

Shirley King, who was born in Wilmington in 1935, has some wonderful memories about the good old days. Like many of us, she misses the influence of railroads, especially the old steam engines.

In the 1940s, when I was a young girl about eight years old, my family lived on Macrae Street in Wilmington near the railroad tracks where the trains came into Wilmington backwards. During that time it was called the Atlantic Coast Line Railroad. They moved to Jacksonville, Florida in the 60s. All the trains were steam locomotives where they put coal in there to run them.

When I was about ten years old, I took my first train ride to New York to visit my grandmother. That was the most joyous time of my life. My cousin went with me and we had a good time.

I remember my father taking me to the railroad station downtown when the circus came into town. It was at the foot of Red Cross Street, where the Railroad Museum is now.

I wish they had kept the train station where it was. It was located on Front and Red Cross Street. At that time they didn't have Front Street open where you could go all the way through. They opened it up when the railroad left Wilmington.

Back then a fish man came through the neighborhood, selling fish from his mule and wagon. It was 25 cents for ten or so fish on a string. And a vegetable man came through on Saturday morning with all kinds of fresh vegetables—collards, turnips, sweet potatoes, etc.—on his old-timey truck. Sometimes he had fresh pork sausage, sliced smoked ham, liver pudding, fatback, etc. You could take ten dollars and buy enough vegetables and meat to last a whole week.

Those two men were the kindliest and friendliest people you would ever meet.

Back then there was a grocery store on just about every corner. My parents could feed a family of seven for about a month for twenty dollars. Rice, sugar, grits was five cents a pound and some was ten cents a pound.

I remember during the war when we had blackouts, like cut all the lights off, turn the radio off and be quiet. I think a siren would go off to let you know that it was time for one. My parents had to get stamps from the government to buy shoes, sugar, clothes and a few other items.

On Saturday night my mother would give us a bath in a number two tub by the heater. She would heat the water in the reservoir on the wood burning stove, the one she cooked on.

We didn't have any luxuries, we only had a radio to listen to. On Saturday nights we would listen to fights and the Grand Ole Opry.

On Sunday mornings we got up, had breakfast and got dressed to go to Sunday school and church, which was about five blocks from where we lived. After church, we would go to the soda shop and get us a five cent cup of soda.

My school, Peabody Elementary, was about five blocks from my house on Sixth Street between Red Cross and Campbell Streets. The grades went from first to fifth. The building is still there as the home of New Hanover County Head Start and Community Action Services.

My uncle used to take my sisters, brothers and me up in the country to visit my aunt and her family. They didn't have inside bathrooms, so we had to go to the outhouse. My aunt made the best biscuits from scratch. They would be on the table in a big bowl and I would sneak in the kitchen and take one or two.

When I was young, that was the best time of my life. Progress is good, but I wish they had left some things like they were.

An Honorary Fireman?
by
Ervin Boswell of Wilmington

Mr. Boswell was born in Wilmington in 1962 and says he grew up in the Fire Department. He didn't share many memories, but he did send a photo of what we assume is a modern Wilmington fire truck.

I started hanging around firehouses when I was eight years old.

Fire trucks had open cabs then, and the firemen slid down the pole.

Back then, they had fireboxes on the corners. If someone actuated the firebox, the bell rang in the control room and all the firemen set off on the fire engines.

Today at age 45, I'm still there, hanging around the firehouses. They have better fire engines, Scott air pacs and EMTs.

I take pictures of firemen, fire trucks and firehouses.

Ervin Boswell at Station #3.

Same Water, Different People
by
Willie Mae Mattocks of Wilmington

Many of us who came up during the good old days often forget how different—and often, how difficult—times were back then. Willie Mae Mattocks provides us with several reminders. Mrs. Mattocks was born in New Hanover County in 1929.

The iceman came on Saturday morning. We would buy a five-cent piece of ice and put it in a box with sawdust to keep food from spoiling.

When you scrubbed floors on your knees, you would use an old cotton Union underwear for a rag to clean the floor. Then we would go and get some white sand and spread it on the kitchen floor when you are cooking so grease would not get stuck on the floor.

On Saturday night, we heated a pot of water and poured it in a tub. Everyone took a bath in the same water.

We had to carry all our water—for drinking, cooking and washing clothes—and for anything else.

We had to walk about a mile for our mail. The post office was in someone's private home.

We carried our lunch bucket to the field. Lots of times we had molasses and cornbread, fatback meat. We ate whatever was in season. Of course we raised chickens and hogs. For Christmas, we would kill a rooster and bake it.

We had our share of picking beans and anything else we could make a dollar for our school clothes.

My grandmother worked for these well-to-do folks. She would bring magazines home and we plastered the walls with them instead of painting. We were too poor to buy paint.

A Tale from the Mountains
by
Hazel Bloodworth of Wilmington

Hazel Bloodworth was born in Asheville in 1915 and grew up on a farm near there. We are sincerely grateful that she chose to share some of her memories for this book.

Hazel Bloodworth.

I was born and raised in Asheville, N.C. and we moved to Wilmington in 1943. I am 92 years young and in good health. My friend Elsie Smiley asked if I would like to share some thoughts and memories about the good old days.

I stayed with my grandparents most of my young life. They had a large farm, consisting of farm gardens, horses, cows, honeybees and sheep.

There was a creek near the farm and my grandfather decided to make a lake with a waterfall that would run his equipment, such as a grist mill, to grind the corn into cornmeal for our family and for the community.

He also placed a big black pot near the water to do our laundry, with two tubs, a scrub board, and one big stick of bluing to make the clothes white. I was nine years old and had to help. A dryer had never been thought of, so a clothesline was hung in a tree to take its place. We used wooden clothespins.

Another spot on the farm was used to make sugar cane molasses. My granddaddy had a machine that was run by a horse going round in circles that squeezed the juice out of the cane. He carried the juice to a big vat to be cooked. It would boil and was stirred with two large paddles. After the syrup was made, the neighborhood gathered to pull and make candy. So much fun!

Hazel Bloodworth, September 20, 1959.

Another exciting day was hog killing day. People in the community would come and make sausage, liver pudding, soap, and hang the hams in the smokehouse to cure for winter.

In those days there was no water in houses. We had a spring and built a house over it to keep meats and milk and butter cool. We built a lazy boy to bring water from the spring for house use. He built a shaft to wind the water and a wire stretched from the house to the spring. Water was brought to the house on the wire.

One other thing I will have to tell you is about our sheep. They were trimmed and the wool was

Hazel Bloodworth.

given to my grandmother to card, and was made into yarn thread on the spinning wheel. The rest of the family knitted the socks. The old spinning wheel was our special antique toy.

I have an apartment in Brightmore and enjoy it very much. The seniors enjoy going to a restaurant nowadays, instead of cooking Sunday dinners and inviting the wagon load of family who used to come on Sunday to enjoy our fried chicken.

Thanks for allowing me to share a bit of my thoughts and memories. Seems like yesterday.

Hazel Bloodworth.

Wilmington's Protective Charm
by
Dorothy Pastis of Wilmington

In this modern world of rapid change, it's refreshing to find an icon that has changed in purpose only little throughout its over one hundred years of existence. Dorothy Pastis, who was born in New York City in 1937, but who grew up in Wilmington, describes Tileston School as a "talisman." We hope it continues to bestow its good luck upon your city's citizens for a hundred more years.

This is meant as a tribute to Tileston School from a former student who was privileged and fortunate for a school of this caliber to be available in Wilmington to educate me.

The school opened in 1872. In 1875, Woodrow Wilson studied there before moving on to Princeton, and eventually to the Presidency of the United States in 1884. Tileston graduated Henry Bacon, who no doubt gazed upon its Italianate architecture before going on to design the Lincoln Memorial. (Note: this is from an article written by John Staton).

In later years, journalist David Brinkley went to Tileston as well as Charlie Daniels. There may be others who have gained fame and hopefully, not notoriety, that others may remember.

Dedicated teachers gave us an exemplary education. We were schooled in math, (without calculators), English, geography, history, art, music, physical education and home economics by educators who knew, loved and enjoyed teaching their respective fields and imparted their expertise with gusto and a sense of sharing. (Attached is a picture of the teachers I knew.)

The administration was innovative. There was a day care on the premises (remember, this was in the early 50s) and the home economics students were given "hands-on" child care training.

There was shop for those wanting to learn a trade. There was distributive education, which allowed students to work half a day in an office or business, giving them responsibility as well spending money. Remember, this was at the junior high school level.

At that time, North Carolina law decreed that young people had to attend school until they became sixteen. A novel approach to control so-called "incorrigible" students, who were all males, was to put them all in one classroom with a very capable teacher in charge. This eliminated their disruptive presence in the other classes. In today's world, the PC world, that would be frowned on. However, I am confident that many of those students (predominately from the area known as "Dry Pond") went on to become successful and worthwhile citizens.

When the school was established in 1872, Tileston's first principal, Amy Bradley, intended it to educate both black and white students. Unfortunately, she had to abandon her original intention. She was a remarkable woman and very ahead of her time.

In 1989, when the school was sold to St. Mary's Church, it seemed that Providence had stepped in and saved this venerable school, which is still being used and is a talisman to the area and to the City of Wilmington.

Cider Hard and Sausage Old
by
Bill Baker of Hampstead

Bill Baker was born in 1932 and raised in the tobacco country near Raleigh. His memories are typical of the time and geography of his upbringing. This one may be a little hard to read, but it's well worth the effort. You won't want to miss it.

I was born on a one-horse farm in Franklin County, North Carolina in 1932. We had no horse, but borrowed a mule for farming.

In the early 40s there was an icebox—a block on Saturday and a half block on Tuesday when it could be afforded in the summer—otherwise, the buttermilk was kept cool by lowering on a rope into the well. The iceman or icemen came in an open flat bed truck with a canvas cover over the ice, backing up to the porch, sliding it off the truck and making that big lift into an icebox. The icebox could accommodate the full block with enough space for a few other items. Two men were necessary to lift the block with tongs into the box.

Use of the icebox was sporadic—summers only—until the house was wired by an uncle for $100 with a 30 amp capacity in the late forties.

I finished 12 years of public school without an electric light. We had kerosene lamps and the brightest was an Aladdin lamp that employed a mantle which, when intact, gave a fairly decent light at the kitchen table.

Ice in the summer time was a luxury that was not always afforded in the late thirties and forties.

On chamber pots: they were for the little people afraid they may fall in the slop jar. This slop jar was kept in a pantry like room off the back porch and used mainly by the females in the house as the males could manage wherever, usually by us boys off the end of the front porch at night. Mother always wondered why her lilac would not grow at the end of the porch. But if there was ice or snow on the porch and you were undressed for bed, the slop jab was not prohibited. Nothing matches the aroma following a bitterly cold night preceded by a meal of fatback, home made biscuits, butter and two or three plates of dried beans with buttermilk, of course.

The once a year venture to Raleigh for the Sunday clothes and school clothes if enough money remained after selling the crops or before repaying the loans to the bank. The suits consisted of a pair of long trousers and a pair of knickers with a matching coat. Usually, you wore the knickers until they could be handed down to a brother and then graduated to the long pants and maybe the jacket would still fit. School clothes for the boys was bibbed overalls and high top shoes or brogans. There were usually two sets of one-piece underwear with short legs and sleeves with button flaps in the back for the obvious. New jackets for most years as growth helped to get new stuff if you happened to be the oldest.

The old farmhouse was built by Great Grandfather in the late eighteen hundreds in three different phases, apparently. The kitchen was added last as the separate one burned many years before my arrival. The house was equipped with carbide gas lamps originally, from the information passed on to me, but the only evidence I know of was the iron pipes in the attic with an outlet in the ceiling. And there was junked equipment present on the premises in my youth, like a metal tank. We later had a tobacco ordering pit on the site of the old gas plant. I have not researched how this thing worked, but the church attended when growing up apparently had the same type lighting.

Mother mopped or used soapy water on the kitchen floor occasionally which would necessitate opening the doors on each side of the room after sweeping the excess water through a hole in the corner of room, probably placed there for that purpose. One Christmas Eve, she had washed this floor and left the doors open. We, my brothers and a neighbor we named Tom Tit, had discovered the cattails in a nearby marsh. The cattails were just right for beating and spreading their little fluffy wings to the wind. The wind was blowing north towards Mother's wet kitchen and proceeded to enter and cover the wet floor. The next thing we knew, this woman, with a yard brush broom, was storming around the corner, leaving us nothing to do but crawl under the house. Except for Tom, who was last seen hightailing it over the hill near the graveyard. Normally, we did not run from Mother, but since this was a group, she apparently decided that mass justice was not warranted and naturally, you did not want to be the first caught. We all made a get-a-way.

Few people today can visualize growing up in a household without electricity, indoor plumbing or running water. Through high school, graduating in 1950, this was our house/home, together with five other siblings, three brothers and two sisters.

Washday consisted of drawing water by bucket from a well, heating some in a cast iron wash pot, transporting by two in washtubs to a bench, using a washboard with lye soap, mostly with the work clothes boiled in the wash pot separately from bedding, rinsing and wringing out by hand, then hanging on a line to dry. In the winter, the clothes would freeze on the line, but eventually dry if the weather was agreeable.

Personal hygiene had limitations since water was drawn from the well, placed in a bucket which became the source for washing, in a separate wash pan. Drinking using a common dipper by whom ever wanted a drink. Or often when outside, drinking from the well bucket that was permanently attached to a chain and pulley.

When small, water in the summer was often heated in one of the wash tubs in the sun. As we became modest, a wash pan was used for the Saturday bath in a room with the door closed alone.

Shaving was in the kitchen at a side table with a small medicine cabinet mirror, water being heated on the wood stove.

Water to the animals confined to a pen had to be carried by bucket to them. The cow had a pasture on which a branch or creek existed most of the time. Hogs had their mud holes and daily bucket of slops which consisted of unused food or unusable food, usually with some type of purchased flour/meal type supplement mixed with the water. Hogs, mules, cow, chickens, etc. had corn also as food. As we grew, we discovered that these animals could and would eat corn without shucking, a dusty, boring job, and being often in charge of these chores, they ate corn in the form it was offered.

The house was heated by the cook stove in the kitchen and a wood stove in one room, usually, and fireplaces in the other two rooms. Normally, only the wood stove and cook stove were fired, making early risers dress hurriedly before starting the fire and everyone else grabbing the clothes for the day and moving to the lighted stove, although it seemed we were heating the stove rather than being warmed by the sputtering fire.

Wood for the stoves was cut on the farm with the cooking wood, we called it stove wood, being pine cut to length and split into rather small stick like pieces that would be placed in the firebox of the cooking stove.

The fire was usually started with kindling (we called it lightwood or the old folks called it liter or something similar) gathered from old pine stumps or pine knots which is essentially what heart pine is known as today. Granddad stated that the farm had these over the entire property when they moved there before the turn of the last century and to clear the land for farming the timber was cut and burned. Some of the timber was used for the house, obviously, as it is heart pine throughout but now owned by nonfamily.

Wood was cut with a two man crosscut saw, cut in lengths of eight to ten feet, hauled to the house by mule and wagon and cut into burning length with a saw powered by the rear wheel of a jalopy constructed by the owner with a shaft with a saw blade probably 18 to 24 inches in diameter on one end and a roller on the other, making contact with the drive wheel when jacked up. Usually a roller table like platform was also included which allowed the operator to push the wood to the saw and in turn move it for the next cut with an assistant taking the cut piece off and tossing it into a loose pile. No safety standards existed that anyone was aware of as this tool could amputate any limb that came in contact with it.

For several years we used a similar setup to grind apples for the making of cider from trees on the farm that had been planted by my great grandfather. The manual cider mill was a two man device with a hopper and handles on each side being turned, as designed, by two men as buckets of apples were poured into the hopper with the resulting pulp falling into slotted and open basket-like forms below. These were moved forward to the press, a screw device with a cap-like structure that fitted into the slotted baskets, squeezing the juice out that was then poured into barrels that was later consumed as cider, vinegar and probably apple brandy at times by the purchasers. To avoid the tough work of turning the mill by hand, a belt was rigged to the wheel of a Model T with the other end around a roller made from a tree on one side of the mill replacing the handle. It made short work of the grinding part, but no faster solution was forthcoming on the pressing part.

My grandma and I were the only ones who liked the hard cider. She also liked old sausage that had been in the smokehouse for several weeks, as I did.

There were few paved roads before the Kerr Scott administration in the 1950's in rural North Carolina. There was only a path - two tracks - through the woods to our farm and another farm beyond ours. There were no passing lanes or turnabouts. The regular roads were scraped/dragged periodically but many ruts existed most of the time and dust when dry which was bad if you lived near the road. And these roads were not for speed, especially if you drove a '33 Chevy that would bounce sideways when encountering severe ruts. Most of these roads were paved in the 50s and we finally got electricity after the co-ops offered to provide it. CP&L, which wanted $50.00 per pole to bring it to the farm prior to that, suddenly were able to provide the service. There was one single overhead bulb in each room with only a few receptacles for lamps and radio. We were finally able to get the electric fridge and a stove, which reduced the labor around the farm for wood cutting. We did not get running water and a washing machine until the mid fifties.

I did not know that a feather bed was for cover until sleeping in German hotels in Berlin. We always used them over the mattress in the winter—works both ways.

Visiting grandparents was a Sunday outing to mother's side of the family. Her father was deceased, causing her to drop out of high school in the ninth or tenth grade to help. There were ten brothers/sisters including her in the family, all older but two. She was born in 1911. Her grandmother was also living there when we visited, her father's mother. She was real ancient to us young kids with the long gingham dress, apron, black lace-up boot type shoes and she could pee standing up without removing or lifting anything which never ceased to amaze the little kids.

Cousins numbered more than twenty of various ages.

Birthday dinner for either Grandma or Great Grandma—I was never sure—required at least three sittings with the men first, then the women and followed by children. All I remember is a huge chicken pie that I did not care for as Mother said I was "curious." I guess it meant that I would not try anything new that looked strange.

The mailman only followed the state roads, not farm paths, which made our mailbox approximately a half-mile away at my other grandparents' place on the road. We always got our paper via the mailman: the *News and Observer*. My grandma who liked cider and sausage would scan the paper before we saw it but I never was sure how well she read. She had an opinion about most people and things. One of her expressions somewhat of a diplomat was, "He does the best he knows, he just don't know much." If the men would not plow the field she thought needed it, she would be out there with the mule and plow herself. She didn't need telephones when she was talking as you could hear her in the evening from our house if she was in her yard.

Bill Baker, the tall one, with brothers, Wayne and Ben, in the early 1940s at their place of birth.

Farming with one mule, breaking the land in the spring, sometimes staying out of school with a one-horse turning plow, taking days for what is done now in an hour or two. Cultivating, chopping, harvesting—all in slow motion when compared—but making do with what one had. Before dawn arising to remove cured tobacco from the barn in order to start another day of filling it with green tobacco. Stripping the cured leaf for market, carefully handling, which later and now is handled with forks into sheets for market.

Good food in the summer and winter after hog killing, and adequate food with biscuits, butter, fatback and beans with some canned or dried foods thrown in. Eating that last bit of cobbler on the table after school, with everyone having a spoon, eating out of the same dish. Dodging the mule leavings in the row when following.

Learning to hit a pitched piece of corn cob with a stick helped with baseball. Kicking the can, ball games with a ball made from twine or filled with cottonseed. Playing paratrooper, jumping from the loft of the packhouse. Corncob wars until a direct hit left the cob imprint. Shooting an air rifle at 'most everything. Swinging from trees in the woods, bent from the top. Picking blackberries and chiggers, looking for wild grapes called bullsies? Riding three to one bike on a dirt road/path, trying to a avoid sand bars.

Corn shucking when the cow needed more food. Pulling fodder (corn leaves) and taking it in when dry (dirty, itching, sneezing job) luckily not pursued every year. Mule and wagon riding around or gathering pine straw for the hog pen and other animals.

Chasing an animal that discovered a way out and cannot find the way back in. Stopping a runaway mule before it destroys the crop and trying not to lose it in the process.

Spending one cent each day at the candy room at school for a BB bat. Taking a biscuit for lunch rather than spend ten cents for lunch. Going barefoot at recess (some came without shoes to school).

Not being aware of racial inequities or housing inadequacies. Black kids passed on the road walking when we rode. Kin and others living in shacks that were barely covering but airy, buggy, rodent infested and just a step above homeless.

Waking up with snow on the covers as the windows were as old as the house. Building a fire in a tin heater for the bath on Saturday in an unheated room and still freezing on the back side.

Working the first paying job at two dollars a day and later during high school for 75 cents an hour.

Having a mother who bore six children at home, worked the garden, helped barn the tobacco and have a big lunch ready also, plus canning soup and vegetables, preserving, drying and keeping us fed and adequately clothed together with Dad and mostly obedient cooperative children.

Obviously, rhetoric takes over when remembering, even when descriptive details are omitted. However, there may be some excerpts that will be useful for publication; and, clarification will be attempted if needed for any part of this letter.

The Deer at the Well
by
Roberta M. Painter of Wilmington

Roberta Painter was born in Boston, Massachusetts in 1940. If you think that only we Southerners had outhouses and flatirons, you need to read this delightful story.

Oh what fun it is to remember the good old days! As a 66-year-old woman, I can remember it all.

I grew up in Philadelphia, Pennsylvania. We had the iceman bringing ice, a party line phone (you had to listen to the number of rings to know if it was for your family), and mailmen delivered mail right to your door. Everyone learned from Dick and Jane to See Spot run. I recently bought sets of Dick and Jane for my grandson.

Everyone passed on hand-me-downs to friends with smaller children, and for toys we had to use our imagination. An old broom was our horse to gallop up and down the street; our fingers were guns for cowboys and

Indians.

My very favorite memory came on Saturday mornings. A little old Italian man would come down the street with his organ and little monkey. The man always had a coat and hat on and the monkey had a red and gold hat and red and gold jacket. My father would give me some pennies and a nickel or two. You handed the coins to the monkey and he would drop them into a cup that he carried. I always looked forward to Saturday mornings just to see the organ grinder and his monkey.

My summers were spent in Lewiston, Maine where my grandfather lived. It was a lot of fun because we had the outhouse, the coal stove, the iron you heated on the stove and we had to get water from the well down a big hill. Fetching water was my job. I would take the bucket and go to the edge of the hill and in the early mornings there would be dozens of deer at the bottom of the hill. As I started down, they would dart away. The hard part was going up the hill with a full bucket but I can still recall how delicious and cold that water was.

We had a lake a mile away and we would go early, take soap and wash in the lake. Afternoons, we had fun swimming in the lake, but for some unknown reason, I still had to take a bath in a tin tub once a week. How I hated those baths. Of course there was a picture of me in the tub which I tore up every year, and when we came back the following year there was that picture again.

We used to gather round the radio and listen to Amos and Andy, Gunsmoke, and other shows while we ate Velveeta Cheese on saltine crackers. My father got one of the first TVs that came out and we would watch Uncle Miltie and wrestling. I think we only had 3 or 4 hours a day of TV time to begin with.

Life was so simple back then compared to the hustle and bustle of today's life. How I wish my grandson could experience such beauty, simplicity and serenity.

A HAM Radio Baby
by
Ellen Dunn Wells of Wilmington

Today, we take instant communication for granted. But back in 1947, in post-war Germany where Ellen Wells was born, almost any kind of communication was near impossible. The problem was getting word of her birth back home to Wilmington. The solution was HAM radio, the precursor to today's cell phone. You don't hear much about HAM radio these days.

My mom, Josephine Brown Dunn, and her parents, Thomas Edwin and Nellie Corbett Brown, and grandparents, are from Wilmington. My dad, Joseph Francis Dunn, was a career Army officer. In the Army, you had to have a hometown. It was Wilmington for me, as all my family was here. Although I grew up all around the world, I did, however, go to school for second grade and seventh grade in Wilmington. I'm a proud graduate of UNC-W.

My mother was on the first Dependent Ship (wives and children of the men stationed in Germany for reconstruction) to go to Europe after World War II in July 1946. My parents were stationed in Frankfurt, Germany. I was born in April 1947 in Frankfurt.

Mr. Donald MacRae Parsley has call number W4FT.

To get word of my birth back to Wilmington wasn't easy. Phone lines were down and there were no computers or cell phones.

Mr. Donald MacRae Parsley, a family friend, lived on Masonboro Sound Road at Live Oaks (the name of his family home). He was a great HAM radio operator and his call number was W4FT. He received my birth announcement from Frankfurt over his HAM radio right there on Masonboro Sound Road. He then got in his car and drove into town to tell my grandparents I was born.

The Obvious Other
by
Mary O. Lange of Wilmington

History (or at least this history) won't record who the absent-minded John Henry in Mary Lange's charming story was. But her story does remind us of a rather common office accessory, and its odious contents, from the good old days. Mrs. Lange was born in Wilmington in 1935, and obviously witnessed a minor—very minor—act of heroism...and suffered the consequences.

When I was employed as his secretary, John Henry was looking toward retirement, while I was a recent 1953 graduate of New Hanover High School.

He was an excellent boss, but had an addiction to cigar smoking, which necessitated an ancient spittoon beside his desk. It always contained some water and, of course, the obvious other.

During my years as his secretary, only one memorable incident occurred regarding the spittoon. One day, curls of smoke began to fill his office and creep out of the doorway. It seems John Henry had put a cigar butt into his full trash can, with fire still aboard. When he realized the predicament, he took the handy water-filled spittoon and outed the ensuing blaze.

If you can imagine the odor we endured the rest of the day—it was even worse!

John Henry was a firefightin' man.

The Girl at the Toilet Goods Counter
by
Walter H. Kelly of Bessemer, Alabama

This is a story about what might be termed today "culture shock," a failed romance and happily, ultimate success. But more than anything, it's a story about friendship, and Walter Kelly, born in 1939, tells it admirably.

The day that my mother, two sisters, and I moved to Wilmington from Bladen County North Carolina in the fall of 1956 was sad for me. I did, however, enjoy the ride on top of our old furniture—one big truckload. My sadness was because I was leaving the rural life that I loved, and I was not so sure if I would like the big city. One thing was sure: I loved the picture shows. That's what the country folk called it.

My great need was a job so I'd have money to go to the Bailey Theater. I'd heard that it was the most expensive and beautiful theater in North Carolina with a spiral stairway, red carpet, fancy toilets, brick inside and out, and seats that were adjustable. I looked forward to many hours of seeing movies at the Bailey. But my problem was getting a job.

I had quit school in the ninth grade. Also, I was as shy as a rat in a cat kennel, and too scared to ask for a job. Nevertheless, my mother's prayers were wholly the reason for the miracle of my getting a job. It was at S.H. Kress and Company, a 5, 10, and 25 cent store, directly across from the Bailey Theater on Front Street.

At Kress's I was introduced to Leonard Williams. He was nice-looking (the opposite of how I felt about myself) and a high school graduate, which was to me like being a god. Kress's was his first job, too. He wanted to be called Leonardo DaVinci Williams because he wanted to get in the movies and decided that would be his movie name.

Leonard was in charge of the stock room at Kress's and taught me how to check-in freight and sweep the floor. He always corrected me when I "put myself down." "Kelly" (he always called me by my last name) "you're doing okay. You'll learn where everything is. Believe me, it won't take no time."

In response to my being ashamed to wear a bathing suit on the beach, he said, "Kelly, you're not so skinny. You just need to get a good tan and the girls will like you." He even put in a good word for me to a girl whom I wanted to be my first real date.

The girl was half German. To hear her speak was as pleasant and thrilling as I thought it would be driving a '57 Chevrolet convertible down Heaven's boulevard. Simply put, her accent was breathtaking—to the point of my being speechless. Moreover, she was cute—but that's not the best word to describe her.

As I delivered merchandise throughout the store, I would intentionally go out of the way by the toilet goods counter where she worked just to hear her voice. "Wow!" But that was that not the word to express my feelings about a girl that pretty. She deserved a silent "gee-whiz" or an unnoticeable gaze—like my peeping over a "Stock Requisition Form" as I was scared that we would make eye contact and I wouldn't know what to do but turn red.

As I said, I was so shy I had abandoned forever the idea of asking any girl for a date. But Leonard got me fixed up with her. It cost

Walter Kelly, on the left, and Leonard Williams at Wrightsville Beach in 1964.

me a dollar for tickets at the Bailey plus popcorn and Cokes and candy. That was before the intermission.

At intermission, I escaped up the famous spiral stairway to the men's room for a smoke break. (I had to keep-up the James Dean image.) Also, it became needful that I check my money situation to see if I could afford her. I couldn't!

Two years later, Leonard persuaded me to join the Air Force with him, but we both failed the entrance exam. Nevertheless, he wouldn't allow me to give up. "Kelly, all you need to do is to get a Thesaurus from the library and study words."

I reminded him that he, too, needed to visit the library in order to pass the exam. His excuse was, "Ah, I could have passed it. But I can't leave Wilmington now. No one at Orton's Pool Room would have any competition."

Within six months, I was in the Air Force. Later, he joined.

Leonard married and had children. And

so did I. Over the years, our families got together on several occasions.

A few years ago, Leonard Williams went to live in his new home in Heaven. You know, he could be driving around that '57 Chevrolet convertible. When I see him again I want to say, "Thanks, Leonard, for being my friend when I needed a friend."

Remembering the Maco Light
by
Clara Jane Murray Hodges of Wilmington

Almost every region boasts a legend of the supernatural but only a few can offer proof…or what appears to be proof. The famous Maco light is real. In addition to this one, several other accounts of sightings are reported in our earlier book, Wilmington Tales. *Clara Jane Hodges, who was born in Pender County in 1935, provides us with an extremely well written example of the spooky light as it once appeared to her in 1948. Perhaps you've seen it, too, if you remembered Old Joe's requirement of silence.*

I was born about seven miles from Burgaw on Murray Town Road. My family moved to Wilmington in February 1941 when I was five years old. I grew up in Winter Park, a suburb of Wilmington. I attended Winter Park School grades one through eight, attended Winter Park Presbyterian Church; and graduated from New Hanover High School in 1953.

I have compiled the history of Winter Park School entitled: *Winter Park School Remembered*. I also have limited edition prints of the school from an acrylic picture I painted.

I hope you enjoy the trip to see the Maco light. I will never forget it myself.

It began with a hayride with a group of teens from Winter Park Presbyterian Church in the late summer or early fall in 1948. I was thirteen years old.

A neighborhood farmer, "Capt'n Dick" as all who knew him well called him, offered to take a group of us teens on a hayride to Maco to see the spooky Maco light. I was delighted to be able to go as it was only for those over 13. I had just reached that age in April.

Most of the group were much older than myself. It was nice to be included with my older sister and her friends. I felt really big and they seemed to accept me.

The truck was full of new hay and there were a couple of blankets just in case we got too chilly while riding in the back of the open pickup. Capt'n Dick was a slow driver so it seemed to take forever to reach that place way across the river. When we turned off the main highway onto a dirt two-rut road, we traveled only a couple of blocks. Capt'n Dick pulled the truck to the left and parked under a big oak tree.

It was about dusk when we arrived and swamp gases were rising from under the trees. We stood and listened to the counselor as it grew a bit darker. We were told to stay together and be very quiet, that the mysterious light did not like noise and would not appear if there was any loud talking or screaming.

So the group of apprehensive teens started to walk down the railroad tracks toward Wilmington. As we walked, some were holding on to one another, while other brave souls pranced on ahead, showing no fear at all.

I was in front of the group, showing that I was not afraid. Guess since I was one of the youngest it seemed the thing to do.

To add to the mysterious atmosphere, we happened upon a graveyard to the right of the railroad tracks. When we spied the tombstones, some of the girls got really scared. Naturally, some of the boys seized the moment to construct all sorts of tales about who was buried in the graveyard. This only added to the tale about "Old Joe Baldwin" looking for his head. That was what the Maco light was all about.

Ever since Old Joe Baldwin had fallen from the train and been decapitated, the light had appeared. The locals said it was he wandering the tracks with a lantern just a-looking for his head which was never found. Thus, we were there to observe the light should it appear.

The light did not always appear. Some would go time after time and never see anything. We were hoping the light would appear, yet; filled with some fear, half-hoping it would not.

As we walked, trying to be quiet, we could see a trestle just ahead. It was now pretty dark and the fog or swamp gas was seen all around. The whole scene was sort of spooky. Some of the "fraidy cats" threatened to turn back because they did not want to walk over the trestle.

About 100 yards from the trestle, someone pointed to a faint light way down the track. We all stopped to see if it was maybe real. Sure enough, there was a glow far away on the evening horizon. We stood, not daring to take one more step toward the trestle. We didn't want to be caught across the trestle and not be able to make it back to the truck really fast.

The glow began to move slowly toward us. We had been told that as long as we were quiet the light would advance. If we made any noise, it would retreat back down the track and fade away.

The light was a good ways on the other side of the trestle, still coming toward us. I was a bit scared but didn't make a sound.

The glow of the light was sort of gold but shrouded in the evening fog. There was a soft halo around it. The fog was illuminated and so, too, were the railroad tracks.

Now the light seemed to be moving faster toward us. We all sensed it would be coming to the trestle very shortly. We huddled together. Some had already started to run back to the truck.

Suddenly one of the girls let out a blood curdling scream. NOW, WE WERE ALL AFRAID! Would the light retreat as was told, or would we all be caught up in the nightly passage of Old Joe Baldwin just a-looking for his head?

The light stopped. Then, as told, it started to slowly move. We were awestruck as it moved faster and faster in retreat and disappeared from whence it had come.

We were so mad at the screamer that we threatened to take her and throw her in the graveyard on the way back.

Needless to say, there wasn't much talking done as we all scurried back to the hay-filled truck. Once in the truck and snuggled under the blankets, we felt safe to discuss what we had seen.

Would we do it again? As far as I can remember, we didn't plan anymore hayrides to see the Maco light. We had seen it and knew it was really there. Besides, it was pretty scary for some!

Scratch Biscuits
by
Juanita E. Gibson of Wilmington

Juanita Gibson was born in 1920 in Sanford, N.C. where she grew up. Her memories may not mean much to the younger generation, but her short rendition of life back in the old days speaks volumes to those of us who also remember those times.

I am an old woman, eighty-six years old. I have used the iceman. I would meet him and get a piece of ice. I have used chamber pots, and an outhouse, too. I remember tin tub

Juanita Gibson, age five.

baths and flypaper and feather beds and biscuits from scratch. I used to make them when I was fifteen years old, and in my married life. It was a hard life. I used to visit my grandparents and I made biscuits for my grandma.

I lived on old dirt roads. We used well water for a long time.

The Cowboys
by
Steven Aviyon Wright of Maury

Steven Wright, who was born in Wilmington in 1962, remembers his first electrical game.

In 1972 when I was ten years old, my parents bought me my first football game. It was five feet long on a very thin tin table. It had 24 plastic men with a vibrator that attached to the tin. You plugged it in and the men just vibed across the table. Back then they didn't have those Play Station, Gameboy and X-box games.

The two teams were the Dallas Cowboys and the Pittsburgh Steelers. Since then, the Dallas Cowboys has been my team. Every time I see them play it brings back memories of my first game.

The Ragged Beggar, Sleeping
by
Hulda A. Willett of Wilmington

What memories will today's children have of their first schools, surrounded by technology, controlled by government mandate and taught by teachers constrained by regula-

Hulda Willett's picture was made in 1942 at Kresses Dime Store.

tions? We believe those memories will never be as fond as those generated by the educational environment described in Hulda Willett's nostalgic story. We salute Mrs. Willett, born in Wilmington in 1919, for her delightful insight (and we thank Mr. Whittier from whom we borrowed the title).

Hulda Willett in 1976.

This is a story about the old Sea Gate School of New Hanover County. The building has been demolished for several years, but the memories of the school and the pupils continue to live on.

This was my first school, and I started in the year 1925 at the age of six. Back in the days of my primary education, there was no kindergarten, Head Start, or pre-school. Children went to school at the age of six, and that was to the first grade.

The first grade at the old Sea Gate School was separate from the main building. It was a one-room white frame building that sat off to the side of the main building.

Our teacher, Mrs. Lee, was a wonderful teacher who wanted us to learn. She did her best to make that possible. She didn't have any discipline problems with us, as we were taught at home to respect our elders and teachers and we all loved her.

The main building was separated into three sections. Each section had a cloak room and a room large enough for two classes. The first section was for the second and third grades. The fourth and fifth grades were in the middle section, and the sixth and seventh grades were in the last section.

There was no auditorium. If there was any special program that involved all the classes, the principal would ring the bell for us to march outside for our activities.

There were no hot lunches because the school had no cafeteria or lunchroom. Everyone brought their lunch from home. Most everyone had a tin bucket with a lid they packed their lunch in. We all had to walk to school, and sometimes it would be raining. The lid on the tin buckets kept our lunches dry and safe.

My lunch consisted mostly of a biscuit and sausage or some kind of meat, or a biscuit with homemade apple butter. Sometimes I would bore a hole in a biscuit and fill it with molasses, or maybe I would take a small container of soup or dried beans left from the night before.

Every day the milk truck brought milk to the school. You could get plain or chocolate. The milk was in half-pint glass bottles and cost five cents. Sometimes I would buy my milk,

Hulda and Jenrett Willett in 1993 at a Stewart Family Reunion.

and sometimes I would bring something to drink from home, or I would get some water from the pump.

The pump was on a cement foundation and on one side of the foundation a place was built and marked with small squares, just large enough to hold a folding metal drinking cup. Each student had a square with his or her name on it, to put their cup. The school didn't supply our cups. It was up to each student to get their own cup.

We had a pump called the pitcher pump. I don't think I have ever tasted better water than the crystal stream that came gushing out of that pump. Sometimes we had to hang on the handle with all our weight to pump the water out of the spout. Many times in the winter, the pump would freeze and scalding water was poured down the pipe to thaw out the ice.

There was no inside plumbing, so the restrooms were on the outside. There was one for the girls on one side of the building, and one for the boys on the other. There were heavy wooden latches on the door, one on the outside and one on the inside. If the door was unlatched from the outside, it was considered to be in use and you had to wait your turn.

When the weather was cold, we used a large wood heater to stay warm. The boys were responsible for bringing in the wood. They had to see that each wood box was filled at the beginning of each day.

There was no janitorial service, so we learned about hard work by helping the teacher with schoolhouse chores, like cleaning the blackboard, dusting the erasers, taking out the trash and carrying water. At the end of each day we had to make sure our room was cleaned for school the next morning.

We learned to love our country by reciting the Pledge of Allegiance each morning. We learned about faith, hope and charity through morning devotionals before school prayer was found to be unconstitutional. I guess we learned pretty much everything we needed, all without the aid of television and computers and the rest of modern educational equipment they have today.

One reason we loved going to school was the joy of recess time. When the bell rang, we had to file out by classes, and in order, but as soon as the door was cleared, the noise and fun began. The boys would play mumbletypeg and marbles while the girls jumped rope, played jacks and hopscotch.

The first grade building was ideal for playing one of our favorite games, anti-over, because we could get the ball over the rooftop of that building.

I think the most popular game we played was called Scrub. It was a baseball game in which both boys and girls took part. We used string balls, made by the pupils by wrapping string around a small rubber ball until it reached the right size, then sewing the entire ball to hold the string wrapping in place. We made our bats from a small hickory limb.

I developed my love for reading in the old Sea Gate School. Every morning the teacher read to us from some good book. Back in the days of the little country schoolhouse, we al had our favorite books that introduced us to "reading, writing and 'rithmatic." One fa-

Hulda and Jenrett Willett in 1995 on their trip to New England.

vorite for parents and teachers alike were small primers designed to introduce us to the letters of the alphabet. I remember how learning to read and write always began with learning the alphabet.

One of my favorite poems by John Greenleaf Whittier is *In School Days*. In it, he speaks of the little country schoolhouse, "Still sits the schoolhouse by the road, a ragged beggar sleeping." The Sea Gate School was not exactly a ragged beggar sleeping, but by the time the new Bradley's Creek School was finished, it had seen its better days.

The day finally came for us to move from the old Sea Gate School to our new school. We took our books and formed a line, and with the teacher leading us, we marched from our old school to the new Bradley's Creek School. Everyone was happy and excited to be in a new, more modern school, with lights and indoor plumbing. We didn't have to go outside to use the restroom or wash our hands. What thrilled us the most was the water fountain. We could drink all the water we needed and not have to pump it.

We were proud of our new school, but at the same time, we were sad, as we were leaving behind a lot of memories we had shared together. I consider the days I spent at Sea Gate School among the happiest of my life.

I will always remember my teachers. Each time I hear the following phrase, I am reminded of them: "One hundred years from now it will not matter what kind of house I lived in, how much money I had in my bank account, what kind of car I drove, nor what my clothes looked like. But the world may be made a little better because I was important in the life of a child."

Hulda Willett in 1986.

Our teachers were very important to us. Every child was special to them, and they were always there for us if we needed help.

I will never forget the sound of that old school bell. The principal rang it when it was time for school to start and end each day. As my memory reaches back through time, its melody I seem to hear again, bringing back to me the clamor and music of that old school bell.

In October 2006, Mr. Sidney Daniels and some more members of the former Sea Gate Volunteer Fire Department dedicated this bell to the Bradley's Creek School, the place where it rightfully belongs.

The Feather Bed, the Rum Runner and the Cobbler
by
Milton H. Domler of Wilmington

Milton Domler was born in Wilmington in 1922, where he lived most of his life. He states, however, that he grew up in the US Navy, a fact you won't find so odd when you read the final paragraph of his story. He is a natural story-teller. Whether you're from Wilmington or Wabash, you'll love these three tidbits from the past. And if you're an old-timer, you'll definitely identify.

Swallowed Alive

I was born and raised in Wilmington. When I was a little boy, my mother took my brother (who was two years my senior) and me out to visit some of my grandparents' family somewhere up close to Rose Hill, N.C. It was to be a weekend trip.

My mom and dad had separated just before I was born, so there would be just the three of us visiting our Uncle (illegible word) and his family. They were very friendly folks, and the conversations were light and everyone was enjoying one another's company.

I was a city-raised kid, and at that point I knew very little about country life. But I was enjoying the folks, and of course, to me at my young age, all the folks were old people from my point of view.

At any rate, evening came on and Mother took my brother Charles and me into the bedroom where we were to sleep. This was very interesting to me. I remember that my mother and my brother grabbed me by the ankles and wrists, swung me a couple of times and tossed me into the middle of the bed. The whole world disappeared! I had been tossed into a feather bed, and the bedding closed in over me. I was so taken over by this affair that I was too frightened to even holler.

Then my mother and brother—who, of course, had planned this little charade—jumped into the bed, one on one side of me and one on the other, and that cover of feathers opened up over my head. They were laughing and I must have turned a little pale because Mother, though half-heartedly, began soothing me and telling me it was all for fun.

Maybe it was. But I have never had a desire for feather beds since then.

A Dry Cleaning Rum Runner

When I was a young man and learned to drive a vehicle safely, I applied for a job in a dry cleaning plant that had placed an ad in the *Wilmington Star-News* for a pickup and delivery man.

The manager took me through the plant and showed me how they processed the clothes. The clothes were slid up wires attached to the ceiling, and bags were slid down over them to protect them. The bags were paper in those days. Plastic had never been heard of.

I considered this to be very interesting. I was learning some very fascinating parts of industry. The manager was a nice man, and I was getting the feeling that he was going to hire me to work in the plant; but he said he would let me have the job of pickup and delivery. Then he introduced me to their van. I was very familiar with the streets and avenues, so I felt comfortable with the job.

We had a special process that was used: we would cover the floor of the van with brown wrapping paper so that no clothes would get soiled. We would put a round turn of twine around the picked up clothes and put the ticket tight within the clothes, and then stack them like stovewood side by side until they were the full width of the van. Then we would start another stack on top of that one. Get the idea?

I was enjoying my job and the folks took to me. I would also go next door sometimes and ask if they needed some dry cleaning. I was well received. The boss was pleased with me.

Everything was mostly routine except I had one customer who always had a cardboard box crammed full, and the flaps on the box were interlocked. But this was an understanding between them and the boss, so I was pleased with it. When their clothes came back, they were hung in the top of the van like all the rest. No big deal.

Then, one Monday, a holiday was coming up and my business was pretty tight. I seemed to be getting a little behind in my schedule. So I hurriedly started around a corner to my right and there was a couple crossing the street. I had to slow down. The van did not have a passenger seat, and on this Monday, I had put the cardboard box on the first layer of clothes behind where the passenger seat would have been. When I applied the brakes, the box kept going and rolled down into the glove compartment area. No big deal. I figured when I stopped at the next customer's house, a block and a half from there, I would straighten it up.

At the next stop, I took the customer's clothes and put them in the van. I then went around to the passenger side, unlocked the door and attempted to lift the box. But it was jammed under the glove compartment. So I took a better grip of it and poof! Out came the clothes…and the whiskey bottles!

I said to myself, "Boy, you have a new profession. You're a rum runner!"

The Shoe Shop Massage

When I was a young boy during the 1920s, there was a building at the corner of 40th and Harnett Streets in an area that was referred to as Brooklyn. It was in the northern part of Wilmington. The building stood on the northeast corner of the intersection, and an inside wall ran down its length, dividing it into two shops. The part next to Harnett was turned into a cobbler shop. The other half was a barbershop.

On the building's inside solid wall on the cobbler shop side there was mounted, on heavy brackets, a long horizontal steel shaft that had several pulleys of different widths. The pulleys had flat, wide surfaces. A drive motor at the back of the shop powered the shaft. Belts from the pulleys drove different kinds of tools or machines like a sewing machine, a buffer machine, a cutting machine, a riveting machine, etc.

This shop was known as Ward's Shoe Shop. Mr. Ward was a very nice man, and could put on half soles, or heels, or whole soles or mend a suitcase. He was well received.

The other shop was the Brooklyn Barbershop and had four chairs in there. The barber chairs were over toward the north side of the shop, and the waiting chairs were up against the dividing wall of the building.

Now, when Mr. Ward would light off the power motor for the drive shaft mounted on the wall, then any of the folks who were waiting to get their hair cut or a shave could get a very good massage sitting in their chair—for free!

I was involved, as a growing boy, for many years with those two shops. It was rather interesting to me, and to anyone else who had sat in those waiting chairs while the shoe shop power was being used.

Growing Up in the Navy

I went into the US Navy before World War II broke out. We were on that north, north Atlantic for two years of raucous seas and cold, caustic weather, and then two years in the Pacific. I was then hospitalized for two years. Had to learn to walk again. I still stagger sometimes.

But I love my God, I love my country and I love my family.

Hits the Spot
by
Frank H. Bowen of Carolina Beach

Frank Bowen's story strikes a philosophical tone as he reminds us of several familiar but forgotten aspects of the good old days. We old-timers can immediately identify with his reflections. Mr. Bowen was born in Pender County in 1933.

In the late nineteen thirties and early forties, farming communities needed a "country store" nearby. This allowed residents to locally obtain necessities such as salt, spices, plow lines, gasoline, feed for livestock and poultry and other supplies rather than their having to travel to town for these items. Depending on the size of the area served by

Frank H. Bowen, age thirteen months, in 1934.

Frank H. Bowen, age eleven, in 1944.

these stores, they were either quite small, containing only very basic items, or very large, including farm, implements, work clothes, seeds and grain and, perhaps, even a pool table or jukebox.

One thing both small and large county stores had in common was that each had a drink box where cold soft drinks were kept for sale. The drink box was about the size of a bathtub and drinks were placed in water around a block of ice to keep them cold. The bottles were segregated according to each manufacturer's product and were identified by the logo on the bottle cap. The drink box had a lid, hinged in the middle for easy access to each end. A bottle cap remover was affixed to each end of the box.

Pepsi Cola was a big item because it contained 12 ounces of soda pop whereas most all other soft drinks contained six ounces. Their jingle was, "Pepsi Cola hits the spot, twelve full ounces, that's a lot, twice as much for a nickel too, Pepsi Cola is the drink for you."

Another item that was common in almost all country stores was a "punch board." These boards were filled with holes about one quarter the diameter of a soda straw. The contents of a hole could be bought from the proprietor of the store for ten cents. The hole would then be punched, using a key, and a number would be revealed. If this number matched one shown on the board that represented a prize, you would win the prize.

I do not recall if any money was offered as a prize (because this would have been considered gambling, which was illegal)

Frank H. Bowen, age six, in 1939.

Frank H. Bowen, age five, in 1938.

but shotguns, watches and similar items were offered as prizes.

If a person could go to the store with a quarter in his pocket, he could buy a Pepsi Cola and get two punches from the board. He usually went home with only a stomach full of soda pop.

Line Dried Laundry
by
Gladys Bowen Thomas of Wilmington

Gladys Thomas was born in Columbia, South Carolina in 1917 and grew up in Burgaw. Her account of a commonplace event back in the 1930s reminds us of the huge difference between the present and the good old days.

In the 1930s, my family lived on a farm in Pender County. Wash day was always on Mondays unless it rained. Mama gathered all the dirty clothes for the family of eight kids, two parents, and Grandma. She set up three fifty-gallon tin tubs on a long bench behind the smokehouse. Nearby was a big, black iron pot — on legs so a fire could be started underneath. Mama filled the pot with water drawn up from the well nearby, then added homemade lye soap. When the water started to boil, she put in the white clothes. With a long wooden pole, she stirred them for about twenty minutes, then with the pole, she moved the hot clothes to the first tub to be scrubbed on the washboard.

After they were scrubbed, the clothes were moved to the second tub to be rinsed by hand. Then they were placed in the third tub and rinsed again. The still warm clothes were given to the older girls to squeeze and hang on the clotheslines with wooden clothespins.

Mama then put the dark clothes in the black pot to boil and repeated the process.

Windy days were best as the clothes flapped back and forth to dry faster.

One summer I picked strawberries at my Uncle Vann's for a penny a quart. I saved my money to buy five dresses that were store-bought, not made of flour sacks, to wear to school in the fall. Our family dog, Alex, saw my dresses flapping in the wind. He jumped up and down and with his sharp nails, he shredded the lower part of every dress he could reach. He only reached mine. BAD DOG!

After the clothes were all washed, my mother let my youngest brother, Frank, play in the last rinse water while she finished up her work. Then she bathed Frank in the tub.

In 1940, I married and moved to town. In 1942, Mama sold the farm and moved to Burgaw where a black woman took the family's dirty clothes to her house, washed and ironed them. Mama died in 1943 and I moved into her house (while my husband was overseas in World War II) to help care for my thirteen-year-old sister and nine-year-old brother. When my husband returned from the war, we bought the house. In 1948 with a baby in cloth diapers, we bought a washer — no dryer.

I still prefer my clothes line dried.

In 1929, my family learned that the one bank in our small town of Burgaw had "busted." The next day, we kids rode the school bus into town and approached the bank building at the corner of Wright and Fremont Streets. We expected to see a big crack down the side and were disappointed when we could not spot it.

Our teacher tried to explain how "busted" meant that the bank had run out of money. Most families lost their savings. Somehow, my old maid aunt managed to get her life savings out and she never trusted any bank after that. She put her money in a Mason jar and buried it in the yard.

In 1935, I was in my freshman year at East Carolina Teachers College. I was required to take "Public School Music" for a teacher's degree, and one requirement of the class was to sing the scales. My day came to sing and I stood up and fainted! That finished my singing career and to this day, I cannot carry a tune.

The Honor System
by
Myrtle Webb Dixon of Wilmington

Myrtle Dixon, who was born in Wilmington in 1934, bases her story on a familiar, and very necessary, service from the past: the ice truck. That icon of former days, however, only helps to tell a far deeper, sometimes poignant, story.

Talking about chasing the ice truck...well, that brings back a lot of memories, the reason being, "Been there, done that."

As a little girl named Myrtle Webb, my parents, Archie and Edna Webb, along with my brother Tommy, lived at that time on Route 1, Wilmington. It's now known as the 84-8500 block of Market Street, and to this day, I still live on the 8400 block of Market Street.

It was in the 1940s and I was six or eight years old. We had no electricity, had the outhouse, battery radio, no phone, Grandma had a windup record player, and our water came from a hand pump on the back porch. I could talk about any of these things, but the old ice truck just rings a special bell with me.

When I was a little girl, we had the icebox on the back porch and we would keep a watch for the ice truck coming down the road. As it approached our house we would flag it down and get that little piece of ice. The iceman would chip the large block of ice with an ice pick until he had chipped us a ten cent piece. Then he would carry the block with his ice tongs to the back of the house and put it in the icebox on the back porch. The ice would last a couple days until the ice truck came again.

As time went on, we learned we could tie a white cloth on the roadside mailbox if we wanted to buy ice from the ice truck. They would know to stop. They would know to stop and leave the ice and we would leave the money on top of the icebox. Seemed like everybody was honest back then and the honor system worked really well.

Myrtle Webb - then - holding someone's baby.

We often refer to those days as the good old days, and in so many ways they were. We didn't have a lot and we were not rich with this world's goods, but really, we were rich and blessed in lots of ways. We truly knew what it meant

Myrtle Webb - now.

to be a family and do everything together.

Several years later, our home was blessed with two more brothers, Ray and Wayne, and two more sisters, Sherry and Kay. As the saying goes, "a big happy family."

Then our daddy passed away and later our mother passed away. Then our brother Tommy passed away. Things have never been the same since we lost them.

I am now 73 years old and I often think back on the precious memories and tears come to my eyes. I can't help but think about those family ties we had, that so many others have never known.

And I think of how special those days of chasing the ice truck really were.

Cotton Wads and Scorched Duds
by
Dianne W. Lynch of Wilmington

Who would ever think that things so annoying back in the good old days would interest us today? But they do, as evidenced by Dianne Lynch's reminder. You youngsters may not appreciate or even understand this story, but those of us who experienced it will smile and nod...and re-live. Dianne was born in Raleigh in 1947.

I am a female and grew up in the 50s in rural Johnston County. One fact was sure — as the youngest of three girls, I had to wear a lot of hand-me-downs. The dresses, shirts and pants weren't so bad, but those darn cotton SOCKS were another matter. The more the socks were washed and hung on the outside line, they were stretched to long lengths. As a solution to this problem, our mom would FOLD the excess length of sock BACK UNDER my toes. I can still feel the discomfort of this "wad" of cotton.

We lived in the country and we walked to school and back home. Sometimes I would remove the socks altogether, but the blisters reminded me to keep them on. If I pulled them up they would be taller than my knees — oh what a sight!

I vowed if I ever had children of my own, that their socks would fit properly. Thank goodness for stretchy socks! The "good ole days" could be pretty terrible.

There were other challenges, growing up in the 50s. Our small farmhouse was heated by one "space" heater. One challenge was to take the heater out of the house during the warmer months.

The heater was large, brown and UGLY. When it was taken out to the barn, all the soot in the pipe would usually fly all over the house. This was quite a mess when we began to clean it up. We didn't own a vacuum and the soot was wiped off (many times).

In the winter months with the heater back in its place, things were usually warm. We had to turn the dial back at night to conserve oil. It was COLD when we awakened in the mornings. We would run to the space heater and throw our school clothes on top or on the two front heater doors to warm them. This made putting our clothes on more comfortable—they were warm. If the heater had heated up too quickly or if we left the clothes on it too long they became scorched. Our wardrobes were limited so we didn't have a lot of clothing choices. If nothing else was available, we wore them to school—scorched and all!

There is a fireplace now where the space heater once stood. The sooty pipe is now covered.

Keeping warm had its challenges, but I still remember jumping up and down, waiting for my clothes to warm up on the space heater.

Last Trip to Utica
by
Lois Basiliere of Wilmington

One of our most satisfying rewards in preparing these books is saving stories that have been passed down through the generations. This tale isn't about Wilmington, or even North Carolina. In it, however, you'll find a parallel to local life that you'll readily recognize, even if you aren't an "old-timer." Lois Basiliere was born in Malone, New York, and has allowed us to forever preserve this gem of American culture.

I got here as fast as I could and I have lived most of my life in North Carolina (39 years now). I recently retired from the New Hanover County School system after 30 successful years. I currently spend time exercising, taking writing classes at Cape Fear Community College, working every other weekend, and spending time with my two children and three grandchildren when they are available.

But, this story is about New York State.

Aunt Goldie was a diminutive and feisty woman. My mother never mentioned, nor did I ever ask, her given name. I expect she was nicknamed "Goldie" for her golden blond locks of hair.

Or, it could have been for her part in accumulating what my mother termed as "a barrel of money" during Prohibition. In fact, my mother said there was so much money that they placed it in coffee cans and buried it in the fields. I fantasize that somewhere along Route II in upstate New York is buried treasure, since no one seems to know what happened to the money after Uncle Wilfred was sent to prison.

I never asked questions; I shut my mouth and listened. Children were to be seen and not heard. I never even knew about the eighteen-month prison sentence until I was grown.

On one occasion, Mom and Dad made a liquor run from Malone to Utica, New York for Uncle Wilfred. I could readily believe that my father would help out his brother this one time; however, I could not imagine my shy and reserved mother ever being part of such an adventure.

Without question, Mom and Dad certainly looked the part. Dad was a handsome man with very dark gray, soulful eyes and dark hair with a slight wave. Mother was a typical flapper; she was 5' 2", had blue eyes and dressed the part of a moll. Please do not misunderstand: Dad was not a gangster, and she was not a prostitute.

Where Uncle Wilfred and Aunt Goldie lived there were enormous trees conveying the impression of large umbrellas of protection over their large stone home in upstate New York. In the kitchen, there was a trap door that was especially convenient the time that a few bootleggers ran into the house and asked Aunt Goldie where to hide. She promptly ushered them through that trap door. The revenuers, or G-men as some dubbed them, were running through the house close behind the culprits. Asking Aunt Goldie where they went, she opened the back door and gestured toward the fields. Off they went, chasing men alleged to be in the fields that were never found.

On what was to be Uncle Wilfred's last trip to Utica, he was caught. He was out plowing the fields. Although Goldie tried to warn him, he knew it was inevitable that he was a goner and he just stood as if frozen. Thus, he went to prison to serve 18 months.

Alcohol was once again legalized soon after in 1933. Utica Club became the beer of choice for many.

Like my relatives, there were millions running or consuming alcohol during Prohibition. I was young when I heard this story and in reaction, I do not believe I possessed any understanding of the fact that it was a crime to consume alcohol, or that my parents were in any way involved in criminal behavior. I responded with awe and wonderment that my parents were cool, had fun and were once young.

I Remember Mimi
by
Peggy Thompson Canady of Wrightsville Beach

This is the kind of story we like to get for our books. We like to remember good, caring folks; we're interested in finding out about interesting and unusual occupations; and we always like to publish tales about people who were well known in their communities. Mimi, the palm reader, was all three of these. Her granddaughter, Peggy Canady, was born in 1948 in Wilmington.

My grandmother (Mimi) was a well known palm reader who lived in the Winter Park

Eunice Thompson Stratford.

area. Her name was Eunice Thompson Stratford, and she was a matriarch who was very forward thinking for her time. She remarried a man much younger and in the arts.

My dad, Charles "Jimmy" Thompson, was an only child and we lived across the street from Mimi. I was her favorite so I attended all the dinner parties and stayed with her constantly.

She had a beach cottage at Wrightville Beach across from what is now the Oceanic Restaurant. We stayed there all summer and enjoyed all the Lumina's activities. Then at summer's end, we would head back to the Park Avenue town home.

Mimi was so well known in the area for her palm reading in the 40s, 50s and 60s that it seemed every other adult I encountered had been to her for a reading at one time or other. They would go on and on about how so many things she predicted came true.

One very prominent member of a Coca Cola Bottling Company family would pull up every week in his chauffeured big black

Wedge and Sledge
by
Carolyn Parrish of Wilmington

Carolyn Parrish, born and raised near Wilmington, is a self-proclaimed country girl who likes the good old days. She heats with wood that she chops herself and has many memories of things that have long ago disappeared. You may recognize many of the folks in her story.

Eunice Thompson Stratford at Wrightsville Beach.

Cadillac. We would scream in delight as we ran to greet my benefactor of many generous gifts to the family, which included a 17 foot motor boat, diamond rings, Hamilton watches and bicycles, among many other things over the years.

I remember the story of the Wilmington Police Department contacting her in reference to a missing person which she helped solve, so at nine years of age, I thought my Mimi held all the great secrets of the world.

She was such a patriotic and giving person. She was always helping out family members in time of need and every Sunday, several servicemen would come to dinner and most became lifelong friends that still stay in contact to this day.

In 1940, when my mother, Elma Thompson, was 18 years old, she was asked to be on one of the Azalea Festival floats.

My father had met her the week before at a Lumina dance and had been swept off his feet. He appeared on every street corner that her float passed, waving and calling her name. My mother can't remember how many corners he ran to, but she smiles and laughs as she tells her story.

I was born December 30, 1953, the daughter of a farmer. I was delivered by Dr. Walker in the old James Walker Hospital in Wilmington.

My childhood doctor was Dr. Oily Crouch, a very well known pediatrician in Wilmington, who practiced with his brother, Dr. Walton Crouch. Dr. Oily Crouch always saved us a coupon to get a free ice cream cone at the Dairy Queen on Person Street. An ice cream cone cost 10 cents at that time.

We got our prescriptions filled at the Rexall Drug Store across from Dr. Crouch's office. We would drink a cherry Coke for five cents at the soda counter.

A friend of mine who lived on Meares Street would buy 100 pound bags of peanuts and his mother and dad would boil them. Then he would put them on his bicycle and go to the shipyard and sell them. With the proceeds from the peanuts, he would buy hamburger meat and his mother would make sandwiches for him to sell at the shipyard for lunch. My friend quit school in the third grade to support his family. He later opened a tire business at 7238 Market Street. His name was Paul Chahoc. Later, he and Leslie Batson opened an auction house, the first one in Wilmington. It was called Les Paul's Auctions and was at 7238 Market Street.

I lived with my grandmother, Mollie Batts, sometimes. After her death, a restaurant called "Mollies" at Surf City was built in her honor by Margaret Godwin Batts and Waymoth Batts of the Godwin Lumber Company.

I remember when we were at Grandmother's house, if the weather was bad or it was nighttime, we used a porcelain chamber pot as a toilet. During the day, we used an old wooden outhouse out at the edge of the field.

We listened to Roy Acuff and the Lone Ranger on radio.

My family had the first phone in our neighborhood. We lived down a dirt road, so it was a fight to get one, but Dr. Crouch helped us get one. I had seizures as a child and a phone was a must. After a while, there were ten families on our line.

I remember that my Uncle Namon Batts would wind Grandmother's clock for her. The clock sat up on the fireplace mantel.

My grandmother always had country ham biscuits for breakfast on barning tobacco days. We had to be up at the table by 5:30 a.m. and in the field by 6 a.m.

We shucked corn by hand to feed the hogs and chickens. We had a hand grinder to take the corn off the cob.

Our mail lady would take our three cents out of the mailbox and put a stamp on the letters for us. Her name was Della Rae King. She was so beautiful and always laughing. On hog killing days at Grandma's house, the mail lady would always stop long enough to eat dinner with us.

Grandmother didn't like children around the hog meat because of cleanliness. My first job at the hog killing was cutting lard into small pieces to fry in a wash pot into cracklings.

We slept in feather beds under so many quilts that we could not move. Grandma would heat bricks on the old wood stove and wrap them in a towel and put them in the bed at our feet in the winter to keep us warm.

I wore bib overalls until I started to school. Then Daddy would let me go to the feed store and pick out the sack of feed I liked the print on for a dress for school and church.

We were never allowed to go skinnydipping.

On barning tobacco days, we would set out a number two washtub in the morning full of water so it would be warm by evening time for our baths. We kept the dirt out of the house this way.

I remember pumping water from the hand pump in the back yard. Some of the other folks who just had wells could keep their milk and butter cool by letting them down into the well by a wooden bucket into the cold water.

We all wore our share of hand-me-downs. The only thing I didn't have to wear were passed down shoes.

My Uncle Herman Welton and Aunt Bernice owned a grocery store on Masonboro Loop Road, at the corner of Masonboro Loop Road and Masonboro Sound Road. They owned a dairy farm behind the country store. A part of their old barn still stands.

I remember on barning tobacco days we would take tobacco sticks and tie twine to them and make us a horse to ride.

When I was five years old, I went to the beach at Topsail Island to watch the men pull in the fish seine (net) by hand. Thousands of pounds of fish would be pulled in by our men. J. H. Lee and Sons would buy them when the men got them up and in the trucks. I fell in the ocean on one of these occasions and my Uncle Namon Batts bent down and lifted me out by my bib overalls. My grandma held me across her knees so my pants would dry in the sun.

I remember the flypaper hung in strips from the ceilings in the food pantries.

When I started school, Dick and Jane was the first book I read. Miss Nellie Howard was my first grade teacher. Her brother worked at a seed store in Wilmington.

My grandmother loved to go downtown

Wilmington to Rhouda Bushes for her seeds and plants.

We did our school shopping on Front Street at the old Efirds Department Store and Greens Department Store at the end of summers when we got paid for working in tobacco. We would eat out at Skinner and Daniels Barbecue on Market Street and see a movie for 25 cents at the Manor Theater.

My sister got a princess ring from Reeds Jewelry from Mr. Zimmerman when she was 14 years old. Mr. Zimmerman had them put it in a real ring box with hinges that would pop open and shut. He had it wrapped up pretty, too.

I guess the worst memory of my life was when I was 11 years old and my uncle found my grandma dead out on the woodpile. She had been chopping wood at the age of 69 and had a heart attack.

Old Dr. Bryant and the black midwives delivered all my aunts and uncles right there at the house. All ten of them.

I raised hogs out on Market Street until two years ago and I still only have wood heat. I still cut my own trees down and split it up by wedge and sledge hammer.

I guess the country and the good old days will always be in me.

The Zoo Keeper's Son
by
Mary P. Duncan of Wilmington

Mary Duncan remembers gooey, gummy and delicious peach cobbler and x-ray machines for small feet in new shoes. Perhaps you will too, when you read her fond description of downtown Wilmington. You might even remember Petunia, Pat and Hootie. Mrs. Duncan, who was born in Wilmington in 1945, ends her story on a romantic note, but doesn't reveal the name of the zoo-keeper's son.

Mary (on left) and Georgia Pappas in the 50s.

I fondly remember the young childhood days back in the 50s. My sister and I would ride bikes, skate and jump rope. We even had a record player for our 45s and 78s.

When I was eight, my uncle bought our first TV. It was a combination TV, record player and radio; it even lasted until the early 70s; then smoke came out of it.

We watched cowboy movies and my grandmother liked the evening soap operas.

We'd often walk over to our cousins' house (we all lived in Sunset Park). Jackson Street wasn't paved between Central and Northern. There was a windmill that was quite interesting to us children.

We attended Greek school twice a week after school. It was located near the community center on Second and Orange, where we learned to play ping pong while waiting. The Greek school was next to the church, under the priest's house. To get our attention, sometimes he would bang his yardstick on the heater. That shocked everyone alert. (The priest was our Greek school teacher.)

Sometimes we went to the YMCA downtown, about on Third and Market. The pool was located way down the stairs. That was where I learned to swim.

At Wrightsville Beach, we'd sometimes go to the lagoon as we called it, near the water tower now. More often, we'd go to Lumina to enjoy the sun and waves. My Yiayia (grandmother in Greek) preferred to go to Carolina Beach and play Bingo. She always wore her black dress after she became a widow, which didn't exactly match beach attire. We'd catch the bus to get there. Even after we finally got a car, Mama used it to go to work.

The Patricia Ann was our grocery. It was at the end of Central Boulevard on Carolina Beach Road. Although small by today's standards, it carried a good variety and also fresh meat and produce.

My grandmother had milk delivered by Echo Farms to the door. The cream was on top of the quart, not mixed and homogenized as it is now.

Georgia (on left) and Mary Pappas.

We had radiators in the house and a steam room out back that held the heater. Somehow, it also heated the hot water, but there never seemed to be enough until my Uncle Victor from up North told us the radiators had to be "bled."

On Saturday mornings we'd often listen to radio. We were members of the Zorro Fan Club, and also the Lone Ranger Fan Club. Other programs we listened to on the radio included Dragnet and Inner Sanctum, with the creaking door sound.

Mama had a record set of Dickens' *Christmas Carol*, which really has great sound effects. Unfortunately, one of the records is broken now.

Across from the Bijou on Front Street was a drugstore, Walgreen's. At their soda fountain, they had the best peach cobbler, with

Sister, Georgia, and Mary behind her in front of Grandmother's house in the mid 50s.

Left to right: Mary Pappas, Sophie and Mary Frankos (cousins) and sister, Georgia Pappas.

pastry that was gooey, gummy and delicious.

Later on when I worked downtown, the highlight of the morning would be break time, when we'd go out for cinnamon twists made fresh at the Dixie Restaurant (not the one on Market Street that was a pool room).

The Bijou and the Manor Theaters had movies such as Flash Gordon (different series). The Manor had a small balcony, I think. There was also the Colony on Market Street and at some point, the Bailey on Front Street. Even Wrightsville Beach had a theater, the Wave, which often showed foreign films.

We shopped at dimestores (Green's, Woolworth's, Kress's, MacClelland's) and at department stores (Belk's and Efird's). There was a Montgomery Ward's catalog store. Downtown had the Diana Shop, the Julia, and the Wonder Shop. Castle Street had the Friendly's and also Halls Drugstore at Fifth and Castle with a soda fountain. In fact, most dimestores had lunch counters.

Georgia (on left) and Mary Pappas with Grandmother, Mary Xanthos.

There was a shoe store downtown that had an x-ray machine so your mama could see if the shoes fit.

Ladies wore hats a lot then, and if you bought one, you'd get a nice round hatbox, often with the name of the store on it. I have some of those which were my mother's.

My great uncle, Nick Johnson, had a newsstand down near the Bijou. We liked to go there and read comic books. He was my grandmother's brother and often ate with us on Sundays. He didn't want us girls to drink anything till after the meal, though. Guess they all thought we were too thin and wouldn't eat enough.

My grandfather had a grill on the corner of Front and Red Cross. A lot of his clientele came from the Coast Line. He also worked in Southport a lot and had had a candy shop there. People called him Jimmy the Greek. My mother and her brothers and sisters had all helped out at times, in Southport.

Sometimes in the hot summer (no one had air conditioning), we'd walk to Greenfield Lake and go swimming. When I was about thirteen, the swimming there ended because we all came home with red bumps. We could still go to the tennis courts next to the lake, though.

Later, there was a zoo with a

Christmas at Grandmother's house at Sunset Beach in the early 50s: Grandmother, Mary Xanthos; Aunt Leona and daughter, Susan Xanthos; great uncle, Nick Carvainis; Mary Pappas; mother, Billie Pappas; sister, Georgia Pappas, uncle, Arthur Xanthos; aunt, Louise, and uncle, Pete Xanthos.

bear, Petunia, and a rhesus monkey named Pat. It was the kiddie zoo and had a little train. There were goats, peacocks, an ostrich, various bantam chickens, sheep, a caged owl, Hootie, and tons of honking geese. Who would know I'd marry the zookeeper's son?

Hazel, Hand-me-downs and Biscuits
by
Nancy Potts of Wilmington

Nancy Potts was born in 1945 in Raleigh but grew up in Carolina Beach. Her poignant memory of a mid-20th century disaster is balanced by other, kinder memories of life typical to that period.

Hurricane Hazel. When I was a child in 1954, I lived at Carolina Beach on the oceanfront on the southern extension. I was in the fourth grade. I remember at dark on October 14, 1954 when the policemen knocked on our door and said that Hurricane Hazel was coming. It was greater than anyone had imagined and it was headed right for Carolina Beach on a full moon tide. We had to evacuate.

My parents didn't know what to do or what to expect. They quickly gathered some items and stashed them in two cars. We drove to Wilmington and stayed at the Cape Fear Hotel.

I can remember hearing the wind roaring and glass breaking from the storefront windows in downtown Wilmington. The hotel was just a few blocks from the Cape Fear River.

When the authorities allowed us to cross the bridge to Carolina Beach the next morning, my mother said that she knew our house was gone. As we approached our lot, I saw an image that I could paint today. The top of our two story beach house was sitting on the sand. The rest was gone. Our piano was found in the lake several blocks over.

I had a three legged cat who had just had kittens. Surprisingly, she was at our lot when we drove up. I always wondered what that cat experienced during the storm.

My parents [names not given] were very strong people and I never knew at that time what a tragedy they had faced. In fact, it was fun in a child's mindset to stay upstairs in a motel where someone let us live for a while.

The drinking water was contaminated and everyone had to boil the water for drinking and cooking. The New Hanover County public health nurse came to the Carolina Beach School frequently to give us vaccinations. We had to line up with our arms out to receive those. I can still see the face of that nurse as she pushed in needle after needle in our arms. I am sure that she hated the process as much as we did.

As an adult, I try to picture myself at the ages that my parents were at the time of Hurricane Hazel. I try to put myself in their shoes. I don't think my feet are nearly the right size for that fit.

Biscuits from scratch. In the 1970s when our family got together, it was a no-brainer that my sister-in-law would make the biscuits. Her product was a huge, soft, cake-like piece of Heaven. She was glad to share her recipe; only there was no recipe on any paper.

Because her biscuits were always perfect, I would stand beside her in the kitchen and do exactly what she did, step by step. Mine were all right, but they never matched the lightness and softness of her biscuits.

What was her secret? Her father would not let her date until she could make biscuits. She said she practiced for hours.

Biscuits from scratch and visiting grandparents. When I was a child in the 1950s, it was a thrill to visit my grandparents who lived in Kenansville, N.C. I really enjoyed seeing my extended family, and especially if Cliff was helping my grandmother in the kitchen. Cliff was a wonderful lady who helped my grandmother with the cooking and cleaning. She made the best biscuits imaginable!

With a child's great interest, I would watch her mix the biscuits in the kitchen. The flour was stored in a pull-out drawer in the lower cabinets in a special bin with a metal lid. I don't know if she used lard or Crisco. We didn't know all about saturated and trans-fats back then.

She would roll out her mixture on the counter and cut out the round biscuits for the oven. If I was lucky, my mother would let me eat some raw dough that was left over. That morsel was heavenly to me and probably led to my loving any bread product that has ever been produced.

When we sat down to eat, I pounced on my biscuit. I learned to make a hole in the center of the biscuit and fill it with molasses. NERVANNA!

Now I am a grandmother and the best I can do are Pillsbury Crescent rolls. They're not bad but they're no match for Cliff's biscuits from scratch. I can't improve on perfection.

Hand-me-downs. I had a cousin who was two years older than I and lived in Goldsboro, N.C. Her mother sent the dresses my cousin had outgrown to my grandmother. My grandmother was an excellent seamstress and could alter the dresses to just my size.

I hated standing still when she placed the pins in my dress. My legs would itch and I would whine very ungratefully that I was having to stand so still.

The finished product was beautiful and my mother and aunt praised the frilly Sunday school dresses that I could wear. As a ten-year-old, I wasn't nearly as thrilled.

However, as I became twelve, the idea of some nice duds coming my way was great.

The only problem was that my cousin stopped outgrowing her youthful dresses and the clothes stopped coming. That was a bummer.

When I had my daughters close together, I spent my time packing and unpacking clothes from the attic so they could get more wear out of the clothes. I should have seen this reaction coming. My third daughter said she didn't think she had ever worn anything new; her clothes were all hand-me-downs from her sisters.

Bringing Home the Paycheck
by
Mildred Packer Navarro of The Woodlands, Texas

Mildred Navarro, who was born in 1928, tells this charming tale of fetching the family paycheck at the tender age of six, square dancing in the 1940s, and of her romance

P. G. Navarro in 1946 standing in front of the Statue to the Confederacy at Third and Market Street in Wilmington.

with a handsome, mysterious Marine whom she married but chose not to identify. (We will wager, however, that his last name is Navarro.)

I was born in Beaver Dam Township in Cumberland County, North Carolina, but I consider Wilmington my hometown. My mom and dad moved to Wilmington when I was six years old and both my mom and dad started working at Spofford Mills.

One of the things I remember so well was going to take the lunch for my daddy when he worked at the mill. I was only six at the time but my mother would send me to pick up my daddy's paycheck because she couldn't go herself. That was quite a responsibility for me.

We lived in a house that was close to the mills. It was called the Molly Baker house, because a lady named Molly Baker had died there.

I remember going to Delgado School and my first teacher there was named Mrs. Redding. The first summer job I got was working at Smith's Shoe Repair Shop on Princess Street which was next to Futrell's Drug Store. Later, when we moved to Maffitt Village, I got started working at Futrell's Drug Store at the soda fountain.

Every morning when I went to work I would catch the bus going into town and I always went to Britt's Doughnut Shop before starting to work. I would get a doughnut and a glass of milk. The cost of one doughnut and a glass of milk was ten cents.

I later went to work at Green's Dime Store as a clerk and later started working at Tom's Drug Store where the pay was better. I worked there at the lunch counter. When I worked at Tom's Drug Store, my younger sister Rachel would meet me when I got off work on Saturdays and I had been paid. We would then go to Saffo's Restaurant to eat. After eating, we would go see a movie at one of the movie theaters; the Carolina or the Manor. After the movies we would go to the Puritan Café and get a Coke while we waited for the bus to Maffitt Village.

When square dancing was started at the Raleigh Building in Maffitt Village, my sister Rachel and sister-in-law Maybelle used to go to them. I loved square dancing and I always

Mildred Packer in 1944.

Spofford Mills Village about 1933. Mildred Packer is standing in front; sister, Emma Rae is holding baby sister Bessie; and Mildred is directly behind her in the back row.

looked forward to going there with them. Rachel and Maybelle didn't dance but they would go with me to listen to the music. Rachel never did learn to dance and Maybelle didn't dance because she was married. My brother Bill worked nights and didn't mind her going to the square dances with me.

One night in December 1945, a young Marine, P.G. Navarro, who was stationed at Camp Lejeune came to the dance hall and asked me to dance. At first I gave him the cold shoulder for I didn't particularly like him. But on the following number I accepted and danced with him.

I recall that after that first meeting I be-

Mildred and Rachel Packer in 1945.

came more acquainted with him and we began dating after I introduced him to my mother and dad and to the family. We used to go to the movies, to the beach, horseback riding, to the carnival at Wrightsville Beach, and bowling. And I especially remember when we went to the Dixie Pig #1 on Carolina Beach Road where he gave me my engagement ring. In June 1946, six months after I'd met him, we were married. We are still together after 60 years.

Caruso in the Groove
by
Millie Solomon of Wilmington

Music of one kind or another has undoubtedly been part of all humanity from the very earliest of times. This delightful piece reminds us that it wasn't until the 20th century that music could be captured and preserved in a "thing," and enjoyed at our leisure, in our homes. Thank you Tom Edison, and thank you Millie Solomon for conjuring up memories of good old crank Victrolas. Winding up those marvelous gadgets gave us a sense of participation, didn't it?

When you reach 90 years, you have experienced many memorable times and events. However, what I'm relating here is more a way of life.

I grew up in New Jersey in an apartment with my sister and parents. We were fortunate to have electricity and even a telephone, but our lives were greatly enhanced by the

Mildred Packer in 1946.

152

introduction of the phonograph.

My father loved the remarkable tenor, Enrico Caruso, and brought home all his records. Our phonograph was the kind you wound up to start, much like the Model T Ford. We would gather around and listen with simple pleasure. After all, what else was there to do? Movies came a bit later in the 20s and opened up a whole new field of adventure. But the phonograph gave us gratification in our home when we wanted it.

The long playing records were often faulty and scratchy, and sometimes you hit a groove that would repeat an aria over and over. Then you had to gently lift the phonograph needle ahead to hear the rest of the record.

As this instrument technically improved over the years and my life moved on beyond school, work and marriage, the phonograph (later called the record player) was always a part of my life and home.

When my son was one year old, we gave him a record player of his own. From then on, as he grew up, he accumulated a collection of records to become a respectable library of music. After college and OCS, he entered the Navy and served as an officer on a ship supplying essential goods and armaments to our Navy in Nam. He taped his favorite records and took them to sea for essential relief of stress.

My children all took music lessons while growing up, but other interests commanded their available time, so none of them can play an instrument today. However, they all attend performances and collect a diversified library of DVDs and any other high tech music that is available for them to listen to. After all, someone has to listen to what talented people perform!

Today, severe hearing loss has made it impossible for me to hear the birds sing, but I still can enjoy a symphony orchestra. So, the great pleasure that music has given my family over these many decades had its inception with one of the simplest and rewarding inventions of the early 20th century: the phonograph.

I'll always remember my dad winding up for a Caruso record!

Seeing This Day
by
Mary Frances Pearson of Wilmington

Mary Pearson was born in New Hanover County in 1924. Those of you who remember the good old days as she does will enjoy her story.

I am the oldest of 15 children. I grew up in New Hanover County near the underpass. There we had to walk the dirt roads or ride the cart and wagon pulled by the horse or the mule.

We had outhouses. There was a time

Christmas, 1981 in Texas: Shelrey, Mae, Mary, George, Regina, Shelrey II and Tina.

Brother, John, Herman, Haskell, Helena, sister and Mary.

Mary F. Pearson.

when would move them to another spot. Sometimes a snake would be around and my father would kill it with a hoe. We used chambers at night and took them out to the outhouse and emptied them in the morning.

We had winding clocks with alarms set to get up in the morning.

I used a tin tub to take a bath in. In the summer we would fill it up with water and put it in the sun to heat the water for a bath.

I went to school when I was six years old. Dick and Jane was my first book to learn to read. I love those books. I have one now I am keeping for history. I am 83 years old and I love books and I love to read.

My mother would make biscuits from scratch. When I was 14 years old I made my first biscuits from scratch. They were my best biscuits. They were big like rolls.

I liked to visit my grandparents. Sometimes you had to go on dirt roads. My grandmother was a good cook. I would have much

Picture submitted by Mary Frances Pearson.

Nieces and nephews: Haskell, Willie, Jr., Gladys, John, George, Mary and Katherine.

fun at her house. During those days I wore the knickers.

Right now I spend a lot of time in books. I go to church and sing with the choir. I love to sing.

I have a friend and we talk about the good old days. It makes you know where you came from and appreciate where we came from.

God has let me live to see this day and I praise God every day.

The Purpose of Little Red Wagons
by
Jay D. Wilcox, Jr. of Wilmington

Some stories can bring on a nostalgic longing that's almost overwhelming. This is one of them. Jay Wilcox describes growing up in Wilmington as "fun." When you read this, you'll agree (if you, too, grew up there in the 40s and 50s) that this description is a tremendous understatement. Thank you, Jay, for sharing your memories of those carefree years.

I was born at Bullocks Hospital on North Front Street in Wilmington on June 28, 1943. I was a "military brat." My father was stationed at Camp Davis, but my mother's family had been in Wilmington since the early 1800s.

I lived in Wilmington on and off from my birth, until my father's military retirement in 1963. I was here during World War II (1943-1945), the Occupation of China (1946-1949), Korea (1950-1952) and vacations (1953-1961). I returned to Wilmington in 1964, made it my home and raised my family here.

Growing up in Wilmington was fun in the 1940s and 1950s for a boy. When I was about four, my uncle made me a train with a string so I could pull it on the sidewalk. All the cars were made out of two by fours with wooden thread spools for wheels. The engine was a Log Cabin Syrup can (shaped like a log cabin with a chimney for a spout) with a Spam can for the coal tinder. Bean cans were used for tank cars and nails for side rails on log cars. I wish I had that train today. My uncle was 92 when he passed away in April 2007.

I remember going to the Bijou Theater on Saturday mornings for nine cents and there would be a double feature, plus cartoons and a serial. These movies had Tom Mix, Hopalong Cassidy, Roy Rogers, Gabby Hayes, and many more. Popcorn was a nickel, so was a soda and a Tootsie-Roll lollypop was a penny. After the movie we would go to Green's Lunch counter.

Hotdogs were ten cents each or three for a quarter and a fountain Coke was five cents.

We didn't have television, cell phones, I-pods, Gameboys or any kind of electronic game. We would gather around the radio in the evening to hear the Lone Ranger or Bobby Benson and the B-Bar-B Riders.

We played outside summer and winter. We didn't have air conditioning. We could go to the YMCA at the corner of Third and Market to swim nude in the indoor pool. We had the beach in the summer. There was also the Boys Brigade at Third and Wooster Streets to play pool and basketball. We would roller skate in the street and sometimes grab hold of a slow moving truck to get to the corner a little faster. Kids back then were safe on the streets. We could ride the bus alone or walk 15 blocks downtown to the movies, without our parents being worried about our safety.

We could roam the streets collecting soda bottles for the two cent deposit and trade them at the corner store for a cold soda or a Popsicle in the summer. We would also collect newspapers and sell them to the fish market for one cent a pound, or sash weights from houses that were being torn down or remodeled to sell for scrap metal. That's what little red wagons were for, hauling a boy's junk. We had to earn our spending money, for the movies on Saturday.

We dug foxholes in my grandmother's backyard to play war. We shot green chinaberries out of slingshots for bullets, and used half-bricks for hand grenades. We would have teams. The good guys "Americans" and the bad guys "Germans or Japanese." We had to take turns being the bad guys.

One day I was a Japanese sniper in a big chinaberry tree. My cousin threw a "hand-grenade" and hit me right between the eyes. I fell out of the tree and landed flat on my back with blood all over my face. My mother saw me fall and came running out of the house. I wasn't hurt, it just knocked the wind out of me, but she told us there would be no more war games. Then, I guess we played cowboys and Indians.

My mother took me to Hall's Drug Store, at Fifth and Castle Streets for a ringworm on my knee. Dr. Hall sat me up on his table in the back room, took out his pocketknife and sterilized it over a gas burner. He then cut along the circle the ringworm had made on my knee. When he was finished, he put some green medicine on the open cut. It burned like fire, but the ringworm died and it healed up without a trace. Doc Hall was not a medical doctor. He was just a pharmacist, but he treated our family for at least two generations.

The circus came to town by train. They would offload all the wagons and animals and parade them down Front Street from the train station at Red Cross Street to Ninth and Dawson Streets where they would put up the big tent. That is where a city water tank is today.

There was also a Christmas parade on Front Street. Santa also came to town by train and rode on a fire truck. Jimmy "Hi-Buddy" Wade would turn on the lights at the "Worlds Largest Living Christmas Tree." At one time he was Wilmington's mayor, and he considered himself the city's ambassador until his death.

We moved back to Wilmington when my father went to Korea. Our car had out-of-state plates on it. My mother was about to put money in the parking meter when Jimmy Wade stopped her. He welcomed her to Wilmington and told her that out-of-state visitors could park free, as Wilmington's guest.

Maybe the city needs to renew this policy.

I could go on and on, but I will stop here.

Remembering Charlie "Barrel" Niven
by
Thurston Watkins, Jr. of Wilmington

Thurston Watkins was born in Wilmington in 1931 and told us that he writes humorous letters to the editor and is a big NASCAR fan.

Charles Duncan Niven (1932-1994) was arguably the best and most exciting three sports athlete ever seen by Wilmington sports fans. Charlie "Barrel" Niven led the nation in basketball scoring in 1954 (38.6) while playing for Wilmington College before it became the University of North Carolina at Wilmington. Sometimes, 25 to 30 percent of Charlie's shots were well past the three point area if it had existed back in the day. This would have pushed the Barrel's nation-leading scoring well into the 40s.

My first memories of Charles Niven go back to the fifth grade at Issac Bear Grammar School. (Strangely enough, this school, built in 1912, became the home of Wilmington College much later.) World War II was under way, and sleepy little Wilmington was being influxed by strange-speaking newcomers from above the Mason-Dixon Line. These new arrivals were children of parents who had moved to our area because of the war. Military installations— Camp Davis at Holly Ridge, Camp Lejeune, Fort Fisher Air Force Facility and Bluethenthal Field (Wilmington Airport)— were being built nearby.

We were about eleven years old when Charlie started to show some of his athleticism that was to bloom years later. During recess, Charlie took it upon himself to be the official Southern hospitality welcoming committee for some of our strangely accented new arrivals. He was in charge of the extracurricular schoolyard activities. Black eyes, bloody noses, and very dirty ripped shirts were the newcomers' initiation fees. This was quite the norm and the beginning of Charlie's fan base.

To clear up the controversy over Charlie's nickname: when he was six or seven, his dad sent him to the barbershop and instructed him to tell the barber, "Clip my head." The barber thought "clip" meant "shave." So he gave little Charlie a slick, shaved head that Telly Sevalas or Yul Brynner would have been proud of.

Charlie started playing basketball at 15th and Dock Street in the backyard of the famous McKoy family. The players were five or six years older than little Charlie. They were Billy Mason, Leonard McKoy, Graham McKoy, Hubert Mckoy, Pluggie Waters, W.A. "Weinner" Brown, Moolie Ayash and Johnny McKoy. Billy Mason became a star at NHHS and later played for Wake Forest. Weinner Brown was a star at NHHS in baseball and was Wilmington's all-time greatest dribbler at NHHS and Wilmington College. He was also the assist man for Charlie Barrel Niven when he led the nation in scoring.

Mutt and Jeff: Thurston Watkins, Jr, (on left) and Charlie "Barrell" Niven in the seventh grade.

When Charlie showed up to play after the barber gave him a spit shine on his rather large head, Moolie Ayash said, "Your head looks just like a barrel." They called him "Barrel Head" at first and then it was shortened to just Barrel.

During this time, Charlie was so short that the older, taller players agreed to let him stand on a barrel near the basketball goal so he could get the ball up to the rim easier. They also called him barrel for that reason.

Barrel Niven and I played first string football in the seventh grade. He played guard and I played end. A slowly developing Charlie played quarterback in the eighth grade but his physical attributes had not arrived yet. He was satisfied to hand the ball off to bigger, faster guys and of course threw me a few touchdown passes that we had worked out on paper the night before the game.

We became best friends and when the sun didn't shine it was rainy day schedule. Charlie and I would change plans from playing two-hand touch in the asphalt street or up to Sonny Jorgensen's where there was a real nice corner lot, to heading to my model airplane building bedroom. In my bedroom closet was a super collection of funnybooks. Charlie and I, and sometimes a friend, Alex Robbins, spent hours digesting wisdom from

Thurston Watkins, Jr. age 24.

this collection. The collection contained two first issue Superman, Batman, Wonder Woman, Human Torch, Plastic Man and Captain Marvel comics. The total collection was well into the hundreds.

Charlie always checked on the rain, hoping for a bit of sunshine.

One day we came in to read a few comics and to our horror, the closet was bare. After recovering from my shock, Mother told us that she had put the comics into the trash and they had been picked up.

Freshman times at New Hanover High School were certainly challenging and the larger, faster guys ruled the roost. Charlie was plenty tough, but was still satisfied to play quarterback in the freshman league. His super running ability hadn't arrived yet and he was content to hand the ball off to the bigger, faster guys. He still threw me a few touchdown passes.

Charlie's super basketball abilities hadn't arrived yet. He played good baseball but didn't seem to like it as well as football or basketball. He rarely practiced baseball.

In my sophomore year I was badly injured in a car wreck. I had to learn to walk all over again. Athletics were out of the question for a long, long time and my thoughts of tagging along with Charlie in sports went out the window.

The great Barrel told me his speed showed up between his junior and senior years at school. He had a good senior year in football, and scored 14 touchdowns, and he was a star on the basketball team.

The AAA Eastern Conference back in the day was made up of seven cities that had only one high school (except Raleigh). The talent pool of athletes on these teams was not as diluted as today where there are almost uncountable high schools in these Eastern Conference cities. In Barrel Niven's day, high schools had their pick of all the athletes from the whole city on one team. Therefore, the records set back then were tougher to come by than the records produced from today's cities with multiple high schools.

Talented athletes were allowed to go to school an extra year and Charlie Barrel Niven complied with the wishes of our sports fans (and our coaches). State championships were probably on our local radar.

Charlie didn't disappoint his fans as the Wilmington Wildcats won the basketball state championship with Sir Charles setting a three game scoring record of 71 points at the tournament.

Wildcat football came up one game short as injuries plagued Charlie's supporting cast and probably prevented the victory. Barrel, however, rolled for 20 touchdowns for the season, with an additional four touchdowns being called back. He scored four touchdowns in the final game of the season against Raleigh, which tied the NHHS record. Mysteriously, he was removed from the game with considerable time to score again.

The baseball team, which really wasn't Charlie's favorite sport, was playing for the state championship. Wilmington had a one run lead in the bottom of the ninth with two men out. An easy roller was hit down to third and guess who let the ball go between his legs and into left field, resulting in our defeat? Adolph Christian "Sonny" Jurgensen, later to become a superstar with the Washington Redskins.

Charlie Niven wasn't through with high school football…not yet. The Barrel was invited to play in the Shrine Bowl game at Charlotte and the "play your favorites" coach was using a single wing offense that Charlie had never played. He was informed that he was to return punts only. When he came in cold to return the first punt on his own 30 yard line, Charlie faked to his left, then did a spin and headed for the opposite sidelines while sweeping around the opposing team of allstars. A Choo Choo Justice-like Niven cleared the whole team and the last man with an angle on the Barrel bumped him out of bounds on the two yard line. The single wing coach allowed Charlie to stay in and take the ball in from two yards out. The 68 yard run was the most exciting play of the day.

The run was on the newsreel between shows at the Carolina Theater. The show filled up all day and night in between shows and the crowd would come alive when the newscaster, Lowell Thomas, said, "Watch New Hanover High School's Charlie 'Barrel' Niven run." The screaming and cheering was so loud, it was like being back at Wilmington's Legion Stadium all over again.

Charlie got invited to Greensboro for the East-West N.C. Allstar game and newspaper articles throughout the state proclaimed the greatness of the western backfield players. Barrel Niven ran wild, including a beauty of a 65 yard kickoff return. The Barrel got the MVP with the great All American Choo Choo Charlie Justice scouting. Choo Choo said Charlie Niven was the best runner he had ever seen and discussed with Barrel the hope of getting him into UNC to take his place.

It didn't work out that way because of academic problems, but with a little politicking and pull by Wilmington's famous coach "Jap" Davis of Duke University fame, Charlie headed to Duke.

Barrel Niven didn't seem to like the composition of the Duke team and spent a lot of time (and nights) with his buddies from Wilmington just down the road at UNC-Chapel Hill. The Duke coach didn't care for this so the Barrel was not on his favorite list.

Case in point: during a scrimmage game between the varsity and freshman teams,

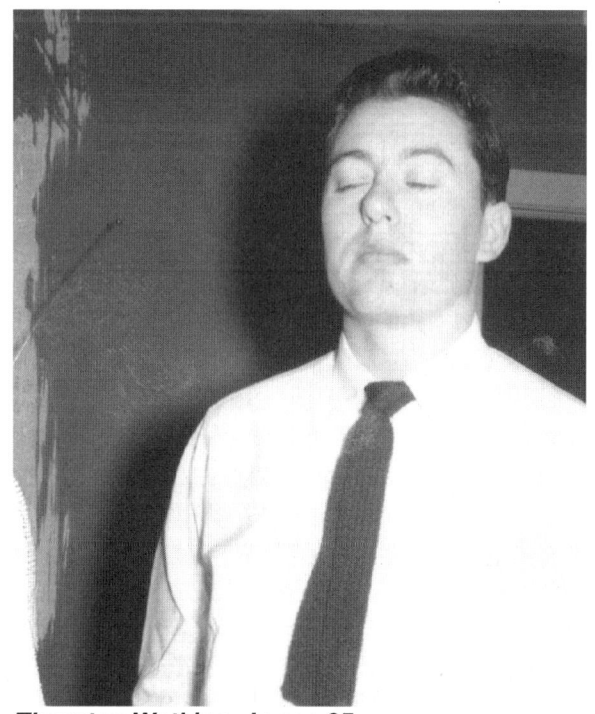

Thurston Watkins, Jr. age 25.

Barrel told the quarterback in the huddle that he could beat the Duke varsity pass defender and to call Charlie's pass play. The Duke coach heard this and the quarterback called Niven's pass play and sure enough, Charlie went for a touchdown. Back in the huddle for the next play, the coach stuck his head into the huddle and said, "Niven, let the quarterback call the plays—if you don't mind."

Charlie was playing freshman ball and when it came time to play his friends over at Carolina, he told the coach he really didn't want to play and that he had some urgent business back in Wilmington. The Duke coach said, "Charlie you have to play, but if you can score three touchdowns before the half, you can go to Wilmington." After his third touchdown, Charlie kept right on running through the end zone and headed to his car and back to Wilmington. Charlie made several touchdowns with the varsity.

A little known fact is that Charlie would go over to the Duke gymnasium where the Duke basketball team was working out and get into some of the scrimmages. Duke had this great All American named Dick Groat, and when the word got around that Charlie the Barrel was "eating Dick Groat up" in scrimmage scoring, trouble showed up in the form of Duke's football coach. When he found out Charlie's basketball escapades, he came over to the gym and announced to the Barrel that he was on a football scholarship and not on a basketball scholarship and to head for the showers. Charlie meant no harm, but he just couldn't resist the competition and a chance to show his stuff.

Charlie had an offer to play in the Canadian Football League for $600.00 per game (big bucks back then) and since he really didn't like the atmosphere at Duke, he left after his freshman year. He had some really good games up there and he was playing against some big time American athletes who had been in the NFL and college stars from the USA, also.

The Barrel became homesick after one season in Canada and answered the call from Wilmington to see what he could do at Wilmington College, the forerunner of UNC-Wilmington. He was in great shape and electricity was in the air. Wilmington sports fans could hardly wait to see if the great Barrel was ready to roll again. [Editor's note: it will become obvious that Niven played basketball at this point.]

In 1951, while playing for Wilmington College, I had a very lucky night against a Chowan College basketball team and scored 30 points as a freshman. I knew my pal Charlie would break my mark with ease and we would joke about how long it would take him to do it. It took only three games.

Charlie Barrel Niven had the greatest basketball season of anyone from Wilmington, including the great Michael Jordan, while at the college level. In 1954, Charlie led the nation in scoring with a 38 plus points per game average. Barrel Niven had a jump shot off the dribble with amazing range. He was a basketball player with the body of a great football halfback.

Charlie also had a drive to the basket that was something to see. The Barrel could dribble with the ball faster than most anyone else could run. He would come dribbling in wide open, something like he did when he was going off tackle in football. He would start elevating to the goal at top speed and put a side spin on the ball that defied the description, "English." Our group said that he didn't put "English" on the ball, he put "French" on it.

The Wilmington College Seahawks made it to the tournament semi-finals and went down to defeat 99-97. Charlie was scorching and set a Campbell College Gym record with a total of 57 points, which included 24 goals and nine foul shots. Charlie played the complete second half without a big toe nail: an opposing player had stepped on it during one of his high speed drives. He was the only player to receive the Most Valuable Player award while playing on a losing team. I have received information from Campbell College that Charlie Niven's 57 points still stands as the record for the gym.

Wilmington College played East Carolina the following year for the Brogden Hall Gym dedication. What a christening of the gym it was. Barrel Niven hit for 42 points, which included 20 foul shots in a row. (That could still be a record for the gym.) The Seahawks won the game 75-70.

Charlie dropped out of school after just a few games and called his record-setting college career a "day." The Barrel wasn't through with basketball by a long shot, and at only 24 years old, there was quite a bit of athletic ammunition left in Charlie's arsenal.

One of Charlie Niven's biggest fans was a guy nemed Henry Parmenter who owned Parmenter Transport. He asked Charlie if he could put together some pretty good local basketball players and form a team.

That was right down the Barrel's alley and he put together Billy Mason of NHHS, Wake Forest and Mens' League of Wilmington fame, locally famous Johnny Edens, Al Black, Jim Hudgins, locally famous dribble master W.A. Brown, myself and sometimes Flo Worrell of Carolina football fame and NHHS and Wilmington College fame.

Henry Parmenter arranged a test game for us with an all-star group down in Nakina, N.C. The Nakina all-stars were supposed to be pretty good, but as it turned out, Niven, Mason, Edens and I each scored 20 points. It was a rout and Henry was very pleased. We called the team the Colonials.

Military teams were very good and admirals, generals and commandants of the Marine Corps would have military personnel transferred to their particular bases for the sole purpose of playing basketball. They had really good players from many big time colleges.

The Cherry Point Flyers came down to play in the NHHS gym on Princess Street and they had a real hotshot guard named Spanbauer. He made 48 points and that was a hard act to follow. Charlie Niven had a better closing act and he hit for 52 points. Our little old team won the game over a team that had beaten the Camp Lejeune Marines, a team with many really good players which included a supposed All-American from Kentucky named Skip Whittaker.

We played the Camp Lejeune Marines at Lejeune and the Kentucky hotshot was guarding the Barrel. Charlie put four fouls on him before the half and Whittaker was mad enough to bite nails when their coach took him out before the half ended.

Before the second half started, Whittaker told Niven, "You can't go but one way, and that's to your right." Cocky Charlie sized him up and said, "I don't need to go but one way against you."

Charlie fouled out Whittaker in the third quarter and scored a respectable 26 points in a losing cause. Mason did not make the

Thurston Watkins, Jr. age 28.

trip with us and could have made the difference.

The Commandant of the Marine Corps came down and paid us a visit in the dressing room. He made a proposal to Charlie to joint up and assured him that all we would be doing was playing ball. Charlie laughed and said, "I can't be in the military. I'm 4-F. I have asthma." If the Commandant had known of the Barrel's football exploits he would have made Charlie some kind of offer he couldn't refuse.

Sadly, good-hearted Henry Parmenter's plane crashed outside of Wilmington and he was killed. The Barrel migrated to the men's league at the downtown Community Center and played quite a few very good years. He did some very good pitching in fast pitch softball and hit over .500 one year. W.A. Weinner Brown beat Charlie out for the batting crown that year.

A few humorous incidents should be recalled. The NHHS baseball team was going out of town to play and the tennis team came along on our 50 MPH bus. Coach Jap Davis was at the wheel and we stopped at a country store for some Nehis and Moon Pies. Fun-loving Charlie stayed on the bus just long enough to hide the tennis rackets in the large baseball equipment bags and then came into the country store for his refreshments. About ten miles up the road from the store, Niven asked some of the tennis players where the tennis rackets were. A commotion of major proportions arose and Niven said, "He thinks he left the rackets back at the store." With tears in their eyes, they tell Coach Jap what Niven said and he stopped the bus and made Charlie tell where he hid them. But this is not the end of the story.

During the return trip, Charlie hollered to the driver, Coach Jap, "Turn on some heat!" The coach continued driving with no heat. Charlie then said, "It's cold back here!" When the heat didn't come on, he took a *Life* magazine apart, piled it up in the bus's aisle and started a fire. The coach saw the glare in the mirror and brought the old bus to a screeching halt. The coach opened the door, asked Charlie to step outside because he was going to throw him under the bus. Needless to say, Charlie refused the offer.

Charlie was usually pretty lucky, and I have a tale about that luck. If it hadn't held, his athletic career could have been over after his junior year in high school.

Charlie didn't excel at water skiing, but one day he asked me to take him skiing with his girlfriend. I said, "Sure," and we were off to the old boat ramp on Waynick Boulevard at Wrightsville Beach. The Barrel wanted to show off a little for his girlfriend. I pulled him up on two skis and I didn't know that fun-loving Charlie was going to cut behind a channel marker the size of two massive telephone poles and then try to zoom out and just miss it. He misjudged the distance and careened off the creosote marker. His shoulder, side and thigh took some really bad abuse. Charlie went flying one way and the skis another. I spun my boat around and sped back to a facedown, floating Barrel Niven. I jumped in and pulled Charlie's head out of the water and he was sobbing with the pain. I think he was slightly embarrassed to have this happen in front of his girlfriend. I started back to the boat with him and astonishingly, he said, "Get me the skis." Black and blue Charlie was ready to go again. If he had hit the marker pole maybe six inches closer to his right side, his day in the sun as a great athlete might not have happened. We kept this a secret and if Coach Brogden had found out about this, I don't wish to even think about it.

Another humorous incident occurred when Charlie, Weinner Brown, John Martin and I made a trip to a Rockingham 500 stock car race. Back in the day, it was quite in vogue to "party" during the whole race when you had a designated driver, so to speak, and that's exactly what we did, with some gusto. There were four rather large gents seated in front of us and they had a large styrofoam cooler between them. My group were all standing on our concrete seats, but the heavy duty gents in front of us were seated with the cooler still full of water, ice and a few beers. They were also sitting on a nice blanket. Barrel Niven lost his balance, fell forward and stepped through the cooler's styrofoam lid. His foot was in the icewater and the lid was caught around his calf. I thought to myself, We are going to be killed right now. As Weinner Brown helped extricate a not so steady Niven, I said, "Charlie, give them twenty dollars for the cooler and blanket, quick!" The Barrel reached in his pocket and happened to have a beautiful, crisp twenty dollar bill.

"King" Richard Petty had a big lead near the end of the race, so we decided to leave with ten laps to go. I didn't think it would be a good idea to walk about three-quarters of a mile next to our ice waterized, heavy duty, very wet friends. We jumped in our big Chrysler and were soon on the way home, 120 miles away.

Over the years, there is no telling how many games I played with my pal, Charlie Niven. I played sometimes with him, but sometimes against him, like in the men's league at the Community Center. When we were both pushing 35 years, we ended up against each other in the finals of the championship game in the men's league. My dad came down to witness this spectacular, as Charlie Niven and W.A. Weinner Brown were two of his favorite people. It was standing room only.

The Barrel had some aces on his team, including a very good Vic Batson of Wilmington College fame. My team had some aces, also, including a very good Flo Worrell and W.A. Brown of Wilmington College fame, and big Danny Parham of NHHS fame. W.A. Brown knew every move Niven had ever made on a basketball court, as he had played as Charlie's assist man when the Barrel led the nation in scoring at Wilmington College. I "sicked" my buddy, W.A. Brown, on my other buddy, Charlie, and it was something to see. Hot Dog Weinner Brown held the Barrel down to 19 points and somehow I lucked up and was the high scorer of the game, which my team won for the championship.

It was a pleasure to see my dad at half court after the game with one arm hugging Charlie and the other hugging W.A. Brown. I called it a day after that game and quit while I was ahead.

When the Barrel died in 1994, the funeral was almost like a 1950-51 reunion. Everybody who was anybody was there and Charlie always did like lots of attention. I told Leonard McKoy, who was Charlie's brother-in-law, that Charlie was still getting plenty of attention right now.

If there is a gridiron or basketball gymnasium on the other side, I'm sure my pal the Barrel will be on the winning team.

The Backseat Pot
by
Barbara Liles of Wilmington

Barbara Liles was born in 1931 in Mississippi and grew up there. These memories are for her grandchildren...and for others who will enjoy this trip back in time.

I've been writing down things I remember so my grandkids will know more about me and the family.

I was born to a butter-maker and a home economist in Starkville, Mississippi. Both parents were college grads. Dad went to Miss State—worked on the college farm daytimes and went to school at night. This was a

Depression program, I think.

As the oldest of three girls, I was, and still am, bossy. But I got better.

My mother's mother baked cakes on a wood stove and sold them. She also sold eggs and fresh chicken (ready dressed) during the Depression.

Farmers didn't have much cash. All my birthday cakes were homemade by my grandmother. I always wished for one of the store-bought ones with white icing. A friend had a party with one and the ice cream was Eskimo Pies. A pink one (strawberry) in each batch rated you a prize.

We had a BIG snow in about 1939. Daddy made a big sled that we used down the hill in front of the school up the street.

I had naturally curly hair, but neither sister did. I gave a number of Toni home perms. Thank goodness things have improved in that department. Frizzy hair was not popular, but curls were.

In the summer of 1941, we took the first family vacation. We didn't travel much. Money was tight and Daddy worked hard. I was ten, Ann was seven and Jane was six.

Mother packed our clothes in dress boxes, one for each of us. We wore our hair in braids pinned across the top of the head, and for the trip, we covered the braids with a bandana so the braids wouldn't have to be done each day. Three little girls took a while.

We stopped in motels that by today's standards were unacceptable: open air camps…screen between the roof and wall…squirrels dropping nuts on the tin roof. We little girls slept fine but Mother didn't!

Driving through the mountains with three little girls, before McDonalds and Hardees were invented, service station bathrooms were the only choices. We carried a gray enamel pot in the back seat. Of course Daddy didn't stop for dumping after each use. You can guess what happened…somebody turned it over! I'll never forget Daddy's comment: "Just a damn chick sale on wheels."

Fifty years ago our son was about ten months old. We moved from Shelby to Elizabethtown. We used cloth diapers, but with a move like this, we decided to try disposables. Chux was what was available. Ben's little bottom did not like the Chux and broke out *very* badly. Thanks to zinc oxide ointment and air exposure, it soon cleared, but *so sore*.

The Doc Who Prescribed Ice Cream
by
Shirley Pope Williams of Wilmington

Again, we are surprised with an unusual and absolutely delightful story from the past! Shirley Williams, born in 1946, remembers a couple of very unusual physicians. We think many of you will remember them, too.

Back in the day when my girls were born,

Shirley Williams with daughters, Rhonda, age three, and Leigh, age two months, in 1967.

Rhonda, age five, and Leigh, age two, in 1969.

Shirley Williams with daughters, Rhonda, age five, and Leigh, age two, in 1969.

in the sixties, doctors' offices were not the big groups I see these days, with their own labs and specialized medicine. My pediatrician of choice was Dr. Auley M. Crouch, Jr. His office was across the street from James Walker Hospital (now James Walker Apartments) where my first daughter was born.

In those days, a checkup was like visiting an old friend. We often sat in the reception area listening as Dr. Auley played his violin between appointments. After the visit, my daughters, Rhonda and Leigh, were given special prescriptions. I found one the other day as I was cleaning out an old cabinet. I don't know how it survived being used. Because this "prescription" could be taken to the Dairy Queen, then located on the corner of Dawson and 17th Street, and exchanged for an ice cream cone. As you can imagine, this made a doctor's appointment less dreaded with the promise of a sweet treat at the end.

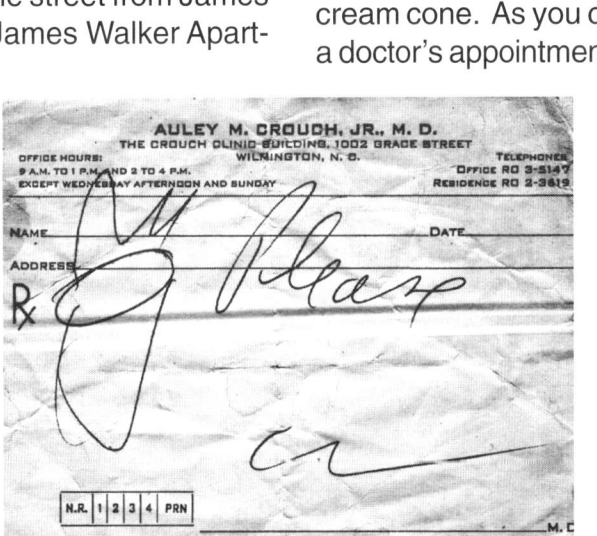

A special "prescription" Dr. Auley would give Shirley's children for a free Dairy Queen ice cream cone.

After Dr. Auley Crouch died, I continued seeing his brother, Dr. Walter Crouch. He was also a very loving and dedicated pediatrician. He later moved his office to Babies Hospital at Wrightsville Beach. It was wonderful to be part of this history, as Babies Hospital has been torn down.

Dr. Walter would examine my child and then before we left, he would have a prayer with us. This was precious to me. I doubt if such a thing could occur these days. I am happy to have these memories of when my children were young.

Iceman and Lumina Farewell
by
Kathleen L. Ellis of Wilmington

Kathleen Ellis has been in Wilmington since the year of her birth, 1927. In this nostalgic reminiscence, she has captured the essence of life in the good old days. Many old-timers will recall the heydays of Greenfield Lake and Lumina, and who can forget the iceman making his rounds on a hot summer day?

As with most of us, the reasons I am where I am today are varied. Here I am at 79 years of age, right where I want to be—in Wilmington, N.C.

How I came to be born here is due to some unrelated happenings long ago. My father's parents (my father's name was Russell Ethelbert Lord) came here from England before he was born. My mother, Jean Scott Lord, an orphaned child in Glasgow, Scotland, was raised from a teenager to a young woman by an aunt, Miss Jean Scott, who never married.

The aunt longed to see again a younger sister, Mrs. William Morton, who had come here years ago to Wilmington with her husband and a daughter and now had three additional children. The trip they made here in 1920 was going to be a "visit," but my mother met my father and they married in 1923. Her aunt returned to Scotland and I was born in 1927 here in Wilmington. I have always lived here.

The Mortons' daughters were Jean Joyce, Mary, Martha and Edith, and their son was William, Jr. Edith married Mike Hall, whose family ran Hall's Drugstore at 5th and Castle for three generations. William, Jr. was also a pharmacist and had his drugstore at 8th and Market.

The young man I would marry in 1950, Hugh Lamar Ellis, came here in 1948 from West Palm Beach, Florida and I thought for sure I would have to move to Florida, but he enjoyed the seasonal weather changes and loved the big shade trees we have. (Ever tried to sit in the shade from a palm tree?) We were very happy right here for nearly 53 years. He died in 2003.

I am so glad we spent our lives here and so happy that all of the memories of my life took place in this area. People seem to think we embellish memories, but mine are real—and simple.

The very ground my house sits on was once Peiffer Airfield, owned by my boss's son, John Colucci, Jr., back in the 1940s. I've been up in small trainer planes which were housed in a hangar here on the lot next door when I was 18 or 19.

There is a lake here in our town, Greenfield. It could be more beautiful as it is not cared for as well as it should be. There is a five mile drive around it, with a few exits to other parts of the area south of town. For 18 years I lived two blocks from this lake. I loved going there better than getting to go to a movie downtown.

The many old cypress trees in the middle of the lake were beautiful, hanging with Spanish moss all over them, but close up, they gave the water around them a sort of brownish shade and not too many chose to bathe that far out. However, weather permitting, you could almost count on a few boys holding their noses and jumping off the dock.

My earliest memory includes a small pavilion out over the lake which was reached by a boardwalk. Sometimes some planned dances were carried on there, but more likely than not, anyone who wanted to do so turned up with their guitar, harmonica or accordion and someone would start dancing pretty soon.

In time, the pavilion disappeared, but the little bridge across the spillway and the waterfall is still there.

There was also on the lake side of the road a natural spring with delicious water. Access to the spring is still available across the street.

One year our city water got terrible (safe, but a strong salt taste), and lots of us made daily trips to the spring, carrying our gallon jugs.

Another year a terrible flu epidemic hit this area and all four of us in my family had been sick. My mother caught my daddy bundling me up in a hat and scarf and every warm piece of clothing I had. She asked, "Where are you taking that child?" He said, "To the lake. It froze over last night and she may never get a chance to see that happen again." I didn't.

I still remember the boys on bikes riding on the ice, sliding all over it, laughing their heads off. It was beautiful. I always have been glad my dad won that argument.

Our other contact with ice in those days was the ten cents worth we had to purchase almost every day to keep milk and other perishables cold enough. It's funny: if you don't know anything else, it's just daily "stuff." But I know my mother was happy when our first electric refrigerator turned out those trays full of ice cubes!

That was, however, the beginning of the end of the ice truck we watched for every day. The truck would stop at a couple of places on the block and the driver would yell, "Iceman!" Someone would appear at nearly every doorway and call back their order. While he was gone to deliver, all of us kids would snatch us a piece of good ol' ice from the back of the truck where he broke his ice supply expertly into ten cent blocks.

Sometimes there weren't enough slivers of ice to go around and somebody would "accidentally" drop a larger piece on the road. We would all get a piece if we behaved. The iceman might fuss but he didn't really care. Sometimes he would even break off a little piece for us himself.

Who knows? Even a child today might enjoy just an old piece of ice as a treat on a hot summer day. Somebody ought to try it.

For several years we had a dear, sweet neighbor, Mrs. Nick Sanders, who became my pal. She had only one son, Herman, who was my younger sister Betty Jean's age and they played together so well. But this lady crocheted beautifully and I used to watch her in awe as she developed those beautiful finished pieces. So she decided that she wanted to teach me as much as I wanted to learn.

I was allowed to buy myself a ten cent metal crochet hook (I still have it) and I went over to her house one afternoon with my hook and a ball of tobacco twine. That dear lady began what was to be many lessons in needlework right on her front steps. I think she enjoyed it as much as I did. She is long gone now, but she is a wonderful memory of someone willing to put off time with a neighbor's youngun.

I think I remember something in our kitchen that evidently not many people remember ever seeing. We heated with coal in our small kitchen stove and a heater in the living room. If there was no special need of the living room stove being fired up, the door between it and the back of the house was kept shut and we dressed, ate, gathered and lived by that kitchen stove. We did have a three-burner gas stove, but Mother didn't use it unless it was necessary. Gas was costly during and after the Depression. But that coal burner in the kitchen had a flat top on it where foods could be heated and the pipe leading up to, through, and out of the ceiling had one section of stovepipe that had an oven made into it—a stovepipe oven! It used the heat that just normally would have gone up and out of the chimney. It was great for making biscuits, coffee cake, roasting sweet potatoes, etc.—keeping warm and cooking nice hot food at the same time. You couldn't beat it. I never have seen another of those ovens since then.

One of the most cherished memories I have is one I was reminded of not long ago. PBS recently featured once again the old film about Lumina, the wonderful old pavilion at Wrightsville Beach which was the center of life there. Not too many of us are still here to speak of boarding the beach car at Front and Princess in downtown Wilmington and riding down the old track and out onto the rails which got it over the waterway and the sound, and then off again and on track down the center of Wrightsville Beach south to the end of the track at Lumina. Even then it was a thrill because everyone knew that it would be only a matter of time till things would change, though no one would have envisioned how much.

Across the tracks from Lumina were a group of modest little cottages called Pomanda Walk. I don't know how they did it in those difficult years, but somehow our parents managed to rent one of those cottages for a week before school started. Dad fished, my sister and I played in the water and the sand, and all of us watched for the arrival of the streetcar bringing the big bands who came to play upstairs in the beautiful ballroom: Tommy Dorsey, Jimmy Dorsey, Kay Kyser, Guy Lombardo, Artie Shaw, and other well known dance bands of the era. And then the dancers themselves would be on a later car—the ladies in their lovely gowns and the fellows all spiffed up.

That dance floor was kept so beautiful, waxed every day, and the folks who danced on it had to wear dance slippers.

For many years this place was used in similar ways. Back when my dad was a young man, he used to assist Mr. John Spellman who set up a booth and took pictures of folks who wanted to save their memories in their finery, or bathing suits, or whatever.

Lumina remained there for many years after World War II, slowly deteriorating as it passed from one owner to another, and was not kept up. Finally it was torn down by a buyer who bought it for speculation as the value of available land increased. Someone should have seen to it that it was not destroyed. In its place stand some of the most unattractive condos ever seen, but that's the way things go. However, no one can take away the memories.

Wilmington and the surrounding areas, including the beaches, have all changed tremendously over the years. Some good, some not so good. And the people keep coming. I guess the word got out: it *is* a great place to live.

The Lost Anchor
by
Sandra Kinlaw Huddle of Shallotte

Although Sandra Huddle didn't provide us any information about her family, she did tell us she was born in Lumberton in 1944. Her memories include a childhood love of water and some wild adventures.

Our family—my parents were Juston and Elizabeth Kinlaw—moved to the Wilmington area in the mid-50s. Our first home was in the Seagate neighborhood. I was in the fifth grade at Bradley Creek School.

The summers were nice, and though we had been told not to go to Bradley Creek, many times my two older brothers, Gail and Gene, and I would slip down to the creek and go over to the sand bar and retrieve some oysters, play in the water and then crab for a while. Often, we would fix oysters along the shore.

It was a fun time for us kids being near the water, plenty of room to ride our bikes. Our younger sister Ann was too young to follow us, and she attended a nursery school nearby.

Halloween was a special time. There were a lot of kids in the neighborhood and we would gather together and cover the area. Our bags were full of goodies when we went home. One of the homes we went to had all of us come in and sing a song before they would treat us. The homes where we went were always fun and polite people.

Things have really changed, and I feel sad that the kids of today do not have that oppor-

Sandra and Ann Kinlaw.

tunity to have the fun we did in those days without being afraid of what might happen.

I remember when Hurricane Hazel came through and the destruction of so much property. We stayed upstairs above Bunky's Grocery and Gas Store. When the hurricane was so strong we could feel the apartment we stayed in sway, we went down and stood at the bottom of the staircase to be closer to the ground and watched the trees sway and many articles being blown down the street. This was our first hurricane to be in and it really made an impression with me. My oldest brother, Gail, loved every minute of it, and looked forward to the next one.

The next house we stayed in was still in Seagate, Peach Street, I think, a two-story house with a balcony upstairs at the back part of the house. In the backyard was a large tree, and across from the back of the house was a shed. My two brothers, Gail and Gene, tied a rope around one of the branches, and a big knot at the end of it. We would go to the balcony and swing from the balcony to the shed, jump down, run up the stairs and repeat the trip. It was fun, we never got hurt, and now as I think about the danger we put ourselves in, we were lucky, we had angels watching over us.

Downtown was really special to me. Sometimes my mother would take me with

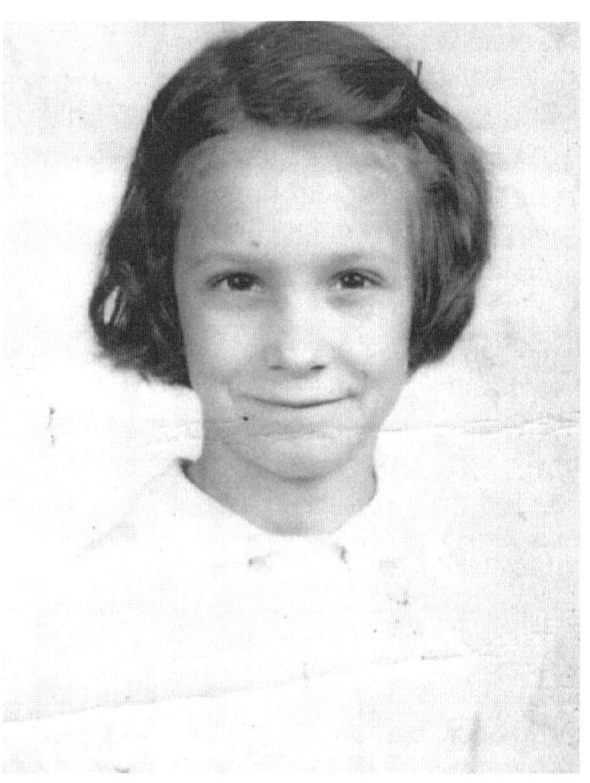

Sandra Kinlaw in the fifth grade in 1955.

her shopping. My dad worked for the Ford Motor Company between Second and Third Street, we would leave early with him and go to Woolworth dime store and enjoy a cup of coffee and a doughnut, just me and my mom. Sometimes my sister Ann would be with us. It seemed like we went into all the shops. One shop, I believe was called the Holly Shop, there we would find such pretty clothes and we would layaway several pieces, then at lunch time we were off to Saunders Drugstore. I know they made the best ham sandwiches. It was quite a day for me. I miss the downtown area with its many shops and dime stores.

Another special attraction for my family was the Azalea Festival parade which we always went to. The year that stood out to me was the year Polly Bergan was queen. She was a beautiful person and added so much to the festival. There were also art shows

Gene, Elizabeth, Sandra and Ann Kinlaw.

downtown that were in a large parking lot that I enjoyed.

My parents found a houise at Masonboro Sound, which we bought. It was on Trails Ends Road, near the water. We were all so excited because we were even closer to the water. My sister Ann told my dad she would go to Whiskey Creek and get him a jar of whiskey every day. Our dad drank at that time, and my sister was too young to know it was only a name, not whiskey in the creek.

We lived a short distance from the water, the end of the road opened up to a large sandy area and water, so very pretty. There were lots of small fishing boats tied to posts. I, with other kids, would go swimming in the water and often stood in one of the many boats and fish. One day a bunch of us kids wanted to go over to the sand bar, so we borrowed one of the small fishing boats and proceeded toward the sand bar. We had no motor, and no oars, but one of the kids, Dick, was along and he would throw out the anchor, pull the boat to it and continue this motion till we were on the sand bar. We all played in the water for some time. Then it was time to head back to shore. We all took our places in the boat and once again Dick began to throw out the anchor. At some time the an-

Elizabeth Kinlaw.

chor was thrown but when Dick began to pull the rope there was no anchor. I and probably others were very worried. How were we going to get back? Only one person was along who could swim, that was Dick. So he jumped out of the boat, took hold of the rope and pulled us to shore. Thank goodness it wasn't a long distance. We never did that again. We really had angels looking over us that day.

It was also here that my other brother, Gene, introduced us to Elvis Presley's music and dancing. Dad didn't think much of that, but it wasn't long before dad and mom would join in and dance with us.

It was at this same location, there were woods behind our house and my brother Gail would take the family while dad was at work and show us the biggest blueberry bushes with the largest bunch of blueberry I had ever seen. It wouldn't take long to fill our buckets and head for home.

To me, Wilmington was a wonderful place to stay, and so many things to do, without paying money for things. We all knew everyone in the neighborhood, it was a time of being laid back and enjoying childhood. There were many trips to Wrightsville Beach, to play in the water and enjoy the white sand, and eye the many items made out of shells at

Ann and Gail Kinlaw.

Sandra Kinlaw in 2001.

Johnnie Mercer's pier.

My family moved to Shallotte in 1958. In 1964 I married. My husband's job kept us traveling in the United States for two years. We now have three grown children. I have kept books for the local Piggly Wiggly. I was an assistant director for the Miss Brunswick County Pageant in 1970 and in 1971. I also worked five years as an assistance secretary for a primary school in Brunswick County. For the last 25 years I have been caregiver for my mother 15 years, and my sister 10 years. Both are now deceased.

One of my enjoyments is playing the accordion. I am active in church. I enjoyed serving as assistant choir director for about 20 years at one church, and then four years as choir director at another, and have been active in the local nursing home with a group that sings once a week. I also am chairperson and treasurer of a local cemetery.

The Judge's Trees
by
Garry McDaniel of Wilmington

Garry McDaniel was born in Wilmington in 1933 and grew up here. He is also a sportsman. Few are the sportsmen who don't appreciate nature, and who aren't conservation minded. Those who aren't, in fact, don't deserve the name. Mr. McDaniel is a true sportsman, as you will see when you read this story. We are proud to publish it and we applaud his sentiments.

I was very happy to read in the *Star-News* this morning that Judge Gilbert and Julian Burnett are making it possible for there to be a 109 acre park on the River Road in the Lords Creek area. I don't think people realize what a wonderful and unselfish gift this is to everyone. I will try to explain it the way I see it.

Back in the 1950s, a friend and I used to hunt crows on the Burnett land off of the River Road which then was really in the country. We hunted crows because we enjoyed the sport and wing shooting as well as being conservation minded. Crows are really smart and you have to outsmart them just to get a shot, and even then they might outmaneuver you for a miss.

Also, according to an article in a NRA Magazine at that time, crows destroyed 65 million duck eggs a year. A duck hunter could more than replace a duck he shot by shooting a crow. We did our part.

One beautiful Saturday, we were coming out of the woods after an early morning hunt and encountered an elderly gentleman on foot who introduced himself as Judge Burnett from Burgaw. He was quite upset because someone had burned some of the trees on his property. We assured him that we were hunting only crows and did nothing to hurt the property. He then gave us permission to continue hunting crows on his property. He only asked in return that if we should see anyone else hunting or hurting his trees, to call the Sheriff's Department and to call him.

He said he only came down here occasionally to check on his trees. He then began to affectionately tell us about his trees as though they were his children. He would point to different trees and groups of trees and tell us what year he had planted them and how much they had grown.

Having always taken trees for granted, I learned a lot from this man. He just walked and looked as though he was totally at peace with his friends.

Then he showed us the sand on the sides of the road which had gone unnoticed, but after sifting through it with his hands a few times, he showed us some small pieces of very old pottery: pipe stems, dishes, cups, and some shark's teeth. Amazing that this had been right under our noses for so many years and we had never looked.

I saw Judge Burnett on quite a few occasions after that. He would always stop and visit. He had a wonderful way of bringing you into his world so that you could share what he felt for the beauty of the land and trees that he loved.

Knowing that Judge Gilbert and Julian Burnett were exposed to the same gifted man that I knew for time, I am not surprised that they would have the same appreciation and want to share it. He would be proud.

Picking Up Coal
by
Charles Hart of Wilmington

Charles Hart was born in 1922 and raised, we believe, in rural Pennsylvania. His series of memories strike right to the core of life during pre-electricity days. If you're over 65, you'll identify with most of them. We're glad he reminded us of the first margarine. Hard to believe you had to mix food coloring with it to make it look like butter, but it sure tasted like lard if you didn't.

I remember the iceman breaking up a piece of ice for us kids. That was a treat.

The first pair of knickers I had, I had to defend myself against my friends.

Our outhouse was a two-seater with a Sears Roebuck and Montgomery Ward catalog. (No toilet paper.)

We had to follow the railroad train carrying coal. When the coal fell to the ground, we would pick it up to heat our house.

We used the same tin tub to have our Saturday night baths that we used to wash clothes in—with a washboard.

We were so happy to get a pair of shoes for Christmas. This made our day.

We had a pump in our yard where we and our neighbors got our water for drinking, bathing and washing clothes.

When I was 11 years old, I broke my wrist. My father gave me our last dollar to go to the doctor. The doctor broke up an orange crate and made splints.

When I grew up, I dated a coal miner's daughter. Her father had to buy everything in a company store and was always in debt.

I remember the little A&P Stores on most every corner with their ugly, black oily floors. But the aroma of that fresh ground Eight O'clock coffee you could never forget. I also remember the Murphy and Woolworth 5 and 10 cent stores where nothing was over a dime.

We had a cobbler in most every town. We called him the shoemaker. He would cut out a piece of leather and nail it to your worn-out shoes and replace the rubber heel. It was like getting a new pair of shoes.

We had no electricity, so my father made what he called a crystal set radio with earphones. We had one station: KDKA. That was it.

We had a gas light that was a flame from natural gas with a flimsy bulb over it. This and homemade candles was what we read by.

I also remember the first margarine. I looked like a pound of lard. I came with four yellow pills and it was my job to mix it and make it look like butter.

My first job was usher in the local theater. I had a black, red and yellow uniform and a flashlight to seat people. The pay was $10.00 a week for seven days.

Those were the good old days. Thank God they're gone.

The Missed Wooden Doll
by
Kristy Dixon of Wilmington

Although she lives in Wilmington now, Kristy Dixon was born, in 1978, in Morganton, N.C. within sight of the Blue Ridge. Sadly, she chose not to reveal the names of the people in her story, and we can only infer that the grandparents she visited lived in or near the mountains. However, what she left out of her story historically is made up for by the contrast she unknowingly presents. Many of the objects and incidents she describes in her story are from a much younger viewpoint than that found in most of the tales in this book. It's interesting and revealing that she considers these things extraordinary, while those of us who grew up during the era that was obviously vanishing when she experienced it considered them normal. Thank you, Kristy, for the contrast.

I remember a few things from when I was young.

My grandparents lived off the interstate. You had to turn right as you exited. It was down a very steep hill that was a dirt road.

I loved to visit because they had so much to do. It seemed that way as a kid. They had dogs, chickens, ducks, rabbits, goats and one really big pig. They never would get rid of it. It grew old and died.

My grandpa had some playhouses built and that was the neatest thing. We had babydolls and kitchen sets in there. We would get water and mud and make mud pies.

Their driveway was all red mud. Out by that, there was an outhouse and on the inside, there was a bench made of wood with a hole in the middle to use the bathroom. I remember not ever wanting to use the bathroom because it smelled.

We washed our hands by a faucet outside.

My cousins lived with my grandparents and we would always have fun playing.

We always got cakes and apple pies from the bakery. They were 25 cent cakes.

My grandpa always wore bib overalls and still does. My dad gets him overalls for Christmas every year. He wears them *every day*.

My great grandpa used to make wooden dolls. I only know this because my dad told me about it. He was going to make me one but he died before he got the chance to make me one.

My great grandmother had a dipper to drink out of and I can remember drinking it— the best water ever. She lived on a dirt road up a mountain. She had a very high hill that was red dirt. One of my uncles used to ride a dirt bike up it and there were wild geese running around in the yard.

My grandparents and great grandma had wood stoves. They sure kept it warm in the house.

My aunt used to take us to the drive in movies. We would go to KFC and ride on the back of the truck. I can't remember what movie it was because it was so long ago. But they had stands right beside the vehicles so you could hear the movie. We would sit on the back and eat and watch the movie.

I also lived in the mountains for a summer. We would go to my cousin's house who lived on a big hill and it was a dirt road all the way up. My (then) brother and cousin put a bike together and rode it down the hill and the bike fell apart and he went flying down the hill and skinned up his left side.

We were all left alone there one day, and it was a trailer full of kids. We decided to walk through the small pine trees (mini Christmas trees) and a couple of us were barefooted. There was a patch of briars all the way down. Some of us carried others on our backs. We heard music playing, so we went to see what it was and we saw an orange car and a blonde man and a black haired man playing a guitar. I still swear to this day it was the Dukes of Hazard guys.

We also had a great aunt who lived in the mountains. She had the best cold water that we drank out of the dipper. She also had a natural flowing small creek that I would love to play in. She also had an old broken down car that we used to play on.

We moved from the mountains when it was time for school to start.

We moved on a dirt road up a small hill. We would walk to and from school. We lived beside a cornfield and a lot of woods. We would always ride our bikes and made clubhouses. My sister and I played hide and seek.

I also pulled up wild onions and I loved to do that.

There's all so much to remember that I can't possibly write down. But there are a couple of other things to write about. One is about the trash pickup. I never knew about trash pickup until I was a teenager. We used to have dumpsters around and I went with my aunt a lot to throw the trash in the dumpsters. We would do what we called dumpster diving. We found a lot of good stuff people threw away. I think that is how I got most of my toys.

I still have a care bear she found me, and it's one of the old ones.

And about the flypaper: my whole family used to have them hanging in the corners of their house to catch flies and they would carry fly swatters around. I thought it was so disgusting just to see all those dead flies.

The Exploring Shoes and the Movie Man
by
Susan Williams of Wilmington

Susan Williams writes about a painful lesson neither she nor her beloved grandfather learned the first time. She also writes about a loving father who also contributed material for this book. Ms. Williams was born in Wilmington in 1971.

Growing up in the 1970s, one of my favorite things to do was to spend the night with my Granddaddy as I affectionately called him. We had a very close relationship, and we always had fun, no matter what we were doing. We were close. He called me Shug. His name was Leo Williams.

In those days Granddaddy lived in Nesbit Courts, which is down by the Cape Fear River

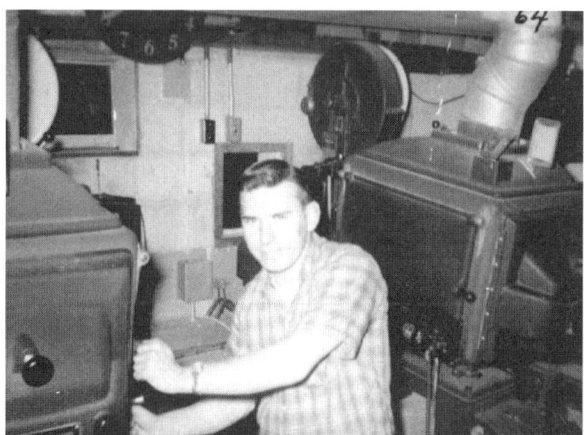

Wrightsville Road Drive-In in 1964 where Cinema 6, opened 1983, was until 2005.

Susan Willams and grandfather, Leo Williams, in 1983.

and the railroad tracks.

We loved to go exploring, so we would get up early when I stayed the night with him and go walking. We'd go down to the river or downtown, anywhere.

Well, one day we were feeling especially adventurous and we decided to follow the railroad tracks further than we ever had before. It was summertime and I had on a pair of flip flops, not the best for exploring, but we were adventurous, or at least I was. Granddaddy had good shoes on.

We walked and laughed and found nature that we thought was newly discovered—by us, of course—and he'd tell me stories about the old days, and we ended up this day going further than we ever had.

Then we heard a train. We looked at each other, not sure we had actually heard what

Susan Willams and grandfather, Leo Williams, in 1983.

we had heard. Sure enough, a train. So off we go, off the tracks and onto the side of the grass and it was nothing but high grass and cactus and sand spurs. And boy, did I start yelling!

Granddaddy asked me, "Shug, what's the matter?" He always called me Shug, because that's what he used to call my Grandmother Paris he loved her dearly and I never did get to know her, as she passed away in 1969 before I was born. I still remember the look on his face, by the way he was smart enough to wear shoes. He helped me get out as many sand spurs as we could, but when you're standing there in about a thousand of them, what can you do? Flip flops cover a little but not a lot and they don't cover legs and the top of feet.

My granddaddy also wore pants a great deal of the time which helped him in a great many circumstances.

At this age—I was nine—I was too old to be picked up and Granddaddy was too old to pick me up, so we had to stand there, him trying to do what he could to help me, and me crying and saying ow ow ow, waiting for that train to pass.

Like all good explorers we survived. Granddaddy cleaned me up.

A couple of weeks went by. We decided to go exploring again on the railroad tracks. Since I once more had only my flip flops with me, Granddaddy had the idea I should bring the bike he had bought me and taught me to ride without training wheels. Sounded fun.

Off we went. The two fearless explorers. But way out once again about where we were once before and lo and behold, what do we hear? A train.

Once again, Granddaddy hops off the tracks and tells me to come on as well. I felt better this time. I have my bike. So I follow Granddaddy off the tracks and I hear a hissss. I look and what do I see? I am sitting in a huge pile of sand spurs and cactus, the biggest cactus you've ever seen in your life. And I have not one, but two, flat tires.

Poor Granddaddy tried to comfort me, but there was no way, because I also had sand spurs in my feet again.

Susan Willams' father, Glenn Williams, a booth manager for Cinema 6, standing in front of a prop for a Stephen King movie, Maximum Overdrive, *in 1986.*

So here we were again, waiting for the train to pass. And I was stuck pushing the bike back to Granddaddy's house with wounded legs and feet.

Granddaddy went out and bought me a pair of exploring shoes the next week.

Susan Willams and father, Glenn Williams, in 2002.

The pain went away but the memory has lasted all of these years and I laugh when I think what our faces must have looked like and when we told that story up until the year my grandfather died in 1988.

Every time we told it we laughed. I remember it like it was yesterday.

My father, Glenn Curtis Williams, was born in 1938, "the same year as Superman," he always reminds me. He always loved movies. When he was only ten, he would walk seventeen blocks to downtown Wilmington to see them.

In 1962, he trained to become a projectionist and began working at all three of Wilmington's drive in theaters, the Skyline, Wrightsville Road and Starway.

Dad and Mom separated a few years after I was born in 1971, and I spent every other weekend with him. There was nothing I looked forward to more because I got to go to work with him.

He would park the car outside the projection room and hook up a speaker to the car window. I had a pillow and a blanket and an endless supply of popcorn and drink. I even got to broadcast through all the speakers when the movies were over.

My favorite was Halloween at the Starway when there was an all night horror movie marathon that lasted until dawn. A cemetery was set up in front of the projection room, and Dad, dressed as Igor, Dracula's sidekick, ran around scaring people. Even with all this going on, he still took time to look after me as I waited in the car.

Word got around in school about my drive in adventures, and occasionally I'd take a friend with me. But mostly this was my time alone with my dad and I wanted to keep it that way.

After the new indoor Cinema 6 six screen theater was built in 1983, Dad became its booth manager, but he also continued to work at the drive ins until they all closed in 1985.

Dad has met many celebrities, including Stephen King (whose autograph he got for me). He was invited to DEG Studios to show a movie for Dino De Larintis. We was given the sheriff badge that Arnold Sscwarzenegger wore in *Raw Deal*. But he has other stories about people who aren't so well known.

One of my favorites is about the little girl who was afraid to watch *Godzilla*. Dad took her to the projection booth and showed her how tiny Godzilla was on the film. That act of kindness defines who my father is to me.

Dad retired in 2005 but he has plenty to keep him busy. He's begun recording his memories onto cassette tapes for his children and grandchildren, and it is so interesting we can't get enough. He is a walking time capsule of movie information. He's shown or seen just about every movie there is.

Years ago, someone nicknamed him "Movie Man." It fits him perfectly even though he's never been in a single movie.

Granny Vann's Bonnet
by
Dianne T. Roof of Burgaw

Dianne Roof, who was born in Clinton, N.C. in 1954, grew up in Wilmington. Her bright story about visiting her great grandmother has a somewhat poignant ending, and it's well worth reading. It'll make you remember, too.

I remember going to my great grandmother's house in Kitty Fork, N.C. It was an adventure every time we went. My great grandparents were Willie and Bessie Vann.

She had a hand crank in the yard to get water from, and one in the house at her sink. We would take turns, my brothers and I, trying to work the "magic" handle that made water appear. My brothers are Robert Edward and Phillip Ray Tew; my sister, Kimberly JoAnn, was a baby at the time.

Granny Vann, as we called her, also had the most comfortable feather beds and pillows.

In the wintertime when Mom and Dad, Robert Eldon and Betsy Butler Tew, and my brothers and I visited from Wilmington, I can remember the fireplace being lit in every bedroom (she had three) so as to keep off the cold.

We used the chamber pots under the bed—it was too cold to go to the outhouse.

We snuggled down into the feather bed, and my mom would pile homemade quilts on top of us. It was a good thing to use the bathroom before we got in the bed, because after climbing in bed and having layers of quilts put on you, you couldn't move.

Some time in the sixties, Granny Vann was killed in an automobile accident. She was on her way to a little store about two or three miles from her house to pick up some Tuberose snuff (I can still remember the smell). There was a tractor-trailer across the road, and Granny didn't see him until it was too late. It was very foggy that morning.

We got word of what had happened and packed up and headed for Kitty Fork. It was about a two hour drive from Wilmington.

Granny's coffin was set up in the dining room. There wasn't a funeral home nearby, and it was tradition to "sit up with the dead." Scared the heck out of me! I was only about ten or eleven years old and didn't quite like the idea.

People came from all over the county and brought food and visited and mourned. Stories were told of how she worked hard in the fields, cropping tobacco, pulling corn or picking cotton.

Granny always wore a sunbonnet like the ones they wore on "Little House on the Prairie."

Sure miss you, Granny.

Five Buttons at the Bijou
by
Douglas R. Flynn of Wilmington

Douglas Flynn was born in Wilmington in 1942, and his story strikes a definite chord for anyone who remembers the universal tradition of Saturday cowboy movies. No child of the fifties and sixties will ever forget the Saturday heroes who taught us lessons in morality and that the good guy always wins. The six-shooters were, of course, necessary props, but they somehow lacked the deadliness of the weaponry portrayed in modern films and television. Today's kids will never know what they missed. Where are you, Roy and Gene?

The good old days are well remembered

if you thoroughly enjoyed the things you did and the places you attended.

As a youngster in the mid to late fifties, I looked forward to each Saturday when I could attend the matinee at the Bijou Theater on Front Street in Wilmington.

During the summer breaks from school, I worked on Hyde Trask's flower farm at Rocky Point. I earned 35 cents per hour. Some of those days I worked 12 to 14 hours.

I saved most of my money for school clothes, but I always allotted myself enough money to see my favorite westerns on black and white film. I remember Roy Rogers, Gene Autry, Lash LaRue and Bob Steele.

Admission was nine cents, which later increased to fifteen cents. Candy bars were a nickel; sodas were ten cents and popcorn fifteen cents.

I remember the soda machine having five flavors: cherry, orange, grape, Coke, and another flavor which I can't remember. When you inserted a dime into the coin slot, a six-ounce cup dropped into a small opening in the door of the soda machine. If you depressed all five buttons at once, the machine would dispense all five flavors. I'm reasonably sure the vendor didn't intend for the machine to do that, but as youngsters, we were always trying to get most out of everything.

I can still see the freshly made popcorn flowing over the sides of the hopper and onto the bottom of the glass-encased container. The aroma was heavenly.

Once I had purchased my box of popcorn, two candy bars and my five-flavor soda, I was ready for the movie. This was the highlight of the week. I would sometimes sit through the same movie twice.

The Bijou Theater no longer stands. It has long been demolished. Each time I pass where it stood, I can still visualize what it looked like. I can almost smell the aroma of the popcorn. They just don't make popcorn like that any more.

Singing in the Swing
by
Maxine Wright of Wilmington

Maxine Wright was born in Wythe County, Virginia in 1930. She has many memories of a childhood in Virginia, about everything from spittoons to washboards...and about a romance that we believe began in Wilmington.

Outhouses: that was where you sat and looked at Sears catalogs and daydreamed. You sometimes sang a song while you waited, and sometimes even talked to yourself. Those were the good old days.

We had to run water in a big washtub and let the sun warm the water so it wouldn't freeze our hands. Then we hung the clothes on the line to dry, but they would freeze before you could get a clothespin in them.

The radio is something else. You could listen to the story and see in your head what you wanted to hear and listen and also dream along with them.

The old wind-up record players sure sounded funny when they ran down. It kept you hopping up and down to keep them going.

On Saturday night we put the big washtub in the kitchen floor with warm water, and we got our weekly bath. The rest of the week we just had what was called a bird bath.

I remember the old spittoons. My grandma kept one behind the heat stove in the living room. She dipped snuff and her lip stood out all the time.

Flypaper hung to keep the flies out of the food. I still have it hung up in my carport. I also still have a wind-up clock and it is dependable.

We all would sit on the back porch using an empty corncob to shuck corn to keep from rubbing our hands raw. This corn we fed to the chickens.

The Dick and Jane book was the first book we learned to read fifty years ago.

My aunt whom I lived with had a feather bed. I had to make that bed up every morning before I went to school. It had to be perfect. I hated that bed.

When I was eight years old the old man who lived down the street came and paid me a quarter to make him homemade biscuits.

We had playtime on Saturday and we would play like we were at the store. We took leaves off a tree. The little ones were five cents. As the money got bigger, so did the leaves. On Sunday, we went to Sunday school and church.

In our spare time, we had to cut wood for the cook stove, cut grass, carry in water and carry out dirty water. We had no running water in the house. We washed clothes on a washboard until our fingers bled. There was no sink and we washed dishes in a dishpan, dried them and put them up. We swept the floor three times a day. We worked in the yard and in the garden. It would have been nice if we could have used leaves off the trees for money like when we were kids.

The home place was nice with the morning glories, snowball bushes and sweetbud trees. That was home.

I used to love to go to Grandma's. She had a warming closet and you could get a jelly biscuit with butter any time and boy, was it good. After school I could come to Grandma's and go out to the apple orchard and get any kind of apple, take it to the front porch and eat it in the swing. Then I would sing.

I always got my sister's clothes but I couldn't wear her shoes. So on Easter I would get a new pair, and they had to be taken care of. I wouldn't get any more for a year. We didn't have a lot of money.

I didn't care for those dirt roads, but I have lived on one for 49 years. Cars fly up and down them and send dirt flying everywhere.

Grandma had a woodshed and I loved playing in it. It had an upstairs and a lot of old stuff, but it was fun. We didn't have anyone to play with, just my sister, brother and me. I was the middle one. Now, at 76, I'm the only one living out of my family.

Kids nowadays don't know how to plan and have fun. They got much more. It was fun when we had to do the best we could with what we had.

' I went on a trip to visit my aunt. I was only supposed to stay a week. I met this handsome guy and we started to date. I told him I had to go home, and he said if I did he would come and get me. So I said, "If you want me to stay I will." I did and when I went home a year later I was married and had a baby boy. That was 52 years ago.

God bless us each and every one.

The Hobo's Letter
by
Rosie Fisher Boyd of Supply

Rosie Boyd has provided us with a delightfully entertaining tale of the good old days, complete with a child's eye view of the Maco Light, skinny dipping and a touch of romance. You'll read about big brother psychology and places like Hood Creek and Rattlesnake Branch. But the visit from the mysterious hobo in the early 1940s stands out as something special. You'll like this one..

I was born at Southport on October 25, 1932. My father, Sullivan B. Fisher, worked at Baldhead Lighthouse. He was also at the CCC camp later at Lillington, N.C. My mother was Mary L. Fisher.

We moved to Aberdeen, N.C. when I was

18 months old. In 1936 my father bought a house and ten acres of land at Maco, N.C. We were all happy to finally have our very own home. It was the first house that really belonged to us.

When we arrived at Maco, we stopped at Newman and Marie Willetts' gas station. When we went inside, I saw this beautiful baby girl, Patsy Willetts, sitting on the counter. Well, to me that was love at first sight. We later became playmates and good friends. Her sister, Glenda (Tink) was born during 1939, another great friend and playmate and we have always remained friends.

As we were leaving the store, I really needed a drink of water, so Mr. Willetts brought me some water in an old tin can. In later years after I grew up, I reminded him of the water he had given me that day in the old can. He laughed and said, "That was no tin can. It was Pasty's chamber."

We had some good times living in Maco and some bad times, also. I seem only to remember the good ones. We had no electricity, televisions, computers, washing machines, etc. Those things were unheard of.

Sullivan and Mary Fisher in the 1950s.

There weren't too many cars around, either, so if you wanted to go anywhere, you either walked or hitchhiked. Sometimes people hitching would stop at our house for a cool drink of water from the old pump on the hill. We didn't have a lot of food, only what came out of our garden, but Mama always gave them food before they went on their way.

One night while my dad was away at the CCC camp, a hobo knocked at our door. He said he just hopped off a train and he was very hungry and tired. The old fellow did look kinda down and out. My mama was a very trusting soul, so she invited him inside and served him some beans, cornbread and some coffee, which was rare to have. We hardly ever had coffee as money was low and you also had to have ration stamps to buy coffee back then as there was a war going on. (My two older brothers, Edward and Samuel, had enlisted in the Army around 1940.)

Well, that hobo's name was James Henry Fox. He informed us that he was no bum, just a poor hobo down on his luck. He stayed with us a week or more and was very helpful. He cut wood for us, worked in the garden and did other things to help us out. Other people in the neighborhood hired him to work for

Sullivan B. Fisher.

Rosie Fisher in about 1958.

them.

After he left, my brother James and I really missed him. He would tuck us in bed at night and tell us hobo stories. He returned a year later for a visit, and later, my mother received a letter from him. I still have the letter he wrote. "I'll see you when the roses bloom again," it read. We never saw or heard from him again. I often wonder whatever happened to that old hobo.

You would have thought Maco a mighty lonesome place back in the 40s, but my brother James and I kept busy. James was two years older than I, so I let him think he was the boss. When we listened to the battery operated radio, I would want to listen to the Lone Ranger, knowing that was what James liked, but I knew if he thought I wanted the Lone Ranger, he would listen to The Shadow, so I always begged to listen to The Shadow. It worked every time.

But when we played Tarzan he was firm that he was Tarzan. Me? I was Cheeta. What happened to Jane?

All of us kids had a great swimming hole, Hood Creek, where we would meet to go swimming. The boys would go skinny dipping and would run and hide when we girls came. We would keep our clothes on, no matter how hard the boys begged us to take them off.

Mama had an old friend who lived a ways up the road named Wennie Pastal. Wennie had a granddaughter named Dorthy. Now, James and I dearly loved Dorthy. She was a great playmate.

We enjoyed going to visit Wennie. She would say, "Come on in, children, beans and bread are on the stove." After eating, we would all go into the living room and bang on the piano. That was beautiful music. Before we left, we would go into her garden and she would send Mama collards. She also had a beautiful flower garden. I think that was why she and Mama were such good friends. They were both big into flowers. I still find some flowers around the old homeplace that Mama sat out all those many years ago.

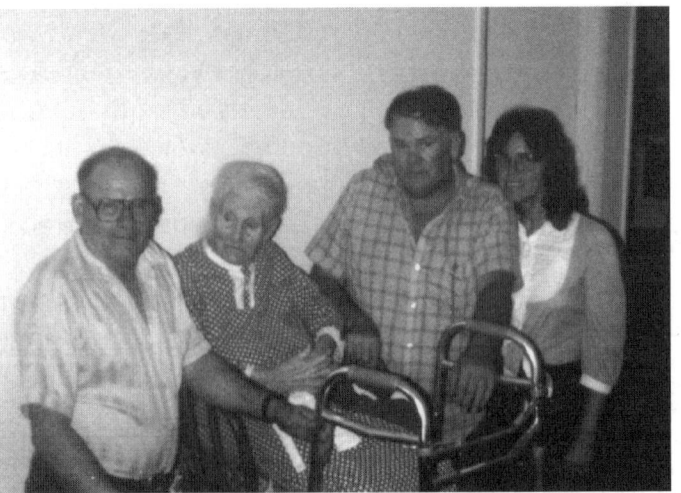
Sam, Mary and James Fisher and Rosie Boyd in 1984.

After leaving Wennie's house we would stop by and see the Costin boys and play a while with them. Later, they would walk partways home with us and we would stop by Rattlesnake Branch for a swim. Still on down the road we would visit the Malpas home and play games with the boys, Wade, George and Lynwood. I forgot just how many children the family had. The baby was Baby Girl Frances. (I recently saw Wade Malpas again, but he really has changed—he looks about as old as myself!)

Well, after leaving the Malpas place we had to hurry home before it got dark. We had work to do. First, we had to cut up lots of wood and take it into the kitchen for the cook stove, and also wood for the fireplace, then rake the yards and burn leaves. Then it was my job to go to the pump and bring water back in the bucket and pitchers to use for supper and breakfast the next morning. Plus, I had to fill up the big bathtub in the yard so that the morning sun would warm it up for me and James to take a bath. That night we just passed around the old basin and washed our feet.

After dark, James and I would go outside and catch fireflies to have during the night for light, as Mama always blew out the lamps at ten o'clock.

The next morning, off to the woods to play.

Rosie Boyd.

Michael Boyd, Rosie's husband.

We would make horses out of sticks, ride down to the creek to our saloon, have a few drinks with Bob Steele, Gene Autry and maybe Roy if he was there. Then over to the railroad to wave at the conductor as the train sped by going to places we wished we could go to.

Sometimes at night, if we were feeling brave, we would sneak out the back door, run through the woods past the old graveyard, and go to the railroad tracks to watch Baldwin's light flash down the tracks and listen to the young men and women up at the crossroads scream with fright at the light. I really think it was just a courting place for them, though. I had my first date there when I was thirteen years old. The boy was Joe Mintz. He leaned over for a kiss and I jumped out of the car and ran all the way home. Needless to say, that was my last date with Mr. Mintz. I wonder whatever happened to him, anyway?

Well, those were the good old days. I will never forget them, and all the fun and friends way back when.

The Things in the Net
by
Ruby Klutz Splawn-Beavers of Wilmington

If you want to see history at its liveliest, you need to read this story. It's one of the most enjoyable accounts of change in a specific location that we've ever had the pleasure of publishing. Without even having to mention that change, Ruby Splawn-Beavers, born 1925 in Rowan County, brings it to life.

My earliest recollection of coming to Carolina Beach from Rowan County where I was born is forever fixed in my mind.

I don't recall the date of the trip because I was very young. (I was born in April 1925.) When we got to the Lumberton/Pembroke area, the Lumber River had overflowed. My dad, Arthur Klutz, got out of the truck and walked ahead to look out the road. My older brother drove until we passed over the flood. To me as a little child, it was very frightening.

When we arrived at Wilmington, we crossed the Cape Fear River on a ferry that landed at the foot of Market Street.

We moved to Carolina Beach in 1930. There were not many jobs during that depression, and my dad fished for a living.

I loved going fishing with him at night to catch flounder. I, of course, always went to sleep in the bow of the little boat, but my dad didn't seem to mind.

He used a net much of his day fishing and I have helped pull the net in and helped pick the fish up off the beach. It was exciting to see the things that came in the net.

We had no truck at the time, so Dad had to remove the backseat out of an old car and haul the fish to Hampstead where there was a fish market.

There were not many children of school age south of the turn bridge over Snow's Cut. At first a Mr. Davis drove the school bus and later, his sons took turns driving.

We of elementary grades through sixth grade went to a three-room schoolhouse in Myrtle Grove. After sixth, we went to Winter Park School for seventh and eighth grades. New Hanover High School was the only high school in the county at that time.

I remember a "northeaster," my dad called it. Now, I know it was a hurricane. It was very frightening to my parents as well as to all us children. That was some time in the 30s.

I remember the huge pavilion that stood in the middle of the boardwalk. It had a bathhouse underneath and a playground in front—not far from the ocean—where I fell from a swing and broke my arm when I was six.

The pavilion served as a dance hall on Saturday night and church on Sunday. I remember being in a Christmas pageant and singing "Away in a Manger" solo.

Later, my grandfather helped build the first church on Carolina Beach that I recall. It was interdenominational and is still open and active at 4th and Cape Fear Boulevard. The name was Community Church but has changed now to Hope Memorial. The Catholics held Mass early and the Protestants came in later to hold their services.

Before that church was built, my grandmother would walk with us kids to a Methodist church that was located near the Cape Fear River. The graveyard is still there and my great grandparents, my parents, brothers and a baby of mine are all buried there.

In the summertime, a Mrs. Osbourne held Sunday School in her house at the corner of Cape Fear Boulevard and Lake Park Boulevard. The house is still there. It is the Cottage Restaurant now.

My great grandparents lived on Cape Fear Boulevard. I remember cutting tender grass from a ditch in front of their house to feed her rabbits that she raised for food. They operated a boarding house and I helped iron linens for my Great Grandma Ludwig.

We had been at Carolina Beach for a little while when my maternal grandparents moved there, too. They were the W. H. Earnhardts. The Earnhardts built a two story house at the corner of Cape Fear Boulevard and 3rd Street. They also operated a boarding house and I loved to help Grandma Earnhardt wash dishes (but I hated the chore at home).

My grandfather owned several cottages in a strip between Cape Fear Boulevard and Hamlet Avenue. We moved into one of the cottages on Hamlet.

The Ludwigs and Earnhardts lived adjacent to each other, for my grandmother was one of the Ludwig's daughters. They had six daughters, Mrs. Mandy Bame, Mrs. Mattie Fisher, Mrs. Edith Sahley, Mrs. Beulah Davis, Mrs. Amy Foster and my grandmother, Lizzie Earnhardt.

I remember the Graystone Inn that was beside a canal that ran through the middle of the town from what is now the yacht basin to the lake. It [probably the canal] has since been covered over.

The Graystone Inn had a dance hall on the roof and often had live bands. I used to watch the ladies in their long evening gowns go with their escorts to the dances. I could hear the music and I dreamed of being grownup and dressing real fine and going to dance the night away.

My dad took us often to Fort Fisher where we played among the trees on a great mound that has since washed away. There was a snack store beyond that mound near the ocean. It was run by a man named Walter Winner.

The Winner name is, and has been, prominent in Carolina Beach as long as I can recall. I remember seeing Mr. and Mrs. Winner at their place of business on the boardwalk. They were the parents of Carl Winner. Carl's son has the Winner Queen and other boats nowadays.

I liked going to Fort Fisher. We found many cannonballs and other artifacts that we did not cherish because we were young. My dad would buy me a coconut cookie and an Orange Crush in the dark bottle. I can almost taste it right now.

There were rides—Ferris wheel, merry-go-round, tilt-a-wheel, etc.—that came to the beach each summer and left after Labor Day. I don't know where they went. Mr. Mansfield had some of those rides. Perhaps they went to fairs, etc.

My oldest brother, Earl, worked for a man named Sam Wright in a shooting gallery at the beach, and after the summer was over they traveled all around to fairs and such. He did that for one or two years.

After the fire, they used to have street dances with live bands and everyone turned out for that.

During the 30s, the beach, Bames Hotel and cottages all were filled during the summer. Every 4th of July was the epitome of business, for the textile companies gave holidays or vacations at that time. Sleeping space was scarce. I remember my mom renting our beds for those few days, and we slept on the floor. We didn't mind, and it meant a little income for my family.

My first job, other than babysitting, was in a souvenir and beachwear shop owned and operated by Ed and Pearl Winner Register. I was a very young teen, but enjoyed meeting people and earning money for school clothes.

The Source of Milk
by
Glenn Williams of Castle Hayne

The title we gave this story will come clear as you read. And we suggest you read it to the end. You'll find as much entertainment here as in your favorite TV program. Glenn

Williams, who was born in 1938 in Duplin County but raised in New Hanover County, recounts some of the most unusual adventures you've ever heard, including an extraterrestrial alien scare and a suspected mad dog.

Rejected for the first grade. The events in this story took place during World War II. In those days, there was a woman who came to people's houses and asked questions of children who were to start the first grade.

Well, I was short for my age of five-and-a-half years, so this lady started asking things like, "Where does the newspaper come from?" I said, "From the newsboy." She said, "Very good." Then she said, "Where does the mail come from?" I said, "From the mailman." She seemed to be very happy with me at this point. I felt like I was on a roll.

Then she threw me a bombshell. She said, "Where does milk come from?" Of course I said, "From the milkman."

I guess I must have said something wrong, because she slammed her books shut and said, "Mrs. Williams, he's not ready for the first grade yet." I said, "What did I do? What did I say?" The lady said, "I'll see you again next year little man."

I could tell my mother was very embarrassed. I asked the lady what the right answer was and she said that milk comes from cows. I said, "What did you expect? I'm a city boy, not a farm boy."

So I was seven years old before I got to the first grade.

A while back I asked my four young grandchildren this same question, and wouldn't you know, they all had the right answer. Now I'm the one who's embarrassed.

The alien mystery. It was around the late 1980s and my brother Leonard had come down for a visit from South Carolina. It was just me and him home at the time; my wife Allie was at work.

I don't know what brought the subject up. It may have been a show on TV, but we started talking about aliens. Leonard and I had always been honest with each other. We would talk about old girlfriends and country music. But this night, my brother seemed to be afraid to talk about aliens. He was in the U.S. Air Force for about 30 years and he seemed to have some knowledge about aliens.

I understand that the Air Force men around the Area 51 at Roswell, New Mexico knew what took place at the crash site. I've seen TV shows that indicated that these men were threatened to keep quiet about what happened. Some of the men were even threatened with death, or something could happen to their families.

My brother seemed to know a lot, but he wasn't talking about it. But he did say he knew some things, and that if he told what he knew he could be fined ten thousand dollars and other things could happen to him.

I told him, "Come on now, I'm your brother and nobody else is here but us." I told him I would not ever say anything about our talk, not even to my wife Allie. But he still wouldn't tell me anything at all.

Now, I knew my brother had been nowhere near Roswell. That is as far as I knew.

By this time he was very uneasy, so I started guessing. I said, "I bet there are spaceships around earth, and they let us live here until they want us for something." I kept talking about different things, and when I got through, he was white as a ghost. He looked at me and said, "You are close. Very close."

I don't remember half the things I said, so I tried to pin him down. But he still wouldn't tell me what part of my talk hit a nerve with him.

For a long time after our talk, I could not remember a lot of the things we talked about. Maybe the aliens messed with my mind and wanted me to forget all about it. I'm still mad at my brother for not telling me about what he knew. Maybe someday I will figure it all out, but if I do, I may be too afraid to tell what I know, just like my brother.

The thirsty mule. Around 1946, when I was around seven or eight, my Uncle Woodrow somehow talked my father and mother into moving to a place called Harels Store, which was not too far from Wallace, N.C. My father had a real neat bicycle with a motor on it. My uncle also talked my father into trading the bike for an old mule so they could do some farm work.

Glenn Williams and his wife, Allie, in 2002.

We also had a cow, so I got to see first hand where milk came from.

My father told me not to mess with the mule. This is something you do not tell a young wannabe cowboy. All I could see was Gene Autry and Roy Rogers on their horses, singing and riding down the canyon. So one day when my father and uncle were out in the fields, I took the mule to our house. The house had a tall porch so I used the porch to jump on the mule's back.

I thought I was headed down some happy trails, but it so happened that there was a deep, old-timey well in the front yard. The mule must have been thirsty, 'cause he went straight to the well. I thought to myself, okay, let him have a drink. And then we'll be on our way.

Well, as you probably know, a well is real deep, so when the mule put his head down to drink I started to slip down toward his neck. I didn't have a saddle. I kept trying to bring his head up, but he kept trying to get water. And I just kept slipping down his neck. I was afraid I was going to fall over his head and into the well.

To this day, I don't know why I didn't just jump off the mule. Maybe I was afraid he would take off and run away. As you might guess, I had no choice but to yell for my mother—which I really didn't want to do because I didn't want her to know I had let the mule out. So I started yelling for help.

Well, my mother came out of the house and pulled the mule next to the porch so I could get off. Of course she told my father what had happened and I got a whipping that night. But in a way I was glad to get the whipping. It was a lot better than being at the bottom of a well.

The mad dog. Another story I remember from Harels Store is when I was real sick with the flu. One night about eight o'clock it was time for my favorite radio show, *Inner Sanctum*. We had never heard of TV in those days. The show always opened with the sound of a real spooky squeaking door, and closed with that sound. The sound was sometimes more scary than the show was.

On this night I was running a high fever, so I had my mother hold my hand as we listened to the show. In the meantime, my father and uncle were walking about a mile to a little country store to get me some bubble gum. We lived way out in the woods and it was a long walk for them.

Well, the next day I still had a high fever. My mother brought my brother Leonard's little bulldog in my room and told me to watch her while she did the laundry out in the front yard in a big black kettle. For some reason, Queenie, the bulldog, started running around my bed, barking and acting all crazy. I stood up on the bed and tried to reach the bedroom door which my mother had shut. Every time I tried to get to the door, Queenie would chase me back to the bed.

So here I was, standing on the bed, when I notice Queenie had something white around her mouth. By this time I was really scared, because I always heard that if a dog had a white mouth it may have rabies, and that you could get lockjaw if the dog bites you.

Along with my high fever, I thought that dog was going to kill me for sure. I started yelling for my mother as loud as I could yell. Thank goodness she finally heard me. When she came into the room, I said, "Mommy, look out! Queenie's foaming at the mouth with rabies!"

My mother started laughing and I thought to myself, What's so funny about this? Then Mom said, "She doesn't have rabies. I gave her some milk a while ago and she still has some on her mouth."

Boy, was I relieved!

There's a moral to this story: Be kind to your dog because someday they may find a way to get even with you.

Skipping school on a Saturday. Now, don't get me wrong: school is okay, but once in a while I felt like I needed a break. We lived at Nessbitt Courts in 1950 and I was twelve years old at the time. I was in the sixth grade at William Hooper School.

My mother always made me a breakfast of grits and eggs and bacon, which I loved and always ate without fail. But if I wanted to skip school, I would sit at the table with my head in my hands and make like I was real sick. My mother knew I must really be sick if I didn't eat. I kept saying, "Mom, I don't feel like going to school today." So after a bit of playacting on my part, she said okay. But she sent me to my room and told me not to come out all day. That was fine with me as long as I didn't have to go to school.

I was thinking that after school was out that day I would be feeling a lot better and that I would go out to play with my friends. But it was not that easy.

About an hour after she sent me to my room, my mother came in to see how I was feeling. She said, "You know today is Saturday, don't you?" I said, "No Ma'am, I did not know that." But I thought to myself, if she knew that, why didn't she say something while I was doing my award-winning playacting?

So I told her I was feeling a lot better. I said, "It's amazing how an hour of rest can perk you up." I also told her I was hungry as a bear, but she said I should wait and save it for dinner. Then I said, "Well, later on I'll go over to my friend's house. That way I'll be out of your hair for a while and give you some peace and quiet." But she said I was not going anywhere that day, or the next day, which was Sunday. She said that I looked like I was real sick that morning, and that she was going to doctor me up all weekend to make sure I would feel like going to school on Monday. And I was put to bed and given all kinds of cold medicines that I really didn't need.

So my little act to skip school sure did backfire on me. I always wonder to this day if my mother knew all along that it was a Saturday.

The moral of this story is if you're going to skip school, be sure it's a school day.

The Green Hornet and Feather Beds
by
Adelaide Scales Ward of Wilmington

In these days of government welfare, it's hard to visualize the tragedy of the Great Depression. And with all our conveniences—cell phones, microwave ovens, super highways, computers—it's hard to imagine the simplicity of life as it once was. Was it better or worse? Before you decide, read this delightful story from Adelaide

Ward, who penned on her handwritten letter, "I don't do computers." Way to go, Adelaide! We understand completely.

I was born in Albemarle, N.C. on February 3, 1924. The Depression descended on this nation and my father lost everything—his money, job and health. We moved to Monroe where my mother's family, the Fairleys, lived, and where we stayed for several years. When I was about five years old, we moved to Raleigh.

I was about nine years old when we moved from one house on Fairview Road to a house on Vance Street. My uncle, Frank Fairley, came to help us move.

We had a lot of snow in those days and I had left my sled at the old house. So my uncle took me to get it. We hooked it up to the back of his Model T and drove a good mile or so. The sled was made of slats and it had snowed the night before and the roads were melted slush. I kept yelling for him to stop and he thought I was having fun! We finally arrived at our new home and I was frozen. I went to the steam radiator to thaw out. My family thought it was funny but I didn't!

I remember the great programs on the radio: the Green Hornet…the Lone Ranger.

And riding and eating on the train was such fun. Too bad we don't have them today.

And feather beds. They were wonderful! You sunk into them, and since we didn't have central heat, boy, were you warm!

We walked to school and rode the bus downtown for a nickel. Even after we moved to Wilmington—I was fourteen years old—we went to the movies for ten cents.

When I was sixteen, I had a part time job for $8.00 a week. I was rich!

I remember when I was going to New Hanover High School, one year the Cape Fear River overflowed. We had water behind the school. Miss Hester Struthers, who taught geometry, had to get across the street in a boat.

The high school had the ROTC in those days. Many of the boys from the senior class went to World War II, and too many did not come home.

They used the building at 2nd and Orange as the USO. My mother used to go and play the piano for the boys.

We had a ration card and I still have it. Sugar, gas, meat—no silver—that was used to make bullets.

I remember Wilmington's trolley on Park Avenue to the beach. It was great when I moved here at age 14. That was the last year the trolley ran—1938. Too bad. It was huge and fun.

I met my husband in high school and we married in 1942 and had three wonderful children. We were very active in civic affairs and in our church. He was a president of the Azalea Festival as was also our son. My husband died in 1999.

Oscar's Money and the Pencil Sharpener
by
Lyman M. Taylor of Ocean Isle Beach

Mr. Taylor was born in 1924 and grew up in Wilmington. We're sure the Wilmington of today scarcely resembles the Wilmington of his childhood, but that early Wilmington is vividly revealed between the lines of his story. This story, however, is not so much about the city as it is about friendship, as you shall see.

I remember an occasion when my friend, Oscar Sewell, met me on Front Street between Dock and Market Streets. He invited me to Tom's Drug Store at the corner of Front and Market Streets, facing Market, for a soda and Nabs (crackers). He finished before I did and suddenly arose from his seat and said he had to go. He left me sitting there with no money, embarrassed, and having to sneak out of the store.

At the time I might have been all of ten years old. The drink may have been a dime and the package of Nabs a nickel. But I had no money.

I recently drove down Front Street, and lo and behold, Tom's Drug Store was still there.

One good turn deserves another. The years passed and I left New Hanover High in 1942 During World War II, got married, worked at N.C. Shipbuilding and joined the Navy. After boot camp and school, I was at the Brooklyn Navy Yard. I was at the Square in downtown New York, when of all people I met Oscar Sewell. I was again without money as my Navy records hadn't yet caught up with me. Oscar, who had just returned from the Guadalcanal battle in the South Pacific, and who had just been paid, asked me if I had any money. "No," I replied. He gave me $20.00.

After the war, I went back and finished high school at New Hanover High and went to work with my brother at Yellow Front Grocery on Fourth Street in Brooklyn. I received a call from guess who? It was Oscar. He was broke and needed money to get to his brother's home in California. I happily responded with $30.00 and Oscar was on his way. I later learned that Oscar joined the Merchant Marine where he captained his own ship.

When I was still a child, my dad, James Luther Taylor, operated a store called Taylor's Market two blocks down the street at 124 South Front Street, between the front gate of the old City Market and the Fish Market, which ran perpendicular to Water Street. The old St. Helena Restaurant was just a few doors down the street and the A&P Store was located on the southwest corner of Dock Street, cattycorner from Beaudabush Flower Shop.

Two or three years before that, when my dad's store was located on the south side of Dock, between Frond and 2nd Streets, I needed my pencil sharpened. I knew that Saleby's Wholesale Produce office across the street had a pencil sharpener. I crossed the street to the office and asked permission to sharpen my pencil. I was told to help myself. When I finished, Mr. Saleby said to me, "Thank you," and I said, "You're welcome." They all laughed at an embarrassed little boy. I'll be eighty-three on the fifth of February, and I'll never forget.

At that time, you must remember, the north bridge on the river had been finished. We paid 35 cents toll fee per car and they were still using the ferry crossing at the foot of Market.

Don't know if it's true or not, but I was told at the time that the reason we had so many brick streets downtown along the waterfront was because a city official had made a terrible mistake in ordering the bricks for the city. He had added too many zeroes to the order.

An Enviable Childhood
by
Anita Jezewski of Castle Hayne

When you read this story, you'll understand its title. Anita (short for Juanita) Jezewski, born in 1939, has marvelously succeeded in painting a picture in words of a childhood—and particularly of a father— that that will keep you reading to the end.

I was about eight years old when my father, Louis J. Bernasconi, opened a grocery store at Wrightsville Beach. The name of the store was Bernie's Frozen Foods which was kind of misleading because he had groceries, fresh vegetables and fruits, and quite a variety of deli products. Realizing this, he changed the name to Bernie's Curb Market. (Bernie was short for Bernasconi, and much easier to pronounce.) The year was 1947.

Daddy would get up at an ungodly—though necessary—hour to get to the Farmer's Market and make the best selections he could of the available fruits and vegetables—by the bushel. He had competition from one other grocery, though not a chain.

Juanita Jezewski and Jimmy in 1941.

Dad's business took off once folks found that he had the freshest produce of the season. When any of the vegetables began to look old or no longer as fresh as they should be, he would bring them home and put them to good use. They were never wasted.

His talent in the food business was only one of many. He loved the business he was in, but there was something he loved more: cooking. He was a wonderful cook. He planned to open a restaurant as soon as his store's profits allowed him to.

He would work all day in the store, and come home and cook supper. Mom helped as did we all with daily chores, but at night, Dad was the chief cook, and what wonderful suppers he concocted.

His talents also extended to growing vegetables for canning. Of course my siblings and I helped with the garden which was quite large. The size alone was daunting—a bit more than a quarter acre—especially when we kids had to do a lot of weeding and harvesting.

Daddy's business continued to be successful and before long, he had a very large customer base.

I remember asking him if I could go with him when he went to the market and he said, "Sure, but you've got to get up with the chickens." Yeah, we had some of those, too, and they got up very early. Mama would wake me at 3:45 AM and we would get to the market about 4:30 AM. Daddy would walk around, carefully look over the produce, pick it up, smell it, feel it, and then decide on what to buy.

After loading what looked to me to be tons of bushel baskets of produce on his truck, we would go to a nearby diner where he would have some coffee and doughnuts. I had the same except with milk. For me, this was a wonderful adventure.

After we left the diner, Daddy would go to Water Street where there were other types of foods for sale. This is where he bought his frozen foods. After that, we would go to the A & P on Third Street near Red Cross and he would purchase a few things there. Then it was on to the store with his purchases.

Some of the produce he bought needed

Jimmy, Joy and Juanita Jezewski in 1946 or 47.

more handling, such as butterbeans. Daddy advertised his store in the *Wrightsville Beach Newsletter*, specifying "Fancy Produce," some of which translated into shelled butterbeans. The beans sold better shelled, so Daddy hired a couple of ladies who lived nearby to help, as did we kids and Mom. We shelled beans, and shelled beans, and then shelled even more beans.

As time went on, Daddy discovered that his customers also loved de-veined and de-headed shrimp. You guessed it: three large wash tubs, one for the shrimp, the other for the cleaned-up version and the last for the final rinsing, and finally packaging in containers to contain the finished product. We were amateurs to start, with both the beans and shrimp, but became very professional, even as kids.

There was another item customers loved: homemade sausage, the Italian kind. Daddy was born in Rome, Italy and was no stranger to Italian sausage. Dad had a grinder already, so he got that out along with the ingredients and the skins for stuffing and proceeded to make what he knew would sell. When the packaging was done, we had the fun of clearing, cleaning and drying.

As a reward, if the evening was still early enough, he and Mom would tell us what a good job we did tidying up the kitchen and announce we were going to the drive-in movie theater on Olerander Drive. That was one of the best treats of all because we were never told in advance. Of course we didn't know it then, but we were being taught that the rewards of good work instill a sense of pride that goes a long way in becoming responsible adults.

Time and good business traits proved to be very profitable in many ways. Daddy's business continued to grow. He had invested in the truck he needed for the store, but wanted to have a car for other occasions. Daddy always hated to owe anyone, so he tried his best not to. Mom and Dad had been married only three years when they moved from Gaffney, South Carolina to Wilmington. Mom told me that they looked around for a while and decided on a house with 14 acres of land about 10 miles from the city. I'm not sure, but I think Daddy paid more than half in cash and the rest in a small mortgage. I remember Mom telling me that the only thing Daddy didn't pay for in total was the store. He borrowed $2,000.00 from a friend to get the business going.

I spent many hours in Dad's store just having fun, especially in the summer. We were allowed to walk down to the ocean (about a block away) and enjoy the water. There was always a lifeguard at the beach and we never went in too far. Part of the time I just enjoyed being at the store, watching the customers, and learning how to ring

Juanita's dad in front of his store, Bernie's Curb Market, in 1947.

Joy, Juanita and Jimmy in 1948 posing in "new" school clothes.

up money on the cash register.

Daddy had a few Italian buddies who came by occasionally and they would speak in Italian. I didn't think about it then, but have always wished we had learned the language as kids. Dad never spoke it at home.

One of the things he did, though not on purpose, amazed some of his customers, especially new ones. He never used his adding machine unless it was requested. He took the customer's groceries (including the produce, deli products, and meats) and one by one, summed up everything in his head, then told them the total. Once his customers became accustomed to his methods, they didn't question the amount but new folks wanted an adding machine tape. The tape always matched the amount he stated, including any tax.

Jimmy, Juanita and Joy in 1945.

Daddy only had a sixth grade education but was brilliant. He designed and built furniture from scratch. He wrote articles for *The Gaffney Ledger* and also for *The New York Times* when he lived in Manhattan. As he stated in an article in the *Ledger*, he had 24 years of experience in planning, altering, remodeling, and manufacturing furniture, fixtures, cabinets, etc. He planned to build our family a new home once he could afford the materials. He drew up the architectural designs himself. The home he designed would have been a round house. Our father died way before he could realize his dreams. Had he been able to build the home, it would have had at least four bedrooms and two and a half baths to accommodate our large family of eight.

Juanita Jezewski in 2002.

Growing up in a large family was a wonderful experience. I can't even imagine any kid being happier than I was. We always had food, warmth, clothes and companionship. We had no television until the 50s, just a radio, but we never lacked for ways to have fun. When we came home from school, we were allowed to have some milk and cookies, go out and play for an hour or so, then do our homework. Then it was time to wash up and help get the table set for dinner. We went to bed early on school nights but on weekends, after our chores, we could go out and play. We got to stay up later which was a special treat to us.

Our playtime usually involved creations of some kind. I remember my brother Jimmy, my sister Joy and I using Daddy's empty bushel baskets and making a playhouse. We had sides, a door and a roof. Inside, we stacked empty square wood crates for furniture and borrowed (without her permission) some of Mom's blue plate china and a few utensils.

When it rained and we couldn't go outside, we would look at catalogs, color, play Old Maid cards or War or just listen to the radio. When the rain stopped, we would go out without our shoes and wade in the ditches which were full of cool water.

Those times were rich with fun and excitement. In fact, I never knew we weren't rich (by society's standards) until later in life. I still don't equate being rich with having money. I know money is needed in order to have a comfortable life, but I have never believed that money can buy happiness.

There could be no way to buy the kind of childhood I had. Though my parents, my older brother Jimmy, and my younger sister Joy are now gone, their memories go on and sustain me in times of sadness.

My parents were wonderful people who worked hard all of their lives. Daddy's store was a marvelous part of growing up. I know one day, God be willing, I'll see my loved ones again. Daddy is probably having a wonderful time in heaven designing furniture and creating sumptuous food to put on Mom's blue plate china.

When I close my eyes, I can recall the wonderful memories of my childhood, sometimes with smiles, and occasionally with tears, and always with thankfulness that I was lucky enough to be born into such an exceptional family.

Mister I Got 'Em
by
Betty Allen Sanders of Hampstead

Betty Sanders was born and grew up in Wilmington. Her date of birth is January 22, 1925. With just a few brief words, she paints a beautiful picture of the past, conjuring up memories far beyond the few she mentions in her story.

Today is my eighty-second birthday.

I remember being seven years old on Ninth Street (between Market and Princess). I remember Old Man Nebetnego coming down the street in his cart pulled by one horse. He sang out, "I got `em! Collard greens, sweet potatoes, turnip greens and rutabagas!" If it was summer, he sang out, "I got `em! Green beans, okra, tomatoes, corn and cucumbers!"

All the children ran after him, calling him "Mr. I got `em," or "Old Man Nebetnego."

There were no automobiles on the street that I remember.

This was 1932. We were visiting our grandparents, who had a wonderful big two story house which they lost in the Depression. When they built this house, Fourteenth Street was the edge of town.

My grandfather, C. F. Willliams, also lost his men's clothing store on Front Street, between Market and Dock Street. He kept his sense of humor and never gave up.

These are my special memories about my wonderful childhood in Wilmington.

The Forecaster
by
Cindy Morrison of Wilmington

Cindy Morrison didn't reveal much of her own history, but her story definitely paints a picture of the Wilmington region during a forgotten era. We're very glad she listened to her husband's grandmother's tales.

My husband's grandmother was Winifred Shepard Morrison. She was born in Wilmington, North Carolina on December 13, 1898. She lived to be 98 and a half years old. She loved to share her memories of Wilmington and also Wrightsville Beach.

Her father was a pharmacist in downtown Wilmington and the family home was located on the corner of 2nd and Nun Streets. On Saturday mornings when Winifred was a child, her father would hitch up the horse and buggy and spend all day delivering medicine to the residents along old Shell Road (which is now Wrightsville Avenue). The road was made out of crushed oyster shell and three tollbooths were set up all along the road. It would take the entire day to travel from 2nd Street to the end of Shell Road and back.

Winifred's father purchased a "beach shack" as she referred to it, or a cottage on Wrightsville Beach around the year 1915. Each summer thereafter, the family would pack up all of their belongings and make the trip to the beach on the trolley car. Her mother would order a 100-pound block of ice to be delivered on the trolley car from Wilmington to Wrightsville Beach. By the time the ice was delivered, it only weighed 50 pounds, having melted in the heat during the trip over. The housekeeper and her young son would go outside with a large metal pan on top of a pull-cart. They would chip the ice into chunks to be placed into the icebox in the kitchen. The children would chase the ice truck in the hopes of getting a small chunk of ice for themselves to cool off on a hot summer day.

It wasn't easy to predict the weather (especially a hurricane) at Wrightsville Beach in the early 1900s. A local resident took it upon himself to be the "Weatherman." When the sky looked threatening and the ocean looked menacing, he would run through each residents' yard yelling, "Storm's a coming!" The residents soon learned to listen to his predictions because he normally was correct. Of course it was not an easy undertaking to pack up your belongings, get on the trolley car and get off the beach in time to beat the storm.

Remembering the Duck Biscuits
by
Margaret Ann Mitchell Faison of Wilmington

Margaret Ann Mitchell Faison was born in Wilmington in 1944 and grew up on the family homestead on Carolina Beach Road. Her story involves a topic very familiar to us old-timers, and it's guaranteed to evoke pleasant memories.

Oh, how I wish I had a few of my mother's biscuits!

During my childhood, my mother, Mary Ann Mitchell, made the best biscuits from scratch. Mother was an excellent cook and she passed on without my getting many of her delicious recipe dishes.

I particularly remember her natural skill of making delicious biscuits from scratch. She used Red Band flour, lard from a cardboard container, milk in glass bottles from Echo Farms, (measurements of ingredients unknown), and her gifted hands. I remember quite well the big bag of Red Band flour, those greasy lard boxes, and the glass milk bottles.

When the time came for biscuits, my siblings and I would stand around the table in our kitchen and watch her skill in action. When she was near the end of making biscuits in the usual round shapes, Mother would always save enough dough to make us biscuits in the shape of ducks.

Excitement grew as we waited for the biscuits to cook in the oven of our enamel white and black wood stove. When they were ready to eat, we would "sop" them with Grandma's molasses, and enjoyed every minute of the "sopping."

This was a dish that was regularly eaten in our home.

Other meals that we ate with Mother's biscuits from scratch included dried lima beans, corn beef with white potatoes, beef liver with rice and gravy, fried and stewed chicken, oyster and clam fritters, baked sheep head (fish), homemade grape jelly, pear preserves, stewed peaches and apples.

Our homestead is still located on the Carolina Beach Road near Wilmington.

My mother passed on in 1999 at the age of 78, but my 94-year-old father, John Allen Mitchell, still lives in our homestead.

Today, I am a retired high school educator, married, and the mother of one adult son.

If I had known yesteryear as I do today, I would never have let my mother pass on without securing her delicious recipe dishes.

When a Penny Was a Treasure
by
Nettie Baker Deasy of Lindenhurst, N.Y.

What was like to be a child in the 1920s and 1930s? Nettie Deasy describes it precisely and compellingly in this wonderful memoir of life in Wilmington during the first half of the 20th century. If there is ever a treasure for historians in the far distant future, it is this story. Mrs. Deasy was born in Wilmington in 1921 and now lives in New York State.

I was born in 1921 in Wilmington and lived in Brooklyn on the north side of the Atlantic Coast Line train tracks. My dad, Walter Baker, worked for the Atlantic Coast Line and Mama, Nellie Baker, like most mamas of that time, stayed home and took care of her family and home.

Mama was active in church and community, a member in lodges and the P.T.A. She participated in the marches for free textbooks in public schools and free milk for needy children. She felt voting was a privilege and spent most election days rounding up the women in our neighborhood to go to the polls.

We had running water but a bathtub was a luxury and we bathed on Saturday in a wash tub in the kitchen. When we did get a bathtub, all the neighbors came to look it over.

Our house was heated by a big pot belly coal stove in the sitting room. We cooked with gas, but there was a small laundry heater in the kitchen for warmth and heating water. Bedrooms had big fireplaces but were used only when someone was sick or when Grandma came to visit. The parlor fireplace was used only on special holidays or when the preacher came to visit.

I had one sister, Emily, who was five years older. We attended Cornelious Harnett School at Sixth and Harnett Street. God bless our teachers! They taught everything. Music was used to teach the times table, parts of speech and Palmer handwriting. For gym class, the teacher opened the windows, put a record on the windup record player and we exercised.

Our school had a play every year and great parties at Christmas, Thanksgiving and Halloween. The highlight of each year was May Day. Every grade offered some form of entertainment and we crowned the May Queen who was chosen by the three upper grade teachers. I was lucky to be chosen May Queen in sixth grade, and that was one of the happiest days of my childhood.

Field day was another big deal. All elementary schools competed at Primbrook

Nettie Baker Deasy in 1940.

Jones Park, with little purple and gold ribbons for winners. (I still have my third place ribbon for some kind of dash.)

Purple and gold were our school colors and we had a great school song. I still remember it.

Sunday was church day and everyone went. There wasn't much else to do because all stores and movies were closed. The drugstore was open in case somebody needed medicine. Sometimes Dr. Madox, the pharmacist, opened the soda fountain for us teenagers after church was over.

In summer, all churches had picnics to Wrightsville Beach. We traveled by trolley car. Mamas were up at the crack of dawn preparing fried chicken, potato salad and coleslaw. The trolley stopped on the way at the icehouse for a big piece of ice. At the beach the men made a big wooden tub of lemonade. That was the best lemonade ever.

Cornelious Harnett School's fifth grade performance for May Day.

Quilting parties were the rage. Mama's church circle would come to our house for a party. The quilt frame would be set up in our parlor for days. Children came with their mamas and we had a ball.

I remember the big to-do when Lindbergh made his solo flight across the Atlantic in 1927. I was six years old and I thought my teacher was making up a story to tell us. But Mama showed me newspaper pictures and convinced me it was real. She also took us to the air show at Blutenthaw Field, now the New Hanover County Airport.

Daddy hand made a radio, so we had one before they were on the market. Neighbors and relatives came every Saturday night for entertainment. As a child, I thought it strange, all sitting quietly looking at this thing. Later, Daddy bought a Philco from Sears and Roebuck.

Before that invention, I remember Daddy playing his banjo and everybody singing in the evenings. My great grandpa told us stories about his childhood, or about the Civil War. Our family played board games and Old Maid cards, and Daddy told stories and drew pictures as he talked. He was a trick artist, and when he finished his story, he would turn the picture upside down and it would be something funny.

Nettie Baker Deasy as May Queen with crown bearer, Alton Croom.

Daddy bought a Ford car and gas was two gallons for 25 cents. He took us for Sunday afternoon rides out Castle Hayne way to see the flower farms.

On Saturday afternoons everyone headed for the Bijou Theater—ten cents if you were under twelve. I think most of us were sixteen before we paid full fare. There was usually a double feature plus Our Gang or a cartoon. We sometimes got the latest episode of Flash Gordon. As we got older, we enjoyed big time movie stars like Gary Cooper, Clark Gable, Ginger Rogers and Greta Garbo. Westerns were also popular. During World War II, I got a chance to meet these stars at Camp Davis when they entertained the troops.

I remember when a penny was a treasure. You could buy a pencil, a big raisin cookie or three Mary Janes. If you saved until you had a nickel, you could buy a Black Cow, a box of candy cigarettes or maybe a sour pickle. At Mrs. Toler's store, you could even stab the pickle for yourself out of that big old barrel.

If you were looking for a wedding gift, an iron skillet or a large coffee pot was your best buy. These could be handed down through the generations. Remember, these were the Depression years.

I remember when children played freely throughout neighborhoods. We played tag, hide and seek, kick the can, baseball, handball, marbles, hopscotch, mumble peg, and we also made up games. Girls played with dolls until they were about nine or ten years old. Then they called it doll collecting. Just about every child got roller skates for Christmas. We proudly wore our skate keys on a shoestring around our necks. I still have my skate key—on the same shoestring (but I'm not planning to go skating).

Girls were taught to sew, embroider and make biscuits from scratch. All children had some kind of work to do about the house or yard. If it wasn't done correctly, you didn't get your allowance. My job was dusting, and I never did it well enough to please my mama. Every time, she threatened to keep my allowance and ended up helping me. I believe she thought I wasn't capable. It worked for me!

Richard and Nettie's wedding day at St. Mary's Church grounds. In the background is the USO at 4th and Ann St.

Before the bridges connected New Hanover and Brunswick Counties, we had a ferryboat. Farmers brought produce by horse and cart on the ferry to the dock at Market Street. Some went to the Farmer's Market and others drove their teams through neighborhoods. They sang as they came down the streets, advertising their wares. They offered fresh vegetables, fruit, eggs, butter, buttermilk, sausage, and even homemade apple butter. Neighborhood vendors also sold fish on Fridays, the fish day for everybody. It was cheaper than meat. Grocery stores were owned and operated by families, who usually lived in back of the store or beside it. It was the same for butcher stores. But everyone was happy when the A&P came in with everything in one store. That was truly the big time.

Memorial Day was special when all veterans marched in the parade. My great grandpa, Richard Reaves, marched in full uniform. Not only did he march, he pushed his buddy in a wheelchair. Both were veterans of the Civil War. The bands played and the streets were jammed with people. When the flags passed, everyone's right hand went over their hearts. They stood in silence, at attention. That was patriotism.

Another big deal was the Feast of the Pirates. The city buzzed with activity and many people dressed as pirates for the parade. Bands played, there were floats, organ grinders with monkeys, clowns and the vendors. At night there was dancing in the streets.

We had great carnivals and real County Fairs. At one fair, I had a chance to ride an elephant. That was exciting! My mama, however, thought it was very un-ladylike.

At Christmastime, we had the lighting of the largest living Christmas tree at Hilton Park. All churches took part in this.

Greenfield Park was the place for Easter egg hunts. In summer, the lake was open for swimming and boating. Around the lake on Hoover Road there was always fishing. Across the street was a zoo. I especially remember the beautiful peacocks.

We thought our city was pretty modern. We had a lot of home deliveries. The postman delivered mail and sometimes a free box of Kellogs Corn Flakes. He also delivered the Montgomery Ward catalogs. A telegram was sometimes delivered from an unknown cousin in Europe, or a death notice. Milk was delivered in glass bottles with cardboard stoppers. Coal was delivered for the pot belly stove, and wood for the laundry heater. Groceries and medicine were delivered by bicycle. When Mrs. Darden, the lady with six children, wasn't feeling well, my mama would call for the doctor on our four-party telephone line. He would show up with his little black bag and deliver her a new baby. I prayed for him to come to our house, but I think Mama was praying he would not.

My high school, New Hanover High, was the only high school in the county. Mr. T.T. Hamilton was our principal. I only saw him at assemblies or graduation. I did see Miss Hattie Strathers often. She patrolled the halls at changing of classes, checking the lengths of girls' skirts. I fondly remember the Debating Club. We did resolve that there is a Santa Claus. I graduated in 1938 at the Legion Stadium because our class was too big for the auditorium. I still have my class ring. It looks like something you might find in a Cracker Jack box. I also have my yearbook. My husband and I attended all class reunions, and we had many.

On December 8, 1941 I was addressing Christmas cards when President Roosevelt announced on radio that we were at war with Japan. I remember the blackouts, rationing, Camp Davis, Camp Lejune, antiaircraft, and the reopening of the old shipyard.

Our city's population explosion forced many families to rent rooms. A lot of people sent invitations to churches and local USOs inviting servicemen and women to join them for Sunday dinner. The USOs had dances and special services for the service people and their families. I was a volunteer at the 4th and Ann Street USO. It was run by the St. Marys Catholic Church. I met my husband at one of the dances. Corporal Richard Deasy made his first visit to the USO there at a Tuesday night dance. He made the wrong turn when he came in and came out on the stage with the band. He stood there, looked over the dance floor, came down the steps and tapped the handsome Marine I was dancing with to break in. He introduced himself and

Wilmington's Greenfield Park in 1939.

Johnny Mercer Pier at Wrightsville Beach in 1940.

we danced. After the dance, we talked a while. We started the next dance, but five other soldiers intruded by breaking in, so when the music stopped we were not together. Soon, I was paged from the office to go to the library, and there he was. When he asked to walk me home I explained we were not allowed to leave with service people. Then he said he would meet me at the corner and I told him I was being picked up by a neighbor. We then went back to the dance floor. He was not the last person I danced with that evening.

When I arrived home that night he was sitting on our front porch talking to my mother. She asked him if he had to go back to camp that night. He told her he had leave until next day at noon and arrangements were made for him to spend the night with our neighbors. Next morning, he was sitting on our porch again when I came out to go to work. I never walked to work but I did that day.

The following Saturday night he was at the dance at 2nd and Orange USO and he did walk me home. Again, he stayed at the neighbor's house, and he was on our porch Sunday morning when I came out to go to church, and we went together. He walked me home afterward, but I did not know that he was one of the five soldiers my mother had invited to dinner that day. All of us went to the park that afternoon.

That evening I had a date with Sergeant Roy Butler, an old friend, who was leaving for Camp Jackson next morning.

The next Tuesday night Corporal Deasy was at the USO dance, and that was the beginning of a 14 month courtship. We were married in St. Marys Church and had our reception in the USO hall. We honeymooned at Wrightsville Beach at the Blockade Runner. Fifty years later, our children arranged for us to celebrate our fiftieth anniversary at Wrightsville Beach at the Holiday Inn. (The Blockade Runner had been destroyed by the hurricane.) At our celebration, we were lucky to have our maid of honor, one usher and the little flower girl. The other eight members of our wedding party were deceased. My dear husband only lived three years afterward.

My husband got his college degree through the GI Bill of Rights. He was the business manager for our school district. I taught school for 35 years, and all five of our children became teachers.

Wilmington has changed so much since 1941. My family lived at 3rd and Harnett Street. Now, all the houses are gone except for the house we lived in and the house next door. My family moved in the fifties to the historical section on the south side of Wilmington. It is our family's residence now, but I spend most of my time in New York.

Most of my neighbors are not natives so they do not care to know their neighbors. The traffic is so heavy I'm afraid to drive out of the neighborhood. We do not even have a grocery store in our neighborhood and the nearest drugstore isn't around the corner. It's okay, though, because my family will see that I have what I need.

I have so many wonderful memories, like pictures of my May Day crowning, field day ribbons, class ring, riding the elephant, swimming in Greenfield Lake, a deck of Old Maid cards and my skate key. Who could ask for more?

I still have the gift of gab. I'm only 85 years old and I plan to stick around for at least another decade. Great Grandpa Richard Reaves did.

The Church in the Wildwood
by
Natalie Hewett Nicholas of Shallotte
From an interview by Karen Dolan

Natalie Nicholas, who now lives in Shallote, was interviewed by Karen Dolan, who did an excellent job of telling Natalie's story. We are grateful to both these ladies for the information provided.

I was born August 4, 1927, in Supply, just the other side of the hospital. I was the baby in the family. I had two older sisters and the sister that was oldest to me was nine years older than I was when I come along. Their names are Lina and Alice. We didn't play too much 'cause they was a lot older than I was. I was sort of a lonely child.

We was raised on a farm and we had neighbors. I went to their house to meet the school bus. We played a ball game before the bus came, softball, not football or baseball. We'd get out there and swing the bat and flip the ball. We wore dresses.

I went to school here in Shallotte. The high school was over there where the grammar school is now. Used to be the high school there and all the grades were there at that school. I graduated in the eleventh grade. I graduated in May, I believe it was 1945, and the year after I graduated it changed to twelve grades.

We had an icebox. We finally got an icebox. And we'd meet the iceman to get a block of ice to put in it. He didn't come every day. We'd get a block of ice and maybe the next time he'd come by, we'd get another block of ice.

We had a garden. We'd get things out of the garden to eat and my sisters and I had to help in the garden. When I come in from school, I had to help get in the firewood. We had a wood stove in the kitchen and we had to fill up the box with wood to start the cooking. We had a little box there we put splinters in to start the fire to cook. We had to do that just about every day. On the side of the cook stove, we had a reservoir and it was hooked on the side of the stove and it heated our water for baths and what have you.

We had a pump. We didn't have running water. The reservoir on the side of the cook stove heated our water. We put it in a tub-like thing and we went in the kitchen to bathe or either in our bedroom to bathe. When I was a kid we only took a bath once a week. We probably had a bath on Saturday night and I reckon washed up the rest of the time. We had a fireplace in the living room and we had to bring in wood for that in the wintertime.

My parents worked on the farm too. There weren't anything to do back then. No jobs. We'd help other people with tobacco. We'd help different ones like that. We got paid just before school started—which was first of September, after the Labor Day. We'd save our money up and buy school clothes and shoes, and my mother sewed. We'd buy material and she'd make dresses for us.

At night I'd have to do my school work. And we had lamps to see by—kerosene lamps. We had Aladdin lamps. We finally got those and they gave a brighter light. It had a little mantel on the inside. It provided a better glow than the other lamps. It was probably in the 30s when we got them.

My daddy used to go to the barn and shuck corn and put it in a big tub and roll it to the house in a wheelbarrow. And that night after supper, we'd gather in the living room and sit around this tub and shell corn and sing songs. Daddy sang the bass part and we'd all sing the other parts. It was kind of a gospel song we'd sing, "Come to the Church in the Wildwood." We'd shell a big tub full and then he'd carry it to the mill the next day to grind for meal to make our cornbread, corn dinners, and so on.

For water, we had to pump by hand and we'd come to get our water and we had to carry a big pitcher in the living room to get our water out of in the night in case we wanted a drink or something. We had an outside john. I was in my teens when we got the indoor plumbing.

There was one man in Supply that had a phone and if we got sick or something, we could go there and they'd call the doctor for us. Some people had a battery radio, but we didn't have one.

We had an old pump organ that we played. I would go to it sometimes. My sister took a little music—not much. She give it up. I'd go to the organ and play, "You Can't Stop Me From Loving You." The knobs on it pulled in and I'd move my hands over the keys and play it, with just one finger, you know.

We got our mail from the post office and our box number was Box Five. I remember that. We'd walk down to the post office; it wasn't far. I don't know whether we went every day or not, but every day or so we'd go to see if we had any mail.

In the summertime once in awhile, we'd get to go to the beach—not often. Back during World War II, I would get with a bunch of girls and there was one man that had a pickup truck that lived close by us. And we'd all get in the back of that, and we'd go to Holden Beach and go across on the ferry to the ocean part. Back during the war, they had a Coast Guard Station at the beach. And they had a horse there. He was in a stable and he was down at the west end of the beach. They used the horse to patrol the beach. And we'd flirt with the boys in the Coast Guard. That must be years ago—about 67 years ago! That's something, isn't it?

When I was a teenager we worked in tobacco and I despised it. It was dirty and it had worms on it—horn worms, green worms, and they'd be about two inches long and they were nasty. We had to pull them off the tobacco as soon we could as they'd eat the tobacco and make holes. And we'd have to go out and worm the leaves and things—throw them down and stomp them.

Just about everybody in my family worked in tobacco. My mother would help some, but most of the time, she would go stay with people. She did practical nursing jobs. She'd go stay with people who got sick and if they passed away, she'd come back home. Sometimes they'd take her different places in the community. They'd come get her 'cause we didn't have a car. We had a mule and cart.

I think there was two grocery stores in Supply—side-by-side. We'd go down and get our groceries. Back then in the forties, they got a theatre here in Shallotte and that had a movie thing where you'd go in the car, you know, a drive-in. That was when I was a teenager, I imagine.

After I graduated from high school, I got a job at H. S. Kress, a dime store. I was a floor walker. I'd get the money from different registers and bring it to the office. I rode the bus back and forth for awhile and then I went and stayed with my cousin up there. So that's about it.

Pretty Decent Folks
by
Frances Blizzard of Beulaville

In the good old days, we were a nation of entrepreneurs. Whether we owned our own land or worked the land as tenants, we were self-employed. And most of us who lived that life usually did turn out to be "pretty decent folks." Frances Blizzard describes that life excellently. Those who aren't already in the know will find out about things like sweeping the yard, tobacco stick horses and how to kill bedbugs. And the talented Frances has provided several quality drawings depicting the good old days.

I was born in 1936 in rural Duplin County. We **[family name not provided]** were tenant farmers. Our landlady owned several tracts of land with a tenant house on each tract. Daddy must have liked to move because I think we lived in every house that lady owned. Each time we moved, the new house would have to be scalded with hot lye water before we moved in to make sure there were no bedbugs or other varmints left living there by the previous tenant. We threw water up on the walls and ceiling and scrubbed the floors with a scrub broom. All the floors, walls and ceilings were unpainted wood so everything was left clean and smelling good.

I don't remember a lot about the work that went on except that Daddy and the boys would be out plowing (with mules and hand plows) or sawing wood for curing tobacco, fireplace wood, and stove wood.

We always had hogs to kill for our meat. They would be killed during the winter. The meat would be salted down on a wide shelf in the smokehouse until it was salty enough to "keep." Then it was washed off and hung

up and smoked.

Sometimes Mama would can some of the fresh lean meat and fresh sausage. There wasn't any way to keep fresh, unsalted meat. The link sausage would be hung up in the smokehouse to air dry. All the scrap meat was saved and cooked so we could use the grease and broth to make lye soap. The soap was cooked outside in a pot, cooled, cut into squares, and laid out to dry. It was used for washing clothes, dishes, and baths.

We always had chickens to lay eggs and to kill for eating. We also had a cow for milk and butter. Corn was carried to the mill to be ground for cornmeal. We didn't buy groceries often and not many when we did. The main things to buy were flour, rice, sugar, coffee, and tea.

I don't remember the iceman coming, but I do remember the fish man. When he came, we would get some butter perch (kind of round, small fish). They were the cheapest. Sometimes Daddy would get a keg of salted mullets. On the occasions that we would have fish, one of the boys would go to the store and get a nickel or dime piece of ice so we could have iced tea with that meal. We'd have to keep the ice wrapped up good so it wouldn't melt so fast.

We grew our own vegetables, starting in February, with potatoes and other things that could withstand the cold weather. Then on Good Friday, we would plant beans and the

rest of the garden. Mama canned what we couldn't eat while it was fresh. If Daddy was curing tobacco at the time, she would put jars of vegetables inside the barn on the sills. They would cook there in the jars. At other times she did her canning on the stove.

Potatoes were put in a bank (a low tent-like place covered with dirt) with an opening for putting them in and taking them out. They would keep there without freezing during the winter.

Some of the chores for the younger children included bringing in wood, feeding chickens, bringing in eggs (for this job, you didn't want to get close to a rooster or setting hen), helping to feed the hogs, and washing dishes. Sometimes we had to shell corn to make some kind of sour mash for the hogs. We swept the yard with a broom made from small tree branches with a lot of twigs on the end. We didn't have grassy yards. If weeds or grass grew, we chopped it before we swept. House brooms were made out of broom straw that grew on ditch banks or laying out fields.

There was not much entertainment for young children. We rode a tobacco stick horse and had a corncob pistol for playing cowboys. Girls played jack rocks—boys had marbles. We liked climbing trees. We played hide and seek and jump rope. We usually had a see-saw and a jump board. For snacks, we would sometimes have tea cakes, but mostly it was a homemade jelly biscuit or a biscuit with a hole punched in it and filled with molasses.

A special treat was mixing sugar and cocoa to make "snuff." But during World War II, when sugar was rationed, we didn't let Mama catch us in the sugar stand. We didn't have a car, so sometimes we could trade somebody a gas stamp for a sugar stamp.

In the summer when the corn was in silks, I would pull an ear and pretend it was a doll. The silks were "hair." When the corn was grown enough to eat, we'd roast some ears in the oven or in the barn furnace if Daddy was curing tobacco. That was really good!

I was the youngest of nine children, six boys and three girls. My six brothers joined the military as soon as they became old enough. The four oldest brothers were all overseas at the same time during World War II. One was killed, one was wounded, and one received a medical discharge after contracting malaria fever in the Panama Canal Zone. The three others retired with twenty-plus years.

We didn't know we were poor when we were young. I thought everybody was living like we were. And looking back, it wasn't such a bad way to grow up. We all turned out to be pretty decent folks!

Past Times
F. Blizzard

Little Cowboy

Past Times
F. Blizzard

Past Times
F. Blizzard